SUBSIDIA
BIB

36

M000308959

STANISŁAW BAZYLIŃSKI

A Guide
to Biblical
Research

GBP
GREGORIAN & BIBLICAL PRESS

Cover: Serena Aureli

© 2009 Gregorian & Biblical Press
Piazza della Pilotta 35, 00187 - Roma
books@biblicum.com

ISBN 978-88-7653-**645**-8

Printed in Italy, June 2009
by Arti Grafiche srl - Pomezia (Rome) - [0.5]

To my students

Table of Contents

Introduction

A year and half after the first release of this work in Italian, both the Spanish and English versions are ready. This volume is based on the second Italian edition (2005) but with more updates.

This English version is the result of five years of teaching the *Introductory Seminar in Methodology* at the Pontifical Biblical Institute in Rome and a continuing dialogue with the students. It addresses their needs on how to approach biblical and exegetical research.

The work is divided into six chapters. The first chapter deals with the primary sources of the biblical text, followed by second chapter which reviews the tools available for biblical bibliographic research. The third chapter presents a panorama of reference works: concordances, synopses, lexicons, grammars, etc. At the conclusion of this chapter there is a brief bibliography on exegetical methods.

Because of the interest students have in literary types in Sacred Scripture, the fourth chapter deals with some of these types. The fifth chapter is intended to help students to surmount many obstacles they encounter in writing an exegetical work. The sixth chapter gives some practical rules in organizing bibliographic citations in footnotes and in a bibliography.

This tool is not exhaustive in dealing with these topics, nor does it include every aspect of biblical studies. During the various revisions and translations of this volume, I have become aware that it is always "a work in progress". In spite of some inevitable lacunae, the reader will find most of the bibliographic indications crucial to his adventure in exegetical research.

Many people have helped in publishing this work. Fr. James Swetnam, S.J., who in the spring of 2003 promoted the project, gave many valuable suggestions and inserted it into the *Subsidia Biblica* series.

He also encouraged me to prepare the English version. Prof. Reinhard Neudecker, S.J., of the Pontifical Biblical Institute, gave me much advice in the area of rabbinic literature. Miss Jo Anne Gibilaro, B.S., Ms. Catherine Steinmann, M.A., and Sister Barbara Sudol, C.S.F.N., D.A., carefully proofread major parts of the draft, whereas Fr. George D. Byers, C.P.M., S.S.L., Rev. Christopher M. Ciccarino, S.S.L., and Rev. Paul Sciberras, S.S.L., read the whole manuscript and suggested improvements in English style and content. Any imperfections are my responsibility.

To them and to all those who participated in the publishing and dissemination of this tool, I am grateful. My hope is that this volume will contribute to the continual enrichment of scientific biblical research and the ability of the student to present his work clearly and carefully.

Author   Rome, March 1, 2006

Introduction to the Second Edition

Requests from readers and advice from reviewers have induced me to undertake a preparation of a new edition, respecting the aims that guided the origin of *A Guide* and sustained its circulation.

As a matter of fact, based on the first edition, I held it appropriate to rearrange the third chapter in which three new sections have been introduced (§ 6 Introductions to the Bible; § 7 Biblical Theology; § 13 Apocrypha), and one section (§ 14 Exegetical Methods) has been amplified considerably. Similarly, the fourth chapter has been enriched with 14 new literary "types". A number of further additions was necessary in some of the passages and notes of the first, second, fifth, and sixth chapters; another, less significant but equally useful, supplement has been incorporated here and there, in order to make the reading easy and facilitate comprehension. Of significance, I suppose, are both the rectification of mistakes and the updating of the existing data in all six chapters. With all these improvements, I entrust to the reader this second edition of *A Guide*, enlarged by a considerable number of pages, in the hope that I have addressed the expectations of the students more efficaciously.

The carrying out of this project would have been unfeasible without the help of my students who spurred me with their theoretical challenges and practical needs, which emerged in courses offered over the past three years. Fr. Russell K. Mc Dougall, C.S.C., SSL, accepted the onus of being the first proofreader of the manuscript. Fr. James Swetnam, S.J., meticulously continued this not easy task and, as the Director of the *Subsidia Biblica* series, he showed great interest in this undertaking and followed it with attention, supporting me in the various stages of its development up to the typographic production of the book.

To them and to all who sustained me in this revising and updating I express my gratitude.

Author   Rome, May 8, 2009

Abbreviations and Symbols

For abbreviations of series, periodicals and rabbinic texts see S. M. SCHWERTNER, *Internationales Abkürzungsverzeichnis für Theologie und Grenzgebiete* / *International Glossary of Abbreviations for Theology and Related Subjects* (*IATG²*) (Berlin – New York ²1992) = *Theologische Realenzyklopädie.* Abkürzungsverzeichnis (Berlin – New York ²1994), integrated by R. ALTHANN, *Elenchus of Biblica 1995-2005* (EBB 11-21; Roma 1998-2008). Other symbols and abbreviations, which do not appear in these works, are quoted below.

A.D.	anno Domini, in the year of the Lord
Aram.	Aramaic
Arm.	Armenian
art. cit.	in the article cited
B.C.	before Christ
c.	century
ca.	circa, about
CD-ROM	Compact Disk - Read Only Memory
cf.	confer, compare
chap.	chapter, chapters
cm	centimeter, centimeters
col.	column, columns
Diss.	dissertation, unpublished thesis for the degree of Doctor
DVD	Digital Video/Versatile Disk
e.g.	exempli gratia, for example
ed.	edidit, ediderunt, edited by; edition
Eng.	English
esp.	especially
et al.	et alii, and others
etc.	et cetera, and so on
Fr.	French

Ger.	German
Gk.	Greek
Hebr.	Hebrew
It.	Italian
Jr.	Junior
Lat.	Latin
lit.	literally
MS; MSS	manuscript, manuscripts
n.	footnote
NB	nota bene, note well
no.	number, numbers
NT	New Testament
op. cit.	opere citato, in the work cited
p.; pp.	page, pages
Pol.	Polish
Port.	Portuguese
prop.	properly
pseud.	pseudonym
rev.	review
Slav.	Slavonic
Sp.	Spanish
Sr.	Senior
sup.	supplement
Syr.	Syriac
tr.	translator, translation
URL	uniform resource locator
v.; vv.	verse, verses
vol. / vols.	volume / volumes
x	per
§	section
/	or; corresponds to
|	caesura, pause
+	and; with
=	equal to
"	inch, placed after a number

I. Primary Sources of the Biblical Text

The purpose of this first chapter is to present selectively some resources for the biblical text in its original languages and in ancient translations.

1. The Biblical Text

The following pages offer brief descriptions of some editions of the biblical text which scholars use in their exegetical analysis.

1.1 *The Hebrew Text*

Preliminary bibliography:

BEN UZZIEL, M., *Kitāb al-Khilaf.* Treatise on the Differences between Ben Asher and Ben Naphtali (ed. L. LIPSCHÜTZ) (The Hebrew University Bible Project Monograph Series 2; Jerusalem 1965).

FRENSDORFF, S., *Die Massora Magna.* I. Die Massora in alphabetischer Ordnung (Hannover – Leipzig 1876, New York 1968).

GINSBURG, C. D., *Introduction to the Massoretico-Critical Edition of the Hebrew Bible* (London 1897).

———, *The Massorah.* Compiled from Manuscripts, Alphabetically and Lexically Arranged (London 1880, 1883, 1885, 1905 = The Library of Biblical Studies; New York 1975) I-IV.

KELLEY, P. H. – MYNATT, D. S. – CRAWFORD, T. G., *The Masorah of Biblia Hebraica Stuttgartensia.* Introduction and Annotated Glossary (Grand Rapids, MI – Cambridge 1998).

LEIMAN, S. Z. (ed.), *The Canon and Masorah of the Hebrew Bible.* An Introductory Reader (LBS; New York 1974).

LIPSCHÜTZ, L., "כתאב אלכלף אלדי בין אלמעלמין בן אשר ובן נפתלי", *Textus* 2 (1962) נח-א = "Kitāb al-Khilaf, the Book of the Ḥillufim.

Mishael Ben Uzziel's Treatise on the Differences between Ben
Asher and Ben Naphtali", *Textus* 4 (1964) 1-29.

MULDER, M. J. (ed.), *Mikra*. Text, Translation, Reading and Interpretation of the Hebrew Bible in Ancient Judaism and Early
Christianity (CRI. II. The Literature of the Jewish People in
the Period of the Second Temple and the Talmud 1; Assen –
Maastricht – Philadelphia 1988).

ROBERTS, B. J., *The Old Testament Text and Versions*. The Hebrew
Text in Transmission and the History of the Ancient Versions
(Cardiff 1951) 1-100, 188-196.

TOV, E., *Textual Criticism of the Hebrew Bible* (Minneapolis –
Assen ²2001).

TREBOLLE BARRERA, J., *La Biblia judía y la Biblia cristiana*. Introducción a la historia de la Biblia (Madrid 1993) 277-313; Eng.
tr. *The Christian and the Jewish Bible*. Introduction to the History of the Bible (Grand Rapids, MI 1997).

WEINGREEN, J., *Introduction to the Critical Study of the Text of the
Hebrew Bible* (Oxford 1982).

WÜRTHWEIN, E., *Der Text des Alten Testaments*. Eine Einführung in
die Biblia Hebraica (Stuttgart 1952, 1988); Eng. tr. *The Text of
the Old Testament*. An Introduction to the Biblia Hebraica
(Grand Rapids, MI ²1995).

YEIVIN, I., *Introduction to the Tiberian Masorah* (SBL.MasSt 5;
Missoula, MT 1980).

1.1.1 Kittel's Edition

R. KITTEL (ed.), *Biblia Hebraica* (Stuttgart 1937).

Although this version was replaced by *Biblia Hebraica Stuttgartensia*, it is still useful for its critical apparatus, which touches
upon many exegetical issues.

The first (Leipzig 1905-1906) and second (Leipzig 1909) editions
of the *BHK* used as their basis the text by Jacob BEN ḤAYYIM: *Biblia
hebraica cum Targum et variis rabbinorum commentariis*. R. Jacob

ben Chaiim Masoram magnam alphabetico ordine digessit et totum opus direxit (Venetiis 1524-1525).

The third edition, 1937, introduced the text of Ben Asher, from the Leningrad Codex B 19a (A.D. 1008 or 1009).

The most important changes in this edition are: a) the larger type face; b) the double critical apparatus; c) the new form of the masoretic text and the insertion of the *masora*, prepared by P. Kahle, which is probably the most important change.

The double critical apparatus is located at the bottom of the page. The first apparatus, just below the main text, uses the letters of the Greek alphabet (α, β, γ...) as footnote references, and offers small variants and less important information. The second apparatus, below the first, marks the footnote references with the letters of the Latin alphabet (a, b, c...), and introduces more important textual changes.

The discovery of the Dead Sea Scrolls, whose contents asked for replacement of former emendations of the MT based on the LXX, as well as the destruction of the printing office in Leipzig, where the type-setting for the printing of the *BHK* were preserved, compelled scholars to prepare a new edition.

1.1.2 Biblia Hebraica Stuttgartensia

K. ELLIGER – W. RUDOLPH (ed.), *Biblia Hebraica Stuttgartensia* (Stuttgart 1967-1977).

It is the fourth edition of *Biblia Hebraica* (*BH*).

The *Codex Leningradensis* B 19a is the textual base of this edition.

The *masora parva* was improved by G. E. WEIL, *Massorah Gedolah, iuxta codicem Leningradensem B 19a* (Romae – Stuttgart 1971, Rome 2001), and placed at the margin of each page. At the bottom of the page, one finds the principal comments of the *masora magna* and the critical apparatus, which includes references both to codices and to versions.

1.1.3 Biblia Hebraica Quinta (BHQ)

A. SCHENKER – Y. A. P. GOLDMAN – A. VAN DER KOOIJ – G. J. NORTON –
S. PISANO – J. DE WAARD – R. D. WEIS (ed.), *Biblia Hebraica
Quinta* (Stuttgart 2004-).

Deutsche Bibelgesellschaft published the following fascicles:
5. *Deuteronomy* (ed. C. MCCARTHY, 2007);
17. *Proverbs* (ed. J. DE WAARD, 2008);
18. *General Introduction and Megilloth* (ed. J. DE WAARD, *Ruth*,
P. B. DIRKSEN, *Canticles*, Y. A. P. GOLDMAN, *Qoheleth*,
R. SCHÄFER, *Lamentations*, M. SÆBØ, *Esther*, 2004);
20. *Ezra and Nehemiah* (ed. D. MARCUS, 2006).

This new project for the publishing of *BH* necessarily emerged
a) after the discovery of new MSS (especially from Qumran; cf. DJD)
and b) because of progress in research relating to the textual transmission of *BH*.

This edition, *Handausgabe* (*editio minor*), prepared for non-
specialist of textual criticism, is however conceived to be a contribution for the eventual publishing of an *editio critica maior* of *BH*.

In anticipation of the whole work in two volumes, the text will be
released in fascicles (until 2015, according to the publisher). Volume
I will include an introduction, explanatory signs, symbols and abbreviations, text and *masora*, critical apparatus. Volume II will contain
explanatory comments on the text and the translation of the notes of
the *masora magna*.

The textual basis of this diplomatic edition is *Codex Leningradensis* B 19a. *BHQ* does not provide a critical Hebrew text, as the history
of the evolution of the *BH* text and that of various traditions are not
sufficiently known so as to give a solid foundation for an eclectic text.
The choice of Codex B 19a is also dictated by a pragmatic motivation:
Deutsche Bibelgesellschaft possesses a typographic version which
has undergone many proof-readings.

As for the *masora*, both the *masora parva* and *magna* are reproduced, though only in basic form, since an exhaustive presentation of the *masora* would require much more extensive work.

The critical apparatus cites only those manuscripts which are important for translation and exegesis, and it includes relevant cases regarding textual transmission. The latter examples derive from the ancient witnesses, namely, the three major Tiberian MSS of the Torah, and two MSS of Neviim and Ketubim, all available pre-Tiberian MSS, and all ancient versions which give evidence for the Hebrew text. The variations derived from those witnesses are judged significant from the text-critical point of view, and may be potentially important for translation and exegesis. Excluded are variants that represent corrections of the style, or periphrastic or haggadic versions. A high value is placed on texts from Qumran and the Peshiṭta while the LXX and the Vg are less cited.

Unlike *BHS*, *BHQ* introduced for the first time a selective commentary on examples mentioned in the critical apparatus and the translation of the *masora magna*, as well as a discussion of the difficult cases of the *masora magna* and *parva*.

1.1.4 The Hebrew University Bible (HUB)

M. H. GOSHEN-GOTTSTEIN et al. (ed.), *The Hebrew University Bible* (The Hebrew University Bible Project; Jerusalem 1995-).

The project began in the 1950s when M. H. Goshen-Gottstein envisioned a new version of *BH*. Initially, the project sought to print the most authoritative MT MSS conjointly with their *masora*. However the publishing was piecemeal, starting in 1975, when the first fascicle appeared with the text of Isaiah.

The work is strictly philological, so that emendations of the MT were not inserted into the apparatus. The textual basis of the *HUB* is the Aleppo Codex, considered to be the most important witness of that branch of the masoretic tradition which became normative among the Jews[1]. The edition has four critical apparatuses, rich in information. The first apparatus quotes the principal versions: the Arabic translation by Saadiah Gaon, the LXX, the Vg, the Peshiṭta, the Targum, and the MT. The second apparatus contains material from both the Dead Sea Scrolls and rabbinic sources. The third apparatus provides information from medieval MSS of the Hebrew text. The fourth apparatus provides small orthographic details, vocalization and accentuation.

To date, three volumes have been published:

> *The Book of Isaiah* (ed. M. H. GOSHEN-GOTTSTEIN, 1995);
> *The Book of Jeremiah* (ed. C. RABIN – S. TALMON – E. TOV, 1997);
> *The Book of Ezekiel* (ed. M. H. GOSHEN-GOTTSTEIN – S. TALMON – G. MARQUIS, 2004).

1.1.5 The Oxford Hebrew Bible (OHB)

This new project of bringing out the Hebrew Bible differs from above-mentioned diplomatic editions (*BHK, BHS, BHQ, HUB*), since this publication should be an eclectic *editio critica maior*. Ronald Hendel, editor-in-chief (University of California, Berkeley), recently presented details of this undertaking:

> R. HENDEL, "The Oxford Hebrew Bible. Prologue to a New Critical Edition", *VT* 58 (2008) 324-351.

---

[1] Cf. I. BEN-ZVI, "The Codex of Ben Asher", *Textus* 1 (1960) 1-16; M. H. GOSHEN-GOTTSTEIN, "The Authenticity of Aleppo Codex", *Textus* 1 (1960) 17-58; D. S. LOEWINGER, "The Aleppo Codex and the Ben Asher Tradition", *Textus* 1 (1960) 59-111; P. KAHLE, *Der hebräische Bibeltext seit Franz Delitzsch* (FDV 1958; Stuttgart 1961) 80-88; I. YEIVIN, *The Aleppo Codex of the Bible*. A Study of Its Vocalization and Accentuation (The Hebrew University Bible Project Monograph Series 3; Jerusalem 1968).

Moreover, three samples of this new edition have been published:

S. White CRAWFORD – J. JOOSTEN – E. ULRICH, "Sample Editions of the Oxford Hebrew Bible: Deuteronomy 32:1-9, 1 Kings 11:1-8, and Jeremiah 27:1-10 (34 G)", *VT* 58 (2008) 352-366.

1.1.6 The Samaritan Pentateuch

A. VON GALL (ed.), *Der hebräische Pentateuch der Samaritaner* (Gießen 1918).

It is an eclectic version of the Samaritan Pentateuch in Hebrew square characters. Its text differs at times from the MT and therefore text critical investigation should precede usage of this edition.

A. TAL (ed.), *The Samaritan Pentateuch*. Edited According to MS 6 (C) of the Shekhem Synagogue (Texts and Studies in the Hebrew Language and Related Subjects 8; Tel-Aviv 1994).

This publication reproduces one of the most important manuscripts of the Samaritan Pentateuch (MS 6 from the synagogue of Shechem, 1204). The work is not intended to be an alternative to the critical edition by A. von Gall, even if it endeavors to make up for its deficiencies such as its eclectic composition and low esteem for the proper character of Samaritan Hebrew. The Hebrew text is printed in square characters, but it has not been provided with a critical apparatus.

1.1.7 Ben Sira

Bibliography:

REITERER, F. V. et al., *Bibliographie zu Ben Sira* (BZAW 266; Berlin – New York 1998).

F. VATTIONI (ed.), *Ecclesiastico*. Testo ebraico con apparato critico e versioni greca, latina e siriaca (Pubblicazioni del Seminario di Semitistica. Testi 1; Napoli 1968).

Being a polyglot, this volume is convenient to use as it provides the text of Ben Sira in four languages: Hebrew, Greek, Latin, and Syriac. The Hebrew text includes the following MSS: A, B, C, D, E, 2Q18, Masada, 11QPsᵃ (col. xxii-xxiii).

The Book of Ben Sira. Text, Concordance and an Analysis of Vocabulary (Jerusalem 1973).

The work is rich in materials since it offers a concordance and a list of lemmas deriving from Ben Sira's MSS. Marginal notes are also included. The presentation of the text follows the LXX sequence of verses. The editors made use of the same MSS as did F. Vattioni.

P. C. BEENTJES (ed.), *The Book of Ben Sira in Hebrew*. A Text Edition of All Extant Hebrew Manuscripts and a Synopsis of All Parallel Hebrew Ben Sira Texts (VT.S 68; Leiden – New York – Köln 1997).

The author attempted to gather and present all existing Hebrew MSS (with MS F); however this edition contains some errors and omissions. See:

> BEENTJES, P. C., "Errata et Corrigenda", *Ben Sira's God*. Proceedings of the International Ben Sira Conference Durham – Ushaw College 2001 (ed. R. EGGER-WENZEL) (BZAW 321; Berlin – New York 2002) 375-377.
>
> MÜLLER, A. R., "Eine neue Textausgabe von Jesus Sirach", *BN* 89 (1997) 19-21.

S. ELIZUR, "קטע חדש מהנוסח העברי של ספר בן סירא" [A New Hebrew Fragment of Ben Sira (Ecclesiasticus)]", *Tarb.* 76/1-2 (2006-2007) 17-28 and

R. EGGER-WENZEL, "Ein neues Sira-Fragment des MS C", *BN* 138 (2008) 107-114.

For the first time, Shulamit Elizur has published and described a sheet of the anthological MS C, from the Genizah (photographs on pp. 25-26). Renate Egger-Wenzel for her part proposed a slightly different reading and offered her arrangement in verses (Sir 3,27; 6,5-10.12-15.18; 20,30-31; 21,22-23.26; 22,11-12.21-22; 23,11; 25,7; 36,24; 37,1-2).

1.2 The Greek Text of the LXX

As for bibliography and introductory information concerning the LXX and other editions of the Greek Bible one can consult the following works:

BROCK, S. P. – FRITSCH, C. T. – JELLICOE, S., *A Classified Bibliography of the Septuagint* (ALGHJ 6; Leiden 1973).

CARBONE, S. P. – RIZZI, G., *Le Scritture ai tempi di Gesù*. Introduzione alla LXX e alle antiche versioni aramaiche (Testi e commenti 1; Bologna 1992).

DELICOSTOPOULOS, A., "Major Greek Translation of the Bible", *The Interpretation of the Bible*. The International Symposium in Slovenia (ed. J. KRAŠOVEC) (JSOT.S 289; Sheffield 1998) 297-316.

DOGNIEZ, C., *A Bibliography of the Septuagint* (1970-1993) / *Bibliographie de la Septante* (1970-1993) (VT.S 60; Leiden 1995).

DORIVAL, G. – HARL, M. – MUNNICH, O., *La Bible grecque des Septante*. Du judaïsme hellénistique au christianisme ancien (ICA; Paris 1988).

FERNÁNDEZ MARCOS, N., *Introducción a las versiones griegas de la Biblia* (TECC 23; Madrid 1979; TECC 64; Madrid ²1998); Eng. tr. *The Septuagint in Context*. Introduction to the Greek Version of the Bible (Leiden – Boston – Köln 2000); It. tr. *La Bibbia dei Settanta*. Introduzione alle versioni greche della Bibbia (Introduzione allo studio della Bibbia. Supplementi 6; Brescia 2000).

JOBES, K. H. – SILVA, M., *Invitation to the Septuagint* (Grand Rapids, MI 2000).
PASSONI DELL'ACQUA, A., *Il testo del Nuovo Testamento*. Introduzione alla critica testuale (Percorsi e traguardi biblici; Leumann 1994) 157-199.
ROBERTS, B. J., *The Old Testament Text and Versions*. The Hebrew Text in Transmission and the History of the Ancient Versions (Cardiff 1951) 101-119, 128-187.
SWETE, H. B., *An Introduction to the Old Testament in Greek* (Revised by R. R. OTTLEY) (Cambridge ²1914).

1.2.1 Göttingen Edition

Septuaginta: Vetus Testamentum Graecum auctoritate Academiae Scientiarum Gottingensis editum (Göttingen 1931-) I-XVI.

The most comprehensive edition of the Greek OT. It presents the Greek text, textual families and groups, and attempts to carefully reconstruct a critical text as close as possible to the original one.

Vandenhoeck & Ruprecht has published the following volumes:

1. *Genesis* (ed. A. RAHLFS, 1926; ed. J. W. WEVERS, 1974); 2/1. *Exodus* (ed. J. W. WEVERS, 1991); 2/2. *Leviticus* (ed. J. W. WEVERS, 1986); 3/1. *Numeri* (ed. J. W. WEVERS, 1982); 3/2. *Deuteronomium* (ed. J. W. WEVERS – U. QUAST, 1977, ²2006); 4/3. *Ruth* (ed. U. Quast, 2006); 8/1. *Esdrae liber I* (ed. R. HANHART, 1974); 8/2. *Esdrae liber II* (ed. R. HANHART, 1993); 8/3. *Esther* (ed. R. HANHART, ²1983); 8/4. *Iudith* (ed. R. HANHART, 1979); 8/5. *Tobit* (ed. R. HANHART, 1983); 9/1. *Maccabaeorum liber I* (ed. W. KAPPLER, ²1967); 9/2. *Maccabaeorum liber II*. Copiis usus quas reliquit W. Kappler (ed. R. HANHART, ²1976); 9/3. *Maccabaeorum liber III* (ed. R. HANHART, ²1980); 10. *Psalmi cum Odis* (ed. A. RAHLFS, ²1967); 11/4. *Iob* (ed. J. ZIEGLER, 1982); 12/1. *Sapientia Salomonis* (ed. J. ZIEGLER, 1962, ²1980); 12/2. *Sapientia Iesu filii Sirach* (ed. J. ZIEGLER, 1965, ²1980); 13. *Duodecim prophetae* (ed. J. ZIEGLER, ²1967); 14. *Isaias* (ed. J. ZIEGLER, ²1967); 15. *Jeremias, Baruch,*

Threni, Epistula Jeremiae (ed. J. ZIEGLER, [3]2006); 16/1. *Ezechiel* (ed. J. ZIEGLER, 1952, [2]1977); 16/2. *Susanna, Daniel, Bel et Draco* (ed. J. ZIEGLER, 1954; ed. O. MUNNICH – D. FRAENKEL, [2]1999).

1.2.2 Rahlfs' Edition

A. RAHLFS (ed.), *Septuaginta* (Stuttgart 1935) I-II.

Since the Göttingen edition has not yet been completed (still missing are the texts of Josh, Judg, Ru, 1–4 Kingdoms, 1–2 Paralipomena, 4 Macc, Prov, Qoh, Cant), exegetes make use of the edition of A. Rahlfs. The first publication of this complete work took place in 1935. Rahlfs reconstructs the text of the LXX based on the A, B, S codices. The critical apparatus is limited to these and a few other MSS.

A. RAHLFS, – R. HANHART, (ed.), *Septuaginta* (Editio altera) (Stuttgart 2006).

This pocket edition corrects errors and typographical mistakes of the previous edition. R. Hanhart inserts some changes of accentuation, in accordance with the criteria on which A. Rahlfs based his reconstruction of the text, and modifies another forms within the text. Similarly, in a moderate way, the critical apparatus was revised. The errors of the collation of manuscripts are corrected and the way of quantifying textual traditions is improved; corrections which derive from textual simplifications are inserted as well as the uncials Q, C and V, and the recensions *O* and *L* with variants in the passages, in which Rahlfs mentions only MS A, B or S.

For a detailed presentation, see:

R. HANHART, "Rechenschaftsbericht zur Editio altera der Handausgabe der Septuaginta von Alfred Rahlfs", *VT* 55 (2005) 450-460.

1.2.3 Brooke's, McLean's and Thackeray's Edition

A. E. BROOKE – N. MCLEAN – H. S. J. THACKERAY (ed.), *The Old Testament in Greek*. According to the Text of Codex Vaticanus, Supplemented from Other Uncial Manuscripts, with a Critical Apparatus Containing the Variants of the Chief Ancient Authorities for the Text of the Septuagint (Cambridge 1906-1940) I-III.

A. E. BROOKE – N. MCLEAN (ed.), *The Old Testament in Greek*. According to the Text of Codex Vaticanus, Supplemented from Other Uncial Manuscripts, with a Critical Apparatus Containing the Variants of the Chief Ancient Authorities for the Text of the Septuagint. I. The Octateuch (Cambridge 1906-1917).

A. E. BROOKE – N. MCLEAN – H. S. J. THACKERAY (ed.), *The Old Testament in Greek*. According to the Text of Codex Vaticanus, Supplemented from Other Uncial Manuscripts, with a Critical Apparatus Containing the Variants of the Chief Ancient Authorities for the Text of the Septuagint. II. The Later Historical Books. III. Esther, Judith, Tobit (Cambridge 1927-1935, 1940).

This edition with an extensive critical apparatus can be used as a valuable supplement to the Göttingen LXX edition, especially in the parts which until now have not been published.

1.3 *The Greek Text of the New Testament*

Bibliography:

ALAND, K. & B., *Der Text des Neuen Testaments*. Einführung in die wissenschaftlichen Ausgaben sowie in Theorie und Praxis der modernen Textkritik (Stuttgart 1982); Eng. tr. *The Text of the New Testament*. An Introduction to the Critical Editions and to the Theory and Practice of Modern Textual Criticism (Grand Rapids, MI – Leiden 1989); It. tr. *Il testo del Nuovo*

Testamento (Commentario storico-esegetico dell'Antico e del Nuovo Testamento 2; Genova 1987).

METZGER, B. M., *The Text of the New Testament*. Its Transmission, Corruption, and Restoration (New York – Oxford ³1992); It. tr. *Il testo del Nuovo Testamento*. Trasmissione, corruzione e restituzione (Introduzione allo studio della Bibbia. Supplementi 1; Brescia 1996).

O'CALLAGHAN, J., *Introducción a la crítica textual del Nuevo Testamento* (Instrumentos para el estudio de la Biblia 3; Estella 1999).

1.3.1 Merk's Edition

A. MERK (ed.), *Novum Testamentum graece et latine* (SPIB 65; Romae ¹¹1992).

The first edition (1933) was based on the *textus receptus I* by H. VON SODEN, *Die Schriften des Neuen Testaments in ihrer ältesten erreichbaren Textgestallt hergestellt auf Grund ihrer Textgeschichte* (Göttingen 1911, 1913) I-II. H. von Soden divided NT MSS into three recensions: K (*Koiné* = Antiochian or Syrian), H (*Hesychian* = Alexandrian or Egyptian), I (*Jerusalemite* = Palestinian).

The fourth and fifth editions (1942, 1944) abandoned von Soden's text, and offered a text based on manuscript evidence, ancient versions, Church Fathers, and critical studies. It contains a useful appendix with textual variants deriving from papyri.

The Latin text reproduces the Vulgate of Sixtus V and Clement VIII, *Biblia sacra vulgatae editionis* (Romae 1592).

1.3.2 The Greek New Testament (GNT⁴)

B. & K. ALAND – J. KARAVIDOPOULOS – C. M. MARTINI – B. M. METZGER (ed.), *The Greek New Testament* (Stuttgart ⁴1993).

*GNT*⁴ has been developed together with NA²⁷ (see below). In comparison with the third edition issued by K. Aland, M. Black,

C. M. Martini, B. M. Metzger, and A. Wikgren (New York – London – Edinburgh – Amsterdam – Stuttgart [3]1975 = NA[26]), the fourth edition contains a revised critical apparatus, which was thoroughly reworked. There were 284 new cases introduced in this version, whereas 273 cases were suppressed.

The goal of this edition is to provide a common basis for inter-confessional translations, restricting and simplifying textual variants to four categories, which are indicated in the first critical apparatus by letters in braces: {A}, {B}, {C}, {D}. These letters show different grades of certitude of the proposed reading: certain, less certain, disputable, and dubious.

The division of readings into these categories is based on the evaluation of variants and readings done by the editorial committee.

For an explanation of the editorial committee's solutions, see:

> METZGER, B. M., *A Textual Commentary on the Greek New Testament*. A Companion Volume to the United Bible Societies' Greek New Testament (Fourth Revised Edition) (Stuttgart [2]1994)

> and, based on this commentary, the work by

> OMANSON, R. L., *A Textual Guide to the Greek New Testament*. An Adaptation of Bruce M. METZGER's *Textual Commentary* for the Needs of Translators (Stuttgart 2006).

In the second critical apparatus, various punctuation-marks existing in the modern translations of the NT are selectively quoted. The readings which most influence the interpretation of the text are included.

The third apparatus includes quotations from biblical and non-biblical passages, cross references and allusions, and other parallel texts.

1.3.3 Novum Testamentum Graece (NA²⁷)

Eberhard & Erwin NESTLE – B. & K. ALAND – J. KARAVIDOPOULOS –
C. M. MARTINI – B. M. METZGER (ed.), *Novum Testamentum Graece* (Stuttgart ²⁷1993).

This is the popular pocket edition of the NT in Greek which Eberhard Nestle published for the first time in 1898. The text is the same as that in the 26th edition, which tried to establish a critical text. This text is also the basis of a number of concordances, lexicons and synopses of the four Gospels. The critical apparatus of this edition was improved with the support of MSS (papyri, uncials, minuscules), versions, patristic citations and lectionaries. Although the apparatus is complex and requires attention in reading, it nevertheless provides a great number of readings without preferring any specific MS. NA²⁷ is considered the best critical version available today.

1.3.4 Nuevo Testamento Trilingüe (NTT)

J. M. BOVER – J. O'CALLAGHAN (ed.), *Nuevo Testamento Trilingüe* (Madrid ⁵2001).

This fifth edition is a reprint of the third (Madrid 1994), which incorporated a large number of papyri that appeared after the publication of the second edition (Madrid 1987). The Greek text of the NT is printed with Spanish translation (positioned at the bottom of the page) and Latin translation (positioned at the upper-right side of the page).

The Greek text comes from the edition by J. M. BOVER, *Novi Testamenti Biblia Graeca et Latina* (Matriti ⁴1959). Bover's text is eclectic and it often deviates from the Alexandrian type, and can be similar to the Western or Caesarean text. The Spanish translation is literal. The Latin column provides *Novum Testamentum et Psalterium iuxta Novae Vulgatae editionis textum* (Città del Vaticano 1974), with its critical apparatus.

The critical apparatus of the Greek text (below the Greek and Latin texts) concisely includes both scholars who defend a particular reading, as well as ancient witnesses that provide evidence in its favor. In continuation with this trilingual edition, J. O'Callaghan published *Nuevo Testamento griego-español* (Madrid 1997), that basically reproduces the text of the third edition of *NTT*, but incorporates the contributions of *GNT*[4] and some changes motivated by his personal studies.

2. Ancient Versions

Due to space restrictions, in this section only some translations (and editions) of the biblical text in Greek, Aramaic, Latin, and Syriac were selected. See, for further research:

> VAN ESBROECK, M., "Les versions orientales de la Bible. Une orientation bibliographique", *The Interpretation of the Bible*. The International Symposium in Slovenia (ed. J. KRAŠOVEC) (JSOT.S 289; Sheffield 1998) 399-509.
>
> METZGER, B. M., *The Early Versions of the New Testament*. Their Origin, Transmission and Limitations (Oxford 1977).
>
> PASSONI DELL'ACQUA, A., *Il testo del Nuovo Testamento*. Introduzione alla critica testuale (Percorsi e traguardi biblici; Leumann 1994) 76-98.
>
> TREBOLLE BARRERA, J., *La Biblia judía y la Biblia cristiana*. Introducción a la historia de la Biblia (Madrid 1993) 315-350, 367-385.

2.1 *Greek*

Aquila, Symmachus, and Theodotion in:

F. FIELD (ed.), *Origenis Hexaplorum quae supersunt, sive, Veterum interpretum Graecorum in totum Vetus Testamentum fragmenta* (Oxonii 1875, Hildesheim 1964) I-II.

C. E. Cox, *Hexaplaric Materials Preserved in the Armenian Version* (SBL.SCSt 21; Atlanta 1986).

E. Klostermann, "Die Mailänder Fragmente der Hexapla", *ZAW* 16 (1896) 334-337.

L. Lütkemann – A. Rahlfs, *Hexaplarische Randnoten zu Isaias 1–16 aus einer Sinai-Handschrift* (MSU 1/6; Berlin 1915) 231-386.

G. Mercati, "Frammenti di Aquila o di Symmachus?", *RB* 8 (1911) 266-272.

——— (ed.), *Psalterii hexapli reliquiae.* I. Codex rescriptus Bybliothecae Ambrosianae O 39 sup. phototypice expressus et transcriptus (CEIBD 8; Città del Vaticano 1958).

A. Schenker, *Hexaplarische Psalmenbruchstücke.* Die hexaplarischen Psalmenfragmente der Handschriften Vaticanus graecus 752 und Canonicianus graecus 62 (OBO 8; Freiburg – Göttingen 1975).

———, *Psalmen in den Hexapla.* Erste kritische und vollständige Ausgabe der hexaplarischen Fragmente auf dem Rande der Handschrift Ottobonianus graecus 398 zu den Ps 24–32 (StT 295; Città del Vaticano 1982).

It is possible to find more information in:

Barthélemy, D., *Les devanciers d'Aquila.* Première publication intégrale du texte des fragments du Dodécaprophéton (VT.S 10; Leiden 1963).

———, "Qui est Symmaque?", *CBQ* 36 (1974) 451-465.

Busto Saiz, J. R., *La traducción de Símaco en el libro de los Salmos* (TECC 22; Madrid 1978).

Fernández Marcos, N., *Introducción a las versiones griegas de la Biblia* (TECC 23; Madrid 1979; TECC 64; Madrid ²1998) 119-162.

Frederick Field's Prolegomena to Origenis Hexaplorum quae supersunt, sive, Veterum interpretum Graecorum in totum

Vetus Testamentum fragmenta (Translated and Annotated by
G. J. NORTON – C. HARDEN) (CRB 62; Paris 2005).

GRABBE, L. L., "Aquila's Translation and Rabbinic Exegesis", *JJS*
33 (1982) 527-536.

HYVÄRINEN, K., *Die Übersetzung von Aquila* (CB.OT 10; Lund
1977).

MERCATI, G., *Psalterii hexapli reliquiae*. I. Osservazioni – Com-
mento critico al testo dei frammenti esaplari (CEIBD 8; Città
del Vaticano 1965).

ROBERTS, B. J., *The Old Testament Text and Versions*. The Hebrew
Text in Transmission and the History of the Ancient Versions
(Cardiff 1951) 120-127.

SALVESEN, A. (ed.), *Origen's Hexapla and Fragments*. Papers Pre-
sented at the Rich Seminar on the Hexapla, Oxford Centre for
Hebrew and Jewish Studies, 25th July – 3rd August 1994
(TSAJ 58; Tübingen 1998).

SILVERSTONE, A. E., *Aquila and Onkelos* (PUM.SL 1; Manchester
1931).

VENETZ, H.-J., *Das Quinta des Psalteriums*. Ein Beitrag zur Sep-
tuaginta- und Hexaplaforschung (CMas.EC 2; Hildesheim
1974).

2.2 *Aramaic*

A. SPERBER (ed.), *The Bible in Aramaic Based on Old Manuscripts
and Printed Texts* (Leiden 1959-1973) I-IV.

Brill, the publishing house of Leiden, issued the following volumes:

1. The Pentateuch According to Targum Onkelos (1959); 2. The
Former Prophets According to Targum Jonathan (1959); 3. The
Latter Prophets According to Targum Jonathan (1962); 4a. The
Hagiographa. Transition from Translation to Midrash (1968);
4b. The Targum and the Hebrew Bible (1973).

It is the best critical edition of the Targumim on the Pentateuch, Josh, Judg, 1–2 Sam, 1–2 Kgs, Isa, Jer, Ezek, Hos, Joel, Amos, Hab, Jonah, Mic, Nah, Hab, Zeph, Hag, Zech, Mal, 1–2 Chr, Ru, Cant, Lam, Qoh, Esth.

A. DÍEZ MACHO (ed.), *Neophyti 1*. Targum palestinense, Ms de la Biblioteca Vaticana. Edición príncipe; introducción y versión castellana (Textos y estudios 7-11; Madrid 1968-1978).

The following volumes were released:

1. Génesis. Edición príncipe, introducción general y versión castellana (1968); 2. Éxodo. Edición príncipe, introducción y versión castellana (1970); 3. Levítico. Edición príncipe, introducción y versión castellana (1971); 4. Números. Edición príncipe, introducción y versión castellana (1974); 5. Deuteronomio. Edición príncipe, introducción y versión castellana (1978); 6. Apéndices (Textos y estudios 20; 1979).

Apart from the Aramaic text, the work includes three translations: Spanish by A. Díez Macho; French by R. Le Déaut; English by M. McNamara and M. Maher. When used for scholarly purposes, the readings of this edition require further verification.

2.3 *Latin*

For information about the Latin versions see, e.g.:

CIMOSA, M., *Guida allo studio della Bibbia latina*. Dalla Vetus Latina, alla Vulgata, alla Nova Vulgata (SuPa 14; Roma 2008) I.

For an evaluative bibliography with a description of Latin translations, see:

BOGAERT, P.-M., "Bulletin de la Bible latine. VII. Première série. Deuxième série. Troisième série. Quatrième série. Cinquième série. Sixième série. Septième série. Huitième série", *RBen* 105 (1995) 200-238; 106 (1996) 386-412; 108 (1998) 359-

386; 110 (2000) 135-155; 112 (2002) 152-175; 114 (2004)
179-201; 116 (2006) 133-163; 118 (2008) 148-170.

2.3.1 Vetus Latina (VL)

*Vetus latina: Die Reste der altlateinischen Bibel nach Petrus Sabatier
neu gesammelt und herausgegeben von der Erzabtei Beuron*
(Freiburg i.B. 1949-).

The whole work will be issued in 27 volumes.

To date, the following volumes have been published: Gen, Ru, Est,
Wis, parts of Sir, Isa, Rom, 1 Cor, Eph, Phil, Col, 1–2 Thess, 1–2 Tim,
Titus, Phlm, Heb, Jas, 1–2 Pet, 1–3 John, Rev.

For those parts in which the Beuron edition is incomplete, it is
possible to use the work by Pierre Sabatier:

P. SABATIER (ed.), *Bibliorum sacrorum latinae versiones antiquae seu
Vetus Italica* (Remis 1743-1749) I-III.

The four Gospels were edited by A. Jülicher and W. Matzkow. In
the second edition of the first three volumes, K. Aland replaced
Matzkow.

A. JÜLICHER et al. (ed.), *Itala.* Das Neue Testament in altlateinischer
Überlieferung. I. Matthäus-Evangelium; II. Markus-Evangelium;
III. Lukas-Evangelium; IV. Johannes-Evangelium (Berlin 1938,
²1972; 1940, ²1970; 1954, ²1976; 1963).

There are also two monographs that contain the text of Maccabees
and Paralipomena:

D. DE BRUYNE (ed.), *Les anciennes traductions latines des Macha-
bées* (AMar 4; [Denée] 1932);

R. WEBER (ed.), *Les anciennes versions latines du deuxième livre des
Paralipomènes* (CBLa 8; Rome 1949).

2.3.2 Vulgate

Biblia sacra iuxta latinam Vulgatam versionem ad codicum fidem... cura et studio monachorum abbatiae pontificiae s. Hieronymi in Urbe ordinis sancti Benedicti edita (Romae 1926-1995) I-XVIII.

It is a critical edition of the entire OT Vulgate. This monumental work, furnished with an extensive critical apparatus, has a great importance for the history of the Vulgate and for the textual criticism of the Bible.

R. WEBER et al. (ed.), *Biblia sacra iuxta vulgatam versionem* (Stuttgart 1969) I-II (in one volume ⁴1994).

This critical edition presents the Latin version of the OT and NT books (protocanonical and deuterocanonical) and, in an appendix the apocryphal texts of the Prayer of Manasseh, 3–4 Ezra, Psalm 151, and the Epistle to the Laodiceans. The fourth edition takes into account the complete critical edition of the OT Vulgate of the Benedictines of San Girolamo, Rome, and revised the apparatus of the following books: Wisdom, the Minor Prophets, 1–2 Maccabees, Titus, Philemon, Hebrews.

Post-Tridentine editions:

> Sixtine: *Biblia sacra vulgatae editionis ad concilii Tridentini praescriptum emendata et a Sixto V. P. M. recognita et approbata* (Romae 1590).
> Sixtine-Clementine: *Biblia sacra vulgatae editionis Sixti Quinti Pont. Max. iussu recognita atque edita* (Romae 1592).

The Vulgate is closely connected with Jerome, who offered to the Latin Church a corrected version of the Latin Bible which replaced versions that had circulated containing errors. However Jerome did not translate every single book: e.g. Bar, Letter of Jeremiah (= Bar 6),

Sir, Wis, 1–2 Macc, (parts of) Esth, while in the NT Jerome revised the existing translations (not VL) of the Gospels.

For more information about the history of the Vulgate see, e.g.:

> BERGER, S., *Histoire de la Vulgate pendant les premiers siècles du moyen âge* (Nancy 1893).
>
> GARCÍA-MORENO, A., *La Neovulgata*. Precedentes y actualidad (Pamplona 1986) 1-125.
>
> KAULEN, F. P., *Geschichte der Vulgata* (Mainz 1868).
>
> PEEBLES, B. P., "Bible. Latin Versions", *NCE* II, 436-457, esp. 439-454.
>
> REICHMANN, V. et al., "Zur Geschichte der Vulgata", *TRE* VI, 178-181.
>
> ROBERTS, B. J., *The Old Testament Text and Versions*. The Hebrew Text in Transmission and the History of the Ancient Versions (Cardiff 1951) 247-265.

2.3.3 Jerome's Iuxta Hebraeos Psalter

J. M. HARDEN (ed.), *Psalterium iuxta Hebraeos Hieronymi* (London 1922).

H. DE SAINTE-MARIE (ed.), *Sancti Hieronymi Psalterivm ivxta Hebraeos* (CBLa 11; Città del Vaticano 1954).

In addition to the introduction by H. de Sainte-Marie (pp. v-lxx), for further information about the *iuxta Hebraeos* Psalter, see:

> ECKER, J., *Psalterium juxta Hebraeos Hieronymi in seinem Verhältnis zu Masora, Septuaginta, Vulgata mit Berücksichtigung der übrigen alten Versionen* (Trier 1906).
>
> ESTIN, C., *Les psautiers de Jérôme à la lumière des traductions juives antérieures* (CBLa 15; Roma 1984).
>
> MARKS, J., *Der textkritische Wert des Psalterium Hieronymi iuxta Hebraeos* (Winterthur 1956).

2.4 *Syriac*

Bibliography:

DIRKSEN, P. B., *An Annotated Bibliography of the Peshiṭta of the Old Testament* (MPIL 5; Leiden – New York – København – Köln 1989).

YOUSIF, P., "Syriaques (Versions). Bibliographie 1955-2000", *DBS* XIII, 828-875.

For further information about Syriac versions, see:

BROCK, S. P., "Translating the New Testament into Syriac (Classical and Modern)", *The Interpretation of the Bible*. The International Symposium in Slovenia (ed. J. KRAŠOVEC) (JSOT.S 289; Sheffield 1998) 371-385.

GORDON, R. P., "The Syriac Old Testament. Provenance, Perspective and Translation Technique", *The Interpretation of the Bible*. The International Symposium in Slovenia (ed. J. KRAŠOVEC) (JSOT.S 289; Sheffield 1998) 355-369.

ROBERTS, B. J., *The Old Testament Text and Versions*. The Hebrew Text in Transmission and the History of the Ancient Versions (Cardiff 1951) 214-228.

TREBOLLE BARRERA, J., *La Biblia judía y la Biblia cristiana.* Introducción a la historia de la Biblia (Madrid 1993) 378-382.

2.4.1 The Old Testament

THE PESHIṬTA INSTITUTE (ed.), *The Old Testament in Syriac According to the Peshiṭta Version* (Leiden 1972-).

This multivolume critical edition is still being published. The type used is unvocalized Estrangelo. The Codex Ambrosianus of Milan, probably from the VII c., is the base text of this edition, because it "is for practical reasons most suitable because of its age, completeness, clear hand and accessibility, and of which there is a facsimile edition prepared by A. M. Ceriani"[2]. Scribal errors and non-original readings in the Ambrosian text were corrected with support of other MSS. The following parts have been published:

> Specimen editionis (*Canticum Canticorum – Tobit – IV Esra*) (ed. J. A. EMERTON – J. C. H. LEBRAM – R. J. BIDAWID, 1966); 1/1. *Praefatio, Liber Genesis – Liber Exodi* (ed. T. JANSMA – M. D. KOSTER, 1977); 1/2. + 2/1b. *Leviticus – Numeri – Deuteronomium + Iosue* (ed. D. J. LANE et al., 1991); 2/1a. *Liber Job* (ed. L. G. RIGNELL, 1982); 2/2. *Liber Judicum – Liber Samuelis* (ed. P. B. DIRKSEN – P. A. H. DE BOER, 1978); 2/3. *Liber Psalmorum* (ed. D. M. WALTER, 1980); 2/4. *Liber Regum* (ed. H. GOTTLIEB – E. HAMMERSHAIMB, 1976); 2/5. *Proverbia – Sapientia Salomonis – Ecclesiastes – Canticum Canticorum* (ed. A. A. DI LELLA et al., 1979); 3/1. *Liber Isaiae* (ed. S. P. BROCK, 1987); 3/3. *Liber Ezechielis* (ed. M. J. MULDER, 1985); 3/4. *Dodekapropheton – Daniel–Bel–Draco* (ed. A. GELSTON et al., 1980); 4/2. *Chronicles* (ed. R. P. GORDON – P. B. DIRKSEN, 1998); 4/3. *Apocalypsis Baruch – IV Ezrae* (ed. S. DEDERING – R. J. BIDAWID, 1973); 4/6. *Cantica sive Odae – Oratio Manasse – Psalmi Apocryphi – Psalmi Salomonis – Tobit – I(III) Ezrae* (ed. H. SCHNEIDER et al., 1972).

N. CALDUCH-BENAGES – J. FERRER – J. LIESEN (ed.), *La Sabiduría del Escriba*. Edición diplomática de la versión siriaca del libro de Ben Sira según el Códice Ambrosiano, con traducción española e inglesa / *Wisdom of the Scribe*. Diplomatic Edition of the Syriac Version of the Book of Ben Sira According to Codex Ambrosianus with Translations in Spanish and English (Biblioteca Midrásica 26; Estella 2003).

This diplomatic edition of Ecclesiasticus, preserved in the most ancient manuscript of the Syriac text (Codex Ambrosianus), tries to

---

[2] P. A. H. DE BOER, praefatio to T. JANSMA – M. D. KOSTER (ed.), *Praefatio, Liber Genesis – Liber Exodi* (OTSy 1/1; Leiden 1977) vii.

fill a persistent absence of a critical edition on the part of The Peshiṭṭa Institute, caused by many difficulties connected with the text of Ben Sira. For their publication, the editors made use of the photolithographic reproduction of the Codex Ambrosianus, prepared by A. M. CERIANI (ed.), *Translatio Syra Pescitto Veteris Testamenti ex codice Ambrosiano sec. fere VI photolithographice edita* (Mediolani 1883) II, 458-485.

2.4.2 The New Testament

P. E. PUSEY – G. H. GWILLIAM (ed.), *Tetraeuangelium sanctum juxta simplicem Syrorum versionem ad fidem codicum, massorae, editionum denuo recognitum* (Oxonii 1901, Eugen, OR 2004).

The critical edition of the Syriac version (Peshiṭṭa) of the Gospel. The text is bilingual Syriac and Latin. For the Syriac the Serto type is used. The text is followed by a list of Syriac codices and by Eusebian Canon tables. The critical apparatus is mixed, as it contains notes of various quality.

The New Testament in Syriac (London 1962).

Edition by R. Kilgour was published using Serto characters by the British and Foreign Bible Society. The text of the Gospel reproduces a revised version prepared by G. H. Gwilliam. Successively, other NT books were added to the Gospels.

II. Bibliographic Research

In this chapter some instruments for preparing a bibliography are briefly presented. Although the difference between that which is traditionally or electronically published is slight, it is advantageous here to categorize items according to their original form. A final section also provides a list of some useful Internet sites, whether or not these have been cited in the previous sections.

1. Printed Resources for Research

1.1 *Elenchus of Biblica (EBB)*

Elenchus bibliographicus biblicus (Roma 1920-1984);
Elenchus of Biblica (Roma 1985-).

Prepared by the Pontifical Biblical Institute, this work contains the most comprehensive biblical bibliography. However, its publication suffers a delay of some years. The most recent volume covers the year 2005.

From 1920 to 1967, the *Elenchus* was included as a part of the periodical *Biblica*, whereas from 1968 onward it has been published separately.

The information is divided in various sections:

> Bibliographica; Introductio; Textus, Versiones, Exegesis totius VT vel cum NT; Libri historici VT; Libri didactici VT; Libri prophetici VT; NT exegesis generalis; Commentarii NT: Evangelia; Actus Apostolorum; Corpus Johanneum; Paulus, alii; Theologia biblica; Philologia biblica; Postbiblica; Religiones parabiblicae; Historia Medii Orientis Biblici; Archaeologia; Geographia biblica; Historia Scientiae Biblicae.

This division does not always permit ready access to the entries. However, this obstacle can be surmounted with the support of the indexes of authors, sites, vocabulary (Akkadian, Greek, Hebrew...), and scriptural citations.

Arrangement of the individual entries. Each entry has a number. Additional information about a particular work can be indicated by a letter: "F" (Festschrift), "D" (dissertation), "E" (editor), "M" (memorial)[1], "R" (review), or "T" (translation).

A *cross reference* between two entries in the same volume is marked, for example, in this way: 240, where the number "240" indicates the position of the entry. The cross reference to an entry which is in a different volume, is quoted, e.g.: 9,5906, where the digit "9" indicates, in this case, the volume number, while the number "5906" is the entry number in that volume.

1.2 *Zeitschrifteninhaltsdienst Theologie (ZID)*

Zeitschrifteninhaltsdienst Theologie (Tübingen 1975-2000).

The Universitätsbibliothek Tübingen released *ZID* in fascicles that provided the titles from both theological and biblical periodicals, and it has kept pace with the publications.

There are two electronic versions of *ZID*:

Zeitschrifteninhaltsdienst Theologie (Tübingen 1997/2-2001) [CD-ROM].

Index theologicus (Tübingen 2002-) [CD-ROM].

From 2001 onward, *ZID* is accessible only via the Internet, since the printed version is no longer published:

http://www.ixtheo.de/zid-curr

---

[1] This reference is situated in the index of names, and it indicates the mention of a person in the title of a work.

1.3 *Neuerwerbungen Theologie und allgemeine Religionswissenschaft (NThAR)*

Neuerwerbungen Theologie und allgemeine Religionswissenschaft (Tübingen 1981-2000).

NThAR was published by the Universitätsbibliothek Tübingen and it offered a list of books which dealt with theological and biblical topics, and was continually updated.

This periodical, also from 2001 onward, is accessible only via the Internet:

http://www-work.ub.uni-tuebingen.de/cgi-bin/theologie.cgi

1.4 *Catalog of the École Biblique of Jerusalem*

Catalogue de la Bibliothèque de l'École Biblique de Jérusalem (Paris 1986) I-XII.

The Dominicans' Library in Jerusalem contains more than 130,000 volumes and 400 periodicals. This patrimony of books presents mostly the contributions of biblical exegesis, archeology, Ancient Near East languages and literature.

The catalog is accessible online:

http://www.ebaf.edu:8080

An electronic version of the catalog is also available:

A Guide to the Catalogue de l'École Biblique et Archéologique Française on CD (ed. S. P. SMITH) (Jerusalem – Oak Harbor, WA 2000) [CD-ROM].

Issued by the École Biblique et Archéologique Française and Logos Research Systems, Inc., this CD-ROM provides a list of titles, which are organized by subjects, books, and authors.

1.5 *International Review of Biblical Studies /*
Internationale Zeitschriftenschau für Bibelwissenschaft
und Grenzgebiete (IZBG)

Internationale Zeitschriftenschau für Bibelwissenschaft und Grenz-
gebiete (Stuttgart 1951-1952; Düsseldorf 1953-1999).
International Review of Biblical Studies (Leiden 1999-).

Initially, this review was published by the Katholisches Bibelwerk
(vol. 1) and subsequently by the Patmos Verlag (vols. 2-45). From
vol. 46 onward, it has been issued by Brill. Each annual volume
includes ca. 2,000 English, German or French abstracts and summaries of articles and books. They deal with the Bible and other literature, as e.g. Qumran, Pseudepigrapha, Non-canonical gospels, and
ancient Near Eastern writings. The single abstracts or summaries are
attainable by means of the index of authors and the detailed table of
contents. From 1980 onward, B. Lang has edited this work that is elaborated by an international team of collaborators. They make use of
over 300 periodicals and series for their summaries. The last volume,
54, covers the year 2007-2008.

1.6 *Old Testament Abstracts (OTAbs)*

Old Testament Abstracts. A Thrice-Yearly Bibliography of Literature
    Relating to the OT (Washington, DC 1978-).
Old Testament Abstracts on CD-ROM (Evanston, IL 1996) [CD-
    ROM].
Old Testament Abstracts on CD-ROM (Ipswich, MA 2005) [CD-
    ROM].

OTAbs is published by The Catholic Biblical Association of America, The Catholic University of America, Washington, DC, and *ATLA*
(see below § 2.3). It contains summaries with short explanation in
English of articles and books concerning the OT and the Ancient Near

East texts, history and archeology, and as well as biblical theology, literature from the intertestamental period and the apocrypha. Currently, this service provides about 40,000 records, and it is annually updated with more than 2,000 new records. The online version is available at:

http://www.ebscohost.com/thisTopic.php?marketID=1&topicID=121

1.7 *New Testament Abstracts (NTAbs)*

New Testament Abstracts (Cambridge, MA 1956-).
New Testament Abstracts. Volumes 29-48 (Cambridge, MA 2004) [CD-ROM].

NTAbs is published by Weston Jesuit School of Theology, Cambridge, MA, in collaboration with *ATLA*. There are short, though useful summaries of articles and books concerning the NT and its historical period. The work focuses particularly on contributions on the NT, Gospels, letters, biblical theology, ancient rabbinic literature, history, and the Greco-Roman period. The database with more than 38,000 records is available at:

http://www.ebscohost.com/thisTopic.php?marketID=1&topicID=180

1.8 *Review of Biblical Literature (RBLit)*

From 1999 onward, the *Review of Biblical Literature* is published annually by the Society of Biblical Literature, Atlanta, and contains reviews of recent biblical studies.
It is available via Internet:

http://www.bookreviews.org

2. Electronic Tools for Research

LUBETSKI, E., "Online Resources for Biblical Studies. A Sampling",
   CurResB 8 (2000) 134-146.
TOV, E., "Electronic Resources Relevant to the Textual Criticism of
   Hebrew Scripture", http://rosetta.reltech.org/TC/vol08/Tov2003.
   html [accessed, January 9, 2009].

2.1 *BILDI*

Bibelwissenschaftliche Literaturdokumentation Innsbruck is a web
site of the Institut für Bibelwissenschaften und Fundamentaltheologie
of the University of Innsbruck:

   http://www.uibk.ac.at/bildi

BILDI lists titles of biblical studies (ca. 134,000 at the end of 2006)
that derive from periodicals and books, and enables one to search by
author, title, subject or biblical quotations, etc. *BILDI* collaborates
with the *Elenchus of Biblica*. The used abbreviations are those of
SCHWERTNER, *IATG²*, integrated by other studies.

2.2 *RAMBI*

רְשִׁימַת מַאֲמָרִים בְּמַדְּעֵי־הַיַּהֲדוּת / *The Index of Articles on Jewish Studies*

Provided by The Jewish National and University Library,
Jerusalem, this service offers a selective bibliography of scientific articles in various fields of Jewish studies and of those related to Israel.
The materials for the bibliography are selected from thousands of
periodicals and from collections of articles in Hebrew, Yiddish and
in modern European languages. *RAMBI* quotes second hand articles
as well:

   http://jnul.huji.ac.il/rambi

2.3 *ATLA*

American Theological Library Association, from 1946, Chicago.

This is a professional association which provides programs, products and services as an aid to theological and religious libraries. The association provides *ATLA Religion Database*, currently with more than 1.4 million records. There are online and CD-ROM versions of this database.

ATLA's service is available for a fee at:

http://www.atla.com

2.4 *BiBIL*

Bibliographie biblique informatisée de Lausanne of the Institut Romand des Sciences Bibliques of the University of Lausanne:

http://www.bibil.net

From 1987 onward, *BiBIL* offers access to biblical titles (ca. 70,000 in the fall of 2005), systematically classified, which can also be searched by subject.

2.5 *BSW*

Biblical Studies on the Web (http://www.bsw.org) presents recent biblical studies. Apart from different remarks and publications on the Internet, it offers an interface that permits one to search some libraries: Online Biblical Articles Library, Library of Congress Online Catalog, Union of Universities in the UK and Ireland, University of Innsbruck; Pontifical Biblical Institute, Rome:

http://www.bsw.org/index.php?l=60 or http://mls.bsw.org

3. Internet Sites

Addresses of some web sites that mostly offer bibliographical information are listed below along with other URLs useful for biblical research.

http://biblioteca.biblico.it
http://www.ebaf.edu:8080
http://opac.ub.uni-tuebingen.de
http://www.uibk.ac.at/bildi
http://jnul.huji.ac.il/rambi
http://www.bibil.net
http://www.bsw.org
http://www.ixtheo.de/zid-curr
http://www-work.ub.uni-tuebingen.de/cgi-bin/theologie.cgi
http://www.atla.com
http://www.bookreviews.org
http://www.sbl-site.org
http://www.ntgateway.com
http://www.bibleresearch-rome.org
http://bibelarbeit.net
http://www.airtonjo.com
http://www.aril.org/Bible.html
http://www.bible-researcher.com
http://www.communiobiblica.org
http://www.acs.ucalgary.ca/~lipton/biblio.html
http://ccat.sas.upenn.edu/~jtreat/rs/resources.html
http://www-user.uni-bremen.de/~wie/bibel.html
http://www.lib.cam.ac.uk/Taylor-Schechter/GOLD
http://www.e-daf.com/index.asp
http://198.62.75.1/www1/ofm/sbf/edit/LAindex.html
http://www.sbible.boom.ru/indexe.htm
http://www.usedbooksearch.co.uk

III. REFERENCE WORKS

In this chapter some works of primary interest for biblical studies are indicated: concordances, synopses, lexicons, grammars, dictionaries, etc. Some of the works cited by J. A. Fitzmyer[1] and J. L. Ska[2] have been used here.

1. Concordances

A biblical concordance is an alphabetical inventory of different words or concepts. The individual entries, placed in their immediate context, are marked by a reference to the books, chapters, and verses. There are two kinds of concordances: a *verbal* concordance (index of words), and a *topical* concordance (index of subjects). From their appearance in the Middle Ages, concordances have been a valued tool, permitting one to find an exact quotation of a passage, or to acquaint oneself, in an organic and complete way, with fundamental biblical ideas or with particularly important topics[3].

1.1 *Traditionally Published Concordances*

1.1.1 Hebrew Old Testament

G. LISOWSKY, *Konkordanz zum hebräischen Alten Testament* (Stuttgart ²1958, 1981).

[1] *An Introductory Bibliography for the Study of Scripture* (SubBi 3; Roma ³1990).

[2] "Bibliografia biblica basilare dell'A.T. / Old Testament Basic Bibliography", http://www.biblico.it/doc-vari/ska_bibl.html [accessed January 10, 2009].

[3] Cf. A. PENNA, "Concordanze bibliche", *EC* IV, 185.

The author used the text of *BHK* to draw up his concordance. All of the verbs and nouns of the Hebrew text are covered; verbs are presented according to conjugation, whereas nouns are grouped on the basis of their function as subject or object of the phrase. Principal prepositions, particles, interjections, numerals are not listed. There is a list of all proper names. The words are translated into German, English, and classical Latin.

S. MANDELKERN, *Veteris Testamenti concordantiae hebraicae atque chaldaicae* (Berlin ²1939; Graz ²1955) I-II.

The best Hebrew and Aramaic concordance. It translates words into Latin; verbs are divided according to their forms, and nouns are reported with the suffixes and prepositions as well.

A. EVEN-SHOSHAN, *A New Concordance of the Bible*. Thesaurus of the Language of the Bible: Hebrew and Aramaic Roots, Words, Proper Names, Phrases and Synonyms (Jerusalem 1990).

This concordance was published in one, two, or three volumes. The author produced an alphabetical catalog of all the words of the Bible, according to the forms quoted in the modern lexicons and not according to the roots. He numbered the occurrences and also listed the prepositions and the syntagmas.

1.1.2 Greek Old Testament

E. HATCH – H. A. REDPATH, *A Concordance to the Septuagint and to Other Greek Versions of the Old Testament (Including the Apocryphal Books)* (Grand Rapids, MI ²1998).

The concordance covers the whole Greek OT with the deutero-canonical books, apocrypha, and the hexaplaric versions of Aquila, Symmachus and Theodotion, drawn from the work of F. Field. It is based exclusively on the MSS A, B, S as well as on MS R, from the Sistine edition: *Vetus Testamentum iuxta septuaginta ex auctoritate*

Sixti V Pont. Max. editum (Romae 1587). For this reason, the references should be compared with the Göttingen edition for possible variants.
Hebrew equivalents of Greek words are numbered. The corresponding reference number indicates a likely Hebrew meaning. This proposed identification should be used with caution. Proper names are listed separately.
Moreover, this edition also contains the contributions by R. A. KRAFT – E. TOV, "Introductory Essay" and by T. MURAOKA, "Hebrew/Aramaic Index to the Septuagint", which is an important tool, indicating all of the various Septuagintal translations from the Hebrew or Aramaic.

1.1.3 Greek New Testament

K. ALAND, *Vollständige Konkordanz zum griechischen Neuen Testament unter Zugrundelegung aller kritischen Textausgaben und des Textus Receptus* (Berlin – New York 1983, 1978) I-II.

This is the most complete, computer-generated concordance of the NT based on NA[26]. Volume I, parts 1-2, lemmatizes words, whereas volume II offers statistics (including *hapax legomena*) and the verbal forms.

H. BACHMANN – W. A. SLABY, *Konkordanz zum Novum Testamentum Graece von Nestle–Aland, 26. Auflage und zum Greek New Testament, 3ʳᵈ Edition / Concordance to the Novum Testamentum Graece of Nestle–Aland, 26ᵗʰ Edition, and to the Greek New Testament, 3ʳᵈ Edition* (Berlin – New York ³1987).

The first (1980) and second edition (1985) are known as:

> *Computer-Konkordanz zum Novum Testamentum Graece von Nestle–Aland 26., Auflage und zum Greek New Testament, 3ʳᵈ Edition.*

Elaborated by the Institut für Neutestamentlichte Textforschung in Münster with the collaboration of H. Bachmann and W. A. Slaby, this concordance is a concise form (in one volume) of *Vollständige Konkordanz* by K. Aland. Twenty-nine of the most frequent words (ἀλλά, ἀπό, καί, μή, ὁ...) are omitted, but there is a list of passages containing them (cf. appendix col. 1*-64*).

W. F. MOULTON – A. S. GEDEN, *Concordance to the Greek New Testament* (Fully Revised) (ed. I. H. MARSHALL) (London – New York ⁶2002).

The user-friendly size, good categorization of the usage of many words, indication of all significant textual variants and quotation of the Hebrew biblical passages quoted in NT Greek are positive qualities of this concordance. Since the former editions are not free from errors, a new revision was necessary. The work began in 1987. Directed by I. H. Marshall, the work of revising was done by graduate students at the University of Aberdeen.

The concordance is based on four editions of the Greek text of the NT: *GNT*⁴; C. VON TISCHENDORF, *Novum Testamentum graece* (Leipzig ⁸1875); B. F. WESTCOTT – F. J. A. HORT, *The New Testament in the Original Greek* (Cambridge – London 1881); A. SOUTER, *Novum Testamentum graece* (Oxford ²1947). Differently from the previous editions (whose citations are taken from the text of B. F. Westcott and F. J. A. Hort), this publication utilized the text of *GNT*⁴, complemented by the cited editions. All words have been checked anew. Superscript numerals indicate a particular usage of a single word. As with earlier publications, there is no presentation of common Greek particles: ὁ, καί, δέ.

P. HOFFMANN – T. HIEKE – U. BAUER, *Synoptic Concordance*. A Greek Concordance to the First Three Gospels in Synoptic Arrangement, Statistically Evaluated, Including Occurrences in Acts / Griechische Konkordanz zu den ersten drei Evangelien in

synoptischer Darstellung, statistisch ausgewertet, mit Berück-
sichtigung der Apostelgeschichte (Berlin – New York 1999-
2000) I-IV.

This work is based on the text of NA^{27}, without its critical apparatus.

The concordances mentioned above indicated the usage of each
word separately. They did not always indicate the idiosyncrasies of an
individual Gospel. In order to achieve this goal, it was necessary to
compile the concordance so as to put before the reader the occurrences
of the words in a synoptic manner: references to the texts and statistics, the material of the Double and Triple Traditions, and the specific
characteristics of each evangelist.

This tool is useful for the study of the vocabulary and style of
a synoptic Gospel and for discovering its redactional interests and
theological purposes.

1.1.4 Targum

J. C. DE MOOR et al., *A Bilingual Concordance to the Targum of the
Prophets* (Leiden 1995-2005) I-XXI.

This bilingual concordance gives a Hebrew equivalent of each
Aramaic word as far as it is possible to establish the correspondence
between them. It is intended as a study, which, in the future – when
a concordance of each existing Targum is available – could help to analyze various relationships between different Targumim. The concordance could help to discover the strata of tradition in the Targum of
the books of the Former and Latter Prophets.

The project was realized with the support of the computer pro-
grammer P. van der Wal at by the Theologische Universiteit van de
Gereformeerde Kerken in Nederland, in Kampen. For the Hebrew
text, the *BHS* was used, whereas for the Targum, A. Sperber's *The
Bible in Aramaic* was used.

Directed by J. C. de Moor and in collaboration with T. Finley,
B. Grossfeld, F. Sepmeijer, E. van Staalduine-Sulman, A. Houtman,
and W. Smelik, Brill has published the following volumes:

> 1. *Joshua* (ed. J. C. DE MOOR, 1995); 2. *Judges* (ed. W. SMELIK,
> 1996); 3-5. *Samuel* (ed. E. VAN STAALDUINE-SULMAN, 1996); 6-8.
> *Kings* (ed. B. GROSSFELD, 1997); 9-11. *Isaiah* (ed. J. C. DE MOOR,
> 2002); 12-14. *Jeremiah* (ed. F. SEPMEIJER, 1998); 15-17. *Ezekiel* (ed.
> T. FINLEY, 1999); 18-20. *The Twelve* (ed. A. HOUTMAN, 2003); 21.
> *Introduction, Additions and Corrections Indices* (ed. A. HOUTMAN –
> J. C. DE MOOR, 2005).

H. J. KASOVSKY, *Oẓar Leshon Targum Onkelos.* Concordance (Based
on the Version of the Targum Onkelos in the Pentateuch of Editio Sabioneta Anno 1557 (Revised by M. KOSOVSKY) (Jerusalem
1986) I-II.

This concordance may be particularly useful for scholarly
purposes. Consultation of this tool requires a good knowledge of
Aramaic/Hebrew.

1.1.5 Syriac New Testament

G. A. KIRAZ, *A Computer-generated Concordance to the Syriac New
Testament According to the British and Foreign Bible Society's
Edition* (Leiden – New York – Köln 1993) I-VI.

This work has roots in the electronic database *SEDRA* (*Syriac
Electronic Data Retrieval Archive*). To build it, the author used:
P. E. PUSEY – G. H. GWILLIAM (ed.), *Tetraeuangelium sanctum juxta
simplicem Syrorum versionem ad fidem codicum, massorae,
editionum denuo recognitum* (Oxonii 1901); unpublished materials
prepared by G. H. Gwilliam and J. Pinkerton (Acts, Jas, 1 Pet, 1 John,
Corpus Paolinum, Heb); J. GWYNN, *Remnants of the Later Syriac Versions of the Bible* (London 1909); IDEM, *The Apocalypse of St. John
in a Syriac Version Hitherto Unknown* (Dublin 1897). Volumes I-IV

contain the concordances of all lemmas; volume V offers proper names and lemmas according to their frequency (part 1); volume VI quotes lemmas according to their frequency (part 2), indexes, lexicographical order of nominal forms under each root, alphabetical list of all lexical words with their roots.

1.1.6 Ben Sira

R. SMEND, *Griechisch-syrisch-hebräischer Index zur Weisheit des Jesus Sirach* (Berlin 1907).

Following the alphabetical order of the Greek text of Sirach, this work offers the index of lemmas in Greek and, if extant, also in Syriac and Hebrew.

D. BARTHÉLEMY – O. RICKENBACHER, *Konkordanz zum Hebräischen Sirach mit syrisch-hebräischem Index* (Göttingen 1973).

The concordance follows the model of G. Lisowsky and K. G. Kuhn for the sequence of lemmas and that of S. Mandelkern for the presentation of each word. The tool is trilingual: Hebrew, Syriac, Greek. It makes use respectively of MSS A, B, C, D, E, M, of Codex Ambrosianus and of the Göttingen edition.

J.-M. AUWERS, *Concordance du Siracide* (Grec II et Sacra parallela) (CRB 58; Paris 2005).

Written in collaboration with É. Proksch-Strajtmann, the book fills out a lacuna of E. Hatch and H. A. Redpath, *A Concordance to the Septuagint*. The concordance includes actually 135 lines of Greek II (an amplified Greek text form of Ben Sira) from J. Ziegler's edition (Göttingen 1965; the lines are numbered according to this edition) and the lines that are known from the concordance by Hatch and Redpath, as well as other variants that were considered important. Attributed to John Damascene, the *Sacra parallela* contain an additional 28 lines, unknown by the Greek tradition, though the Latin tradition knew 15 of them. The numbering of the *Sacra parallela* is based on the edition of the Benedictines of San Girolamo, Rome. All 456 lemmas follow the arrangement of Hatch and Redpath.

1.1.7 Qumran

K. G. KUHN et al., *Konkordanz zu den Qumrantexten* (Göttingen 1960).

The work presents in alphabetical order lemmas of biblical and non biblical texts, found at Qumran up to the publication year of the concordance.

M. G. ABEGG Jr. et al., *The Dead Sea Scrolls Concordance.* The Non-Biblical Texts from Qumran (Leiden – Boston 2003) I/1-2.

Long-awaited, this work covers the whole qumranic material published in the series *Discoveries in the Judaean Desert* and also texts from the first and eleventh cave, published elsewhere. The individual words are analyzed from the linguistic point of view and placed in their context. The two parts (one: *alef–mem*, two: *nun–taw*) report the occurrence of about 134,000 words (with an English translation) listed in alphabetical order, not in that of the roots.

1.2 *Electronic Concordances*

BibleWorks 8.0 (Norfolk, VA 2008) [CD-ROM/DVD].

Software *BibleWorks* uses the text of *BHS, GNT*[4] (or NA[27]) and, for the LXX, A. Rahlfs' edition.

The second revision of *BibleWorks* 5.0 added the following works:

> L. KOEHLER – W. BAUMGARTNER – J. J. STAMM, *The Hebrew and Aramaic Lexicon of the Old Testament.* The Complete and Unabridged Fourth Edition (Leiden 2000) [CD-ROM];
> W. BAUER, *A Greek-English Lexicon of the New Testament and*

Other Early Christian Literature (Edited and Revised by F. W. DANKER) (Bellingham, WA ³2002) [CD-ROM].

BibleWorks 6.0 contains the Greek text of the NT by C. von Tischendorf with its entire apparatus; the works by Josephus Flavius with morphological analysis and English translation; the NT in Syriac (Peshiṭta), in square Hebrew characters and in Estrangelo; the various Targumim with morphological analysis; *Gesenius' Hebrew Grammar*; *Introduction to Biblical Hebrew Syntax* by B. K. Waltke and M. O'Connor; sectarian MSS from Qumran with morphological analysis; and the apostolic Fathers in Greek.

The improvement of this exegetical and biblical research software is now in its seventh edition (*BibleWorks* 7.0), which offers a new user interface, more Bible versions and reference tools.

Among other items, new databases contain: *A Greek-English Lexicon of the Septuagint* by J. Lust, E. Eynikel and K. Hauspie with the collaboration of G. Chamberlain; *Textual Commentary on the Greek New Testament* by B. M. Metzger; *A Concise Hebrew and Aramaic Lexicon of the Old Testament* by W. L. Holladay; *Greek Apostolic Fathers*, the morphological parsing by A. Gieniusz; *Textkritik des Neuen Testaments* by C. R. Gregory; *Works of Philo* (Greek Text, Morphology, and English Translation) edited by P. Borgen, K. Fuglseth, R. Skarsten.

For an additional fee, other modules are available. Among the databases are: the 9th Revised Edition of *A Greek-English Lexicon* by H. G. Liddell, R. Scott, H. S. Jones and R. McKenzie; *Greek Grammar of the New Testament and Other Early Christian Literature* by F. Blass, A. Debrunner and R. W. Funk; M. Zerwick's *Biblical Greek*; *CNTTS Critical Apparatus* of Center for New Testament Textual Studies in New Orleans; *Exegetical Dictionary of the New Testament* by H. Balz and G. Schneider; *Theological Dictionary of the New Testament (Abridged)*, edited by G. Kittel and G. Friedrich, and abridged by G. W. Bromiley.

In the fall of 2008 *BibleWorks* 8.0 was issued. Besides new search possibilities, the software adds more translations of the Bible (at present, there are more than 190 in the base package) and more than twenty other tools. It is worth mentioning, among them, H. von Soden's Greek New Testament, Vulgata Clementina 1598 with Glossa Ordinaria, OT apocrypha in Greek with morphological analysis and English translation (by C. Evans, or by R. H. Charles), two English translations of biblical and sectarian Qumran texts (*Dead Sea Scrolls. A New Translation* by M. O. Wise, M. G. Abegg Jr. and E. M. Cook; *The Dead Sea Scrolls Bible*. The Oldest Known Bible Translated for the First Time into English by M. Abegg Jr., P. Flint and E. Ulrich). The last, corrected edition of *A Grammar of Biblical Hebrew* by P. Joüon and T. Muraoka has been included along with *Greek Grammar beyond the Basics*. An Exegetical Syntax of the New Testament by D. B. Wallace, and other books. The morphological analysis of the Hebrew Bible has been improved and the Greek New Testament Diagrams has been completed.

A broad spectrum of contents and a more extensive search capability makes *BibleWorks* 8.0 a highly regarded electronic concordance.

For more information on this software, see:

http://www.bibleworks.com

Accordance 8 (Altamonte Springs, FL 2008) [CD-ROM/DVD].

Accordance for the first time was released in 1994 for Mac OS. This software is both a biblical concordance and a digital library destined to reach a larger audience. For this reason, OakTree Software, Inc. elaborated different commercial offers: Starter Package; Library Collection; Catholic Collection; Jewish Collection; Scholar's Collection. The latest two collections are particularly useful for Bible students and scholars who can personalize them selecting the necessary components among the remaining offers as well.

As *BibleWorks* 8.0, *Accordance 8* uses the text of *BHS*, *GNT*[4] (or NA[27]) and, for the LXX, A. Rahlfs' edition, and furnishes modern Bible translations (mostly English), lexicons, grammars, commentaries, dictionaries, maps and other tools. In addition to them, *Accordance 8* supports searching the Hebrew and Greek text for forms and lemmas.

A comprehensive comparison of the content of both programs is beyond the goal of this presentation. However, a brief signaling, as an example, of some *Accordance 8* features is reasonable. In it, the critical apparatus has been added to the text of *BHS* and NA[27]. Moreover, the software furnishes the Hebrew text of Ben Sira with grammatical analysis by M. G. Abegg Jr. and C. Toews along with an English translation; early Hebrew inscriptions with grammatical analysis and translation by W. Schniedewind; Greek NT papyri and some uncial MSS (א, B, D, W) with morphological analysis provided by A. Koivisto.

In the library division, the user can find inter alia: B. PORTEN – A. YARDENI, *The Textbook of Aramaic Documents from Ancient Egypt* (Jerusalem 1986-1999) I-IV, with morphological analysis and English translation; W. W. HALLO – K. Lawson YOUNGER Jr. (ed.), *The Context of Scripture*. Canonical Compositions, Monumental Inscriptions, and Archival Documents from the Biblical World (Leiden 1997-2002) I-III; E. JENNI – C. WESTERMANN (ed.), *Theological Lexicon of the Old Testament* (Peabody, MA 1997) I-III; D. N. FREEDMAN et al. (ed.), *The Anchor Yale Bible Dictionary on CD-ROM* (Bellingham, WA 2008) [CD-ROM]; C. SPICQ, *Theological Lexicon of the New Testament* (Peabody, MA 1994) I-III; G. F. HAWTHORNE et al. (ed.), *Dictionary of Paul and His Letters* (Downers Grove, IL – Leicester 1993); J.-L. CUNCHILLOS – J. P. VITA – J. A. ZAMORA, *Ugaritic Data Bank / Recurso electrónico*. Los textos (Novallas 2003) [CD-ROM]; Word Biblical Commentary and more other works.

Though *BibleWorks* 8.0 certainly offers a vast amount of modern Bible translations and slightly more numerous grammatical resources,

nevertheless, the analogous capacity of searching along with the morphological analysis and a much more developed digital library branch
are highly esteemed qualities of *Accordance 8*.

For detailed and full information, see:

http://www.accordancebible.com

1.3 *Statistical Data*

R. MORGENTHALER, *Statistik des neutestamentlichten Wortschatzes*
    (Zürich – Frankfurt a.M. 1958).

The work includes tables with statistical data of different kinds:

> a) A vocabulary of words in the NT according to their frequency
>   in books or in groups of books;
> b) Special words (pronouns, prepositions, composite verbs with
>   single or double prepositions and with prefixes, foreign
>   words);
> c) Words and vocabulary of each book;
> d) Different forms (nouns, verbs, proper nouns, adjectives, ad-
>   verbs, etc.) of each book;
> e) Numerical frequency of single words for each book of the
>   NT.

R. MORGENTHALER, *Statistische Synopse* (Zürich – Stuttgart 1971).

This synopsis offers statistical data for each tradition: Mark,
Q source, proper material of Matt, Luke, Mark, the materials of the
Double and Triple Traditions.

2. Synopses

A synopsis gathers parallel passages (of Gospels or other books) in synoptic tables, arranged in parallel columns or in some other way. This facilitates a comparison of the data[4].

2.1 *Gospels*

K. ALAND, *Synopsis quattuor Evangeliorum*. Locis parallelis evangeliorum apocryphorum et patrum adhibitis (Stuttgart [13]1988); Eng. tr. *Synopsis of the Four Gospels*. Greek-English Edition of the *Synopsis quattuor Evangeliorum* (New York – London [6]1983).

The work is based on the text of NA[26]. Compared to previous versions, this synopsis introduces extensive changes in the critical apparatus, which is more aligned with the tradition of Nestle – Aland, without identifying itself with it. Headings of single passages are quoted in German, Latin and English. The most important parallels from NT apocrypha and from some Church Fathers are given for a number of passages. K. Aland followed Matthean arrangement in the laying out of the parallel passages. This choice forced him to use references to indicate passages located in different places. The appendices contain the Coptic Gospel of Thomas and the texts of some Church Fathers (Papias, Justin, Irenaeus, et al.)

The English bilingual edition adopted the translation of the *Revised Standard Version*. The English apparatus includes variants of this version as well as those of the *American Version* and *Revised Version*. In the Greek section, the apparatus of NA[26] is used. It is extended, however, to include the recently discovered papyri and uncial MSS.

---

[4] G. LASSERRE, *Les synopses: élaboration et usage* (SubBi 19; Roma 1996), proposes a methodological reflection on synopses.

M.-É. BOISMARD – A. LAMOUILLE, *Synopsis graeca quattuor Evangeliorum* (Leuven – Paris 1986).

The synopsis essentially uses the Greek text of the Alexandrian tradition, preserved in MSS B, S, C, L, but adds, at times, witnesses from the Western text. The work respects the arrangement of each Gospel, but cites parallel passages, particularly when these are arranged differently from other Gospels. The critical apparatus is limited to the cases in which the chosen text differs from that of NA[26].

A. HUCK – H. GREEVEN, *Synopse der drei ersten Evangelien mit Beigabe der johanneischen Parallelstellen / Synopsis of the First Three Gospels with the Addition of the Johannine Parallels* (Tübingen [13]1981).

H. Greeven completely reworked the twelfth edition of 1975, which was a reprint of the ninth edition of 1936. As the base of his synopsis, H. Greeven proposes a new and personal recension of the Greek text of the Gospels. The apparatus correctly quotes variants of other critics.

A. POPPI, *Sinossi quadriforme dei quattro vangeli*. Greco-italiano. I. Testo (Padova [2]1999).

The volume has developed the content of the first edition: *Sinossi dei quattro vangeli* (Padova 1992). Modified in some points, the Codex Vaticanus is the basis of the publication. *GNT*[4] is used for comparison. The work is composed of four parts; each uses one Gospel (Matt, Mark, Luke, John) as a main text. This guiding text is then accompanied by parallel passages from the other Gospels. The Italian translation faithfully follows the Greek text. Different underline styles (dashed, continuous or dotted) emphasize the materials of the Double and Triple Traditions, and the minor agreements between the Gospels.

A. POPPI, *Nuova sinossi dei quattro vangeli*. Greco-italiano. I. Testo (Padova 2006).

Even though this work is fundamentally based on two previous synopses by the author, some relevant changes have been inserted. The *Nuova sinossi* is ca. 190 pages shorter than the *Sinossi quadriforme*. The cursive presentation of each Gospel was abandoned and the pericopes are arranged chronologically: Johannine and Lukan Prologue, the Gospels of the Infancy, public ministry, revelation of the cross, passion and resurrection. The Codex Vaticanus B remained the textual basis of this edition. In it, the author took into account new scientific acquisitions. The critical apparatus is simpler, because it is limited to the most important manuscripts and it does not indicate differences between the Codex B and the *GNT*. Finally, the graphic appearance has been changed. More types of underscores and vertical lines have been used, as well as grey backgrounds to indicate relationships between the gospel passages.

F. NEIRYNCK, *The Minor Agreements in a Horizontal-line Synopsis* (SNTA 15; Leuven 1991).

The list of minor agreements was compiled at the request of G. Strecker, chairman of the Colloquium on the Minor Agreements which took place in Göttingen from 26 to 28 July 1991. The synopsis uses the NA[26]. In 109 paragraphs, the parallel passages of Matt, Mark and Luke are arranged horizontally, and indicate, by means of different kinds of underlining, the words which coincide.

For more information on individual cases of minor agreements, see:

> NEIRYNCK, F. et al., *The Minor Agreements of Matthew and Luke against Mark with a Cumulative List* (BEThL 37; Leuven 1974).

J. CERVANTES GABARRÓN, *Sinopsis bilingüe de los tres primeros evangelios con los paralelos del evangelio de Juan* (Instrumentos para el estudio de la Biblia 4; Estella 1999).

The biblical text is presented in parallel columns in Greek and Spanish. The Gospel of John is inserted into the synopsis from the 18th chapter onward. The Greek text is that of NA^{27}, incorporating contributions of GNT^3 and NTT^2. The Spanish translation is the author's. He provided the synopsis with a short critical apparatus.

2.2 *Q Source*

S. SCHULZ, *Griechisch-deutsche Synopse der Q-Überlieferungen* (Zürich 1972).

This publication of 106 pages completes an extended analysis (pp. 508) of the Q source issued by:

> S. SCHULZ, *Q – Die Spruchquelle der Evangelisten* (Zürich 1972).
>
> Divided into three parts: a) it describes the state of research on the Q source; b) it analyses the Q source according to source criticism; c) it systematically arranges the pericopes, focusing on the kerygma of the Judeo-Christian community included in Q.

In Greek and German, the synopsis offers the text attributed to Q in the form preserved in Matthew and Luke. S. Schulz follows the order of the text which corresponds to that given in his monograph, which is neither Matthean nor Lukan.

J. S. KLOPPENBORG, *Q Parallels*. Synopsis, Critical Notes & Concordance (Foundations & Facets. New Testament; Sonoma, CA 1988).

Even if this tool does not represent a critical study of the Q source, it might help with reconstruction and inquiry. The bilingual synopsis, Greek-English, indicates the verbal and non-verbal agreements between Matthew and Luke, the Q text as generally accepted; and the Q text, probable and possible. Biblical passages are furnished with critical notes. The volume provides a Greek concordance of Q (pp. 207-238).

P. HOFFMANN – C. HEIL, *Die Spruchquelle Q.* Studienausgabe Griechisch und Deutsch (Leuven 2002).

Between 1989 and 1996 a team of 42 European and North American scholars worked on an exact reconstruction of Q. The results of their activity were published in:

> J. McConkey ROBINSON – P. HOFFMANN – J. S. KLOPPENBORG, *The Critical Edition of Q.* Synopsis Including the Gospels of Matthew and Luke, Mark and Thomas with English, German, and French Translations of Q and Thomas (Leuven 2000); Sp. tr. *El documento Q en griego y en español.* Con paralelos del evangelio de Mc y del evangelio de Tomás (Biblioteca EstB 107; Leuven – Salamanca 2002).

> It is a fundamental tool for the study of the Q source. In the introductory part, J. M. Robinson describes the history of the research on Q and presents the synopsis (pp. xix-cvii). At the end of the book there is also a brief Q concordance (pp. 563-581).

P. Hoffmann and C. Heil offer, instead, a study edition (*Studienausgabe*) for general usage which synoptically provides the reader with the Greek text and a German translation of Q, along with a good introduction to the history of the research and to the criteria of the reconstruction of the text.

See also:

> C. HEIL, *Lukas und Q.* Studien zur lukanischen Redaktion des Spruchevangeliums Q (BZNW 111; Berlin – New York 2003).

> This monograph presents the ancient Q source as it appears in Luke. Since it is an old theological and historical Judeo-Christian document, originating in the Galilean-Syrian area, Q makes the most ancient tradition on Jesus accessible. The reception of Q in Luke is described and evaluated in the light of Lukan theology and of its adaptation for Hellenistic listeners. The work points out the differences between Luke and the first Judeo-Christians.

F. NEIRYNCK, *Q-Parallels*. Q-Synopsis and IQP/CritEd Parallels (SNTA 20; Leuven 2001).

This is a new edition of the synopsis issued previously in the same series: *Q-Synopsis*. The Double Tradition Passages in Greek (SNTA 13; Leuven 1988) and of its revised edition with appendix: *Q-Synopsis*. The Double Tradition Passages in Greek (Revised Edition with Appendix) (SNTA 13; Leuven 1995).

The work is composed of two parts: the first presents the passages of the Double Tradition according to the Lukan order, whereas the second part proposes a critical reconstruction of Q. For this purpose, contributions of the International Q Project and *The Critical Edition of Q* by J. M. Robinson et al. are placed in parallel.

2.3 *Pauline Letters*

A. PITTA, *Sinossi paolina* (Cinisello Balsamo 1994).

This pioneer synopsis in Italian is useful for studying all Pauline letters (the epistle to the Hebrews excluded). The book is arranged in twenty-four sections which synoptically present subjects deriving from the letters.

R. REUTER, *Synopse zu den Briefen des Neuen Testaments*. I: Kolosser-, Epheser-, II. Thessalonicherbrief. II: Die Pastoralbriefe (ARGU 5-6; Frankfurt a.M. – Berlin – Bern – New York – Paris – Wien 1997-1998).

Volume I indicates, in vertical columns, the parallel texts from Col, Eph and 2 Thess, whereas volume II presents parallels from the Pastoral Letters. The Greek text is that of NA[27].

2.4 *Chronicles and Samuel–Kings*

P. VANNUTELLI, *Libri synoptici Veteris Testamenti seu Librorum Regum et Chronicorum loci paralleli quos hebraice graece et latine critice edidit* (SPIB; Romae 1931).

This work presents, in 240 paragraphs, the parallel passages of Samuel–Kings and Chronicles; the Hebrew text is on the left-hand page, with the Greek text is on the right-hand page. At the bottom of the Hebrew text (*BHK* of 1905-1906) the Latin Vulgate is cited (edited by T. HEYSE – C. VON TISCHENDORF, *Biblia Sacra Latina* [Lipsiae 1873]) along with relevant quotations from the *Antiquities* by Josephus Flavius (edited by B. NIESE, *Flavii Iosephi opera* [Berolini 1888-1895]). The Greek text of the LXX, from the edition by H. B. SWETE (ed.), *The Old Testament in Greek* (Cambridge 1905-1909), has a critical apparatus. The work makes the study of the text and its redaction easier, indicating gaps of parallel passages and the different vocalization of words.

J. KEGLER – M. AUGUSTIN, *Synopse zum Chronistischen Geschichtswerk* (BEAT 1; Frankfurt a.M. – Bern – New York – Paris ²1991).

Essentially, it is a reprint of the first edition (BEAT 1; Frankfurt a.M. – Bern – New York – Nancy 1984) in a new layout.

This work was conceived for German students. The authors chose the Chronicles as their main text, placing it in the right column, whereas the left column includes the texts of Samuel–Kings. At times, in a central column, there are the other OT parallels. Each biblical passage is in Hebrew. The passages are divided into units suggested by form criticism. The same authors also published a German version of this synopsis:

> *Deutsche Synopse zum Chronistischen Geschichtswerk* (BEAT 33; Frankfurt a.M. – Bern – New York – Paris – Wien 1993).

J. C. ENDRES – W. R. MILLAR – J. B. BURNS, *Chronicles and Its Synoptic Parallels in Samuel, Kings, and Related Biblical Texts* (Collegeville, MN 1998).

The synopsis offers the English text of the books mentioned in the title, dividing the text, according to the literary order, into four blocks: the genealogies, David, Solomon, the divided kingdom. Within each unit, the biblical text is presented in sections or in pericopes. For some texts, the *New Revised Standard Version* is used. For others a new translation is provided by editors.

2.5 *Ben Sira*

P. C. BEENTJES (ed.), *The Book of Ben Sira in Hebrew*. A Text Edition of All Extant Hebrew Manuscripts and a Synopsis of All Parallel Hebrew Ben Sira Texts (VT.S 68; Leiden – New York – Köln 1997).

It presents all available Hebrew MSS. The same passages which appear in two or three different MSS are put into parallel columns.

F. V. REITERER et al., *Zählsynopse zum Buch Ben Sira* (Fontes et Subsidia 1; Berlin – New York 2003).

This work helps to solve the difficulty of the different numbering of verses of Ben Sira. In 11 parallel columns, it arranges synoptically various editions and translations of Sirach, indicating the similarities between them.

2.6 *Other Synopses*

U. VANNI, *Apocalisse e Antico Testamento*. Una sinossi (Pro manuscripto ad uso degli studenti) (Roma ⁴2000).

Composed for Italian students, the synopsis offers a literal translation of the Apocalypse. The text is divided into pericopes and is placed on the right-hand pages. On the left-hand pages, the OT passages which refer to the Apocalypse are cited. For the selection of the OT texts, the author made use of information included in NA[26] and in other modern studies.

K. KOCH – M. RÖSEL, *Polyglottensynopse zum Buch Daniel* (Neukirchen-Vluyn 2000).

Important for the study of the complicated history of the text of Daniel, the synopsis covers the whole book and reproduces in five columns the texts from: MT, Peshiṭta (in square script), Theodotion, LXX, Vg, complete with a critical apparatus which cites different witnesses.

J. SIEVERS, *Synopsis of the Greek Sources for the Hasmonean Period.* 1–2 Maccabees and Josephus, War 1 and Antiquities 12–14 (SubBi 20; Roma 2001).

It is the first synopsis, inclusive of 1–2 Macc, which is put in parallel with the passages of *The Jewish War* and *Antiquities of the Jews* by Josephus Flavius. The work is a basic tool for the literary and historical analysis of the included passages. The body of the work is divided into three parts which, in Greek, are placed in parallel: 1) 1 Macc 1,10–7,50; 2 Macc 4,7–6,11; 8,1–15,39; *War* 1.41-45; *Antiquities* 12.237–12.412; 2) 1 Macc 8,1–13,42 and *Antiquities* 12.413–13.214; 3) *War* 1.50–357 and *Antiquities* 13.215–14.491.

S. GĄDECKI, *Grecko-łacińsko-polska synopsa do Pierwszej i Drugiej Księgi Machabejskiej* (Prymasowska Seria Biblijna 19; Warszawa 2002).

This trilingual synopsis (Greek-Latin-Polish) of 1–2 Macc provides, in parallel columns, the Greek text of the LXX (ed. A. Rahlfs), the Latin text of the Vg (ed. B. Fischer), and the Polish translation of these texts. Other sources – among them the *Antiquities* by Josephus

Flavius – are quoted in Greek and Polish, whereas passages from the *War* and *Against Apion* by Josephus Flavius, as well as texts by Polybius, Livy, Justin, Plutarch, Appian of Alexandria, Dan 7–12, *Ethiopian Book of Enoch* 90, Tacitus, Sallust, *Testament of Abraham* and *Megillat Taᶜanit* are provided in Polish.

C. J. WAGNER, *Polyglotte Tobit-Synopse*. Griechisch – Lateinisch – Syrisch – Hebräisch – Aramäisch. Mit einem Index zu den Tobit-Fragmenten vom Toten Meer (AAWG.PH 258 = MSU 28; Göttingen 2003).

This synopsis presents the textual traditions of the Book of Tobit. In the first part, on the left-hand pages, there are in parallel columns the Greek texts (G I, G II, G III), whereas, on the right-hand pages, are located the Latin (VL, Vulgate) and Syriac translations (Peshiṭta). The fragments of Tobit in Greek, Latin and Syriac, which are present also in 4Q196–200, are highlighted in blue. The Hebrew and Aramaic fragments of Tobit are arranged in proper order in the second part. At the end of the synopsis there is an index of Hebrew and Aramaic passages from Qumran with Greek and Latin parallels.

D. HOLLY, *Comparative Studies in Recent Greek New Testament Texts*. Nestle-Aland's 25th and 26th Editions (SubBi 7; Rome 1983).

The first part presents a synopsis registering the differences (accentuation, additions, punctuation, errors, lexical changes, etc.) between the twenty- fifth and the twenty-sixth edition of the Greek NT of Nestle – Aland. The complete list of all sixteen types of changes is given in the second part. The third part provides, for the respective editions, statistics derived from these changes.

3. Lexicons

3.1 *Hebrew, Aramaic*

F. BROWN – S. R. DRIVER – C. A. BRIGGS, *A Hebrew and English Lexicon of the Old Testament* (Oxford 1906).

The volume has been reprinted many times with corrections and reissued as:

> *The New Brown-Driver-Briggs-Gesenius Hebrew and English Lexicon with an Appendix Containing the Biblical Aramaic* (Peabody, MA 1979).

There is a complete electronic version:

> F. BROWN – S. R. DRIVER – C. A. BRIGGS, *A Hebrew and English Lexicon of the Old Testament* (Unabridged) (Oak Harbor, WA 2000) [CD-ROM].

The lexicon covers the biblical text in Hebrew and Aramaic, listing the words by their roots. At times, a second examination of the etymological proposals and translations is necessary. Biblical passages are cited abundantly.

W. BAUMGARTNER et al., *Hebräisches und aramäisches Lexikon zum Alten Testament* (Leiden 1967-1996) I-V + sup.; Eng. tr. *Hebrew and Aramaic Lexicon of the Old Testament* (Leiden 1994-2000) I-V; Pol. tr. *Wielki słownik hebrajsko-polski i aramejsko-polski Starego Testamentu* (Prymasowska Seria Biblijna 30; Warszawa 2008) I-II.

There is an English version on CD-ROM:

> *The Hebrew and Aramaic Lexicon of the Old Testament.* The Complete and Unabridged Fourth Edition (Leiden 2000) [CD-ROM].

W. Baumgartner was assisted by L. Koehler, B. Hartmann and E. Y. Kutscher. After the death of W. Baumgartner in 1970, the work was guided by B. Hartmann, who had the assistance of P. Reymond and J. J. Stamm. At the present time, it is the best complete Hebrew lexicon for the study of the OT.

Two abbreviated versions of this lexicon was published:

> HOLLADAY, W. L., *A Concise Hebrew and Aramaic Lexicon of the Old Testament, Based upon the Lexical Work of L. Koehler & W. Baumgartner* (Leiden 1971);
> REYMOND, P., *Dictionnaire d'Hébreu et d'Araméen Bibliques* (Paris 1991); It. tr. J. A. SOGGIN et al. (ed.), *Dizionario di Ebraico e Aramaico Biblici* (Roma 1995); the second Italian edition of 2001 has been augmented by the *Dizionario dei nomi biblici, dei nomi di luogo e dei lemmi di incerto significato* (pp. 501-594), prepared by F. Bianchi.

L. KOEHLER – W. BAUMGARTNER, *Lexicon in Veteris Testamenti libros* (Leiden ²1958) = *A Bilingual Dictionary of the Hebrew and Aramaic Old Testament.* English and German (Leiden 1998).

The meanings of lemmas and their discussion are in German and English. The Aramaic part is better than the Hebrew.

W. GESENIUS, *Hebräisches und aramäisches Handwörterbuch über das Alte Testament* (ed. U. RÜTERSWÖRDEN – R. MEYER – H. DONNER) (Berlin – Heidelberg – New York – London – Paris – Tokyo ¹⁸1987-) I-V.

It is a new edition of the seventeenth edition of W. Gesenius' lexicon (1915) which takes into account the most recent developments in Semitic philology. The first part (1987) covers the letters א-ב; the second (1995) ג-ד; the third (2005) מ-כ; the fourth (2007) פ-נ; the fifth (2009) ש-צ. In drawing up the third part, J. Renz took the place of U. Rüterswörden. The fourth and fifth parts were prepared by H. Donner.

D. J. A. CLINES, *The Dictionary of Classical Hebrew* (Sheffield 1993-) I-VI.

This is a new kind of lexicon concerning linguistic principles. Its major concern is the use of words in the language, particularly standard usage in written texts. It applies the adage *verba valent usu*, which may be paraphrased: "the meaning of the words depends on their usage in the language". Another novelty of this dictionary is the extension of the examined texts: the Hebrew Bible (without the parts in Aramaic), Ben Sira, MSS from Qumran and similar texts, inscriptions and other occasional texts. The publication has reached the letter *pe*.

F. ZORELL, *Lexicon hebraicum et aramaicum Veteris Testamenti* (Romae 1940-1954).

It is a more modest lexicon than the previous ones. Among its qualities are the inclusion of vocabulary from the Hebrew text of Ben Sira, along with many precious observations. It is written in Latin. After the death of F. Zorell, in 1947, professors of the Pontifical Biblical Institute completed the work. The Biblical Aramaic part was published separately by E. Vogt.

E. VOGT, *Lexicon linguae aramaicae Veteris Testamenti documentis antiquis illustratum* (Roma 1971).

This excellent Biblical Aramaic lexicon covers the entire Aramaic vocabulary of the OT. Individual terms are explained through those words present in the Aramaic text of the Bible, as well as contemporary and later Aramaic usage. An up-dated English translation is being prepared by J. A. Fitzmyer.

J. LEVY, *Wörterbuch über die Talmudim und Midraschim* (Berlin – Wien [2]1924, Darmstadt 1964) I-IV.

This most important vocabulary for the Talmudic and rabbinic literature was completed with the assistance of H. L. Fleischer. Based on this lexicon, M. Jastrow subsequently compiled his simpler dictionary. The importance of this work is founded upon abundant attestations and passages, translated into German by the author himself. It provides important information on many concepts, and its second edition furnishes additions by L. Goldschmidt.

G. H. DALMAN, *Aramäisch-neuhebräisches Handwörterbuch zu Targum, Talmud und Midrasch* (Göttingen ³1938, Hildesheim – New York 1967).

This Hebrew and post-biblical Aramaic lexicon is useful for the study of the Hebrew and Aramaic text from Qumran.

M. JASTROW, *A Dictionary of the Targumim, the Talmud Babli and Yerushalmi, and the Midrashic Literature* (London – New York 1886-1900).

Containing more references to rabbinic and targumic literature makes it a better work than G. H. Dalman's lexicon; however, it can cause some difficulties for beginners since the words are frequently given in *scriptio plena*.

This dictionary is available online at:

http://www.cwru.edu/univlib/preserve/Etana/JAST.DICv1/JAST.DICv1.html

R. ALCALAY, *The Complete Hebrew-English Dictionary* (Enlarged Edition) (Massada 1990).

This dictionary, at least partially, can be used for rabbinic literature as well.

M. SOKOLOFF, *A Dictionary of Jewish Palestinian Aramaic of the Byzantine Period* (Dictionaries of Talmud, Midrash and Targum 2; Ramat-Gan 1990).

This new dictionary of the Jewish Palestinian Aramaic replaces Dalman and Jastrow. The lemmas in general are not vocalized.

M. SOKOLOFF, *A Dictionary of Jewish Babylonian Aramaic of the Talmudic and Geonic Periods* (Dictionaries of Talmud, Midrash and Targum 3; Ramat-Gan – Baltimore – London 2002).

This dictionary is useful for students and scholars of the Jewish Babylonian Aramaic dialect (III-XI c.). Furthermore, it indicates the relationships of lemmas between this Aramaic dialect and the other dialects, such as, Syriac and Mandaic. The entries are usually vocalized, whereas the quotations within them are not. Syriac words are printed in Estrangelo. This work includes good indexes: citations from the Babylonian Talmud; the Geonic writings; writings of Anan; incantation texts and others.

A. TAL, *A Dictionary of Samaritan Aramaic* (HO 50/1-2; Leiden – Boston – Köln 2000).

These two volumes (having continuous pagination) systematically cite the literary texts in Samaritan Aramaic and writings in "Neo-Samaritan Hebrew", a spoken language, which is a combination of Aramaic and Hebrew strongly influenced by Arabic.

S. A. KAUFMAN – J. A. FITZMYER – M. SOKOLOFF (ed.), *The Comprehensive Aramaic Lexicon* (Baltimore).

According to the editorial plan of the John Hopkins University Press, the publication of this new lexicon will cover all dialects from all periods of Old Aramaic. The work, still in production, will include epigraphic material which, until now, has not been seen in Aramaic dictionaries. The lexicon will also provide data from recent scientific discussions. For further information, see:

http://cal1.cn.huc.edu/info.html

3.2 *Greek*

W. Bauer, *Griechisch-deutsches Wörterbuch zu den Schriften des Neuen Testaments und der frühchristlichen Literatur* (ed. K. & B. Aland) (Berlin – New York ⁶1988); Eng. tr. W. Bauer – F. W. Danker – W. F. Arndt – F. W. Gingrich, *A Greek-English Lexicon of the New Testament and Other Early Christian Literature* (Chicago – London ³2000).

The best dictionary of NT Greek. Besides the meaning of the individual lemmas and their presence in the NT, it provides a brief history of the Greek word with the support of Greek literature, the LXX, papyri, and later Greek literature. It also includes bibliographical references. The lexicon in based on the twenty-sixth edition of Nestle – Aland.

There is also an English version on CD-ROM:

> W. Bauer, *A Greek-English Lexicon of the New Testament and Other Early Christian Literature* (Edited and Revised by F. W. Danker) (Bellingham, WA ³2002) [CD-ROM].

An index of BAGD lists biblical passages:

> J. R. Alsop, *An Index to the Revised Bauer–Arndt–Gingrich Greek Lexicon* (Grand Rapids, MI ²1982).

F. Zorell, *Lexicon graecum Novi Testamenti* (Parisiis ³1961).

When it was released for the first time in 1911, it was the only lexicon of the NT that included material from the papyri. It is limited to NT writings. No ancient Christian writers are cited. The third edition includes almost forty pages of bibliography.

J. F. Schleusner, *Novus thesaurus philologico-criticus: sive, lexicon in LXX et reliquos interpretes graecos, ac scriptores apocryphos Veteris Testamenti* (Lipsiae 1820-1821) I-IV.

This thesaurus of more than 2,500 pages covers vocabulary specific to OT Greek. The description of the entries is not its main point of interest. Rather the stress is laid on Hebrew equivalents. In 1994, the publisher, Brepols, made an anastatic reprint of the second edition of 1822, issued in three volumes in Glasgow. It includes an introduction by J. Lust.

J. LUST – E. EYNIKEL – K. HAUSPIE, *A Greek-English Lexicon of the Septuagint* (Stuttgart 1992, 1996) I-II.

Since the work by J. F. Schleusner is not easy to find, one can make use of this more recent lexicon, as well as the others mentioned below, which are all more readily available. If entries are studied elsewhere, the proper bibliographical notes are given. In 2003 the Deutsche Bibelgesellschaft has issued a revised edition in one volume.

J. H. MOULTON – G. MILLIGAN, *The Vocabulary of the Greek Testament, Illustrated from the Papyri and Other Non-Literary Sources* (London ²1957).

This book appeared in 1930. The dictionary confines itself to the Greek lemmas of the NT which are attested by non-literary papyri and other non-literary sources (inscriptions, etc.). At times, it points out the ordinary usage of NT Greek words in extra-biblical texts. New discoveries in Greek philology since 1930 make critical use of this lexicon indispensable.

T. MURAOKA, *A Greek-English Lexicon of the Septuagint*. Chiefly of the Pentateuch and the Twelve Prophets (Louvain – Paris – Dudley 2002).

The dictionary represents essentially an enlarged version of the previous *A Greek-English Lexicon of the Septuagint* (Twelve Prophets) (Louvain 1993). It covers the entire Pentateuch and the Twelve Prophets with about 4,500 lexemes. About 1,500 lexemes

from other LXX passages are given in anticipation of the future publication of the dictionary covering the entire LXX. The textual basis
of this lexicon is the critical Göttingen edition, with some later
changes. Apart from morphology, translations of lemmas and lists of
occurrences, Hebrew equivalents from which the Greek words derive
are proposed.

H. STEPHANUS, *Thesaurus graecae linguae* (Genevae 1572) I-V.

The Genevan edition of this first complete vocabulary of the Greek
language is currently not easy to find. More readily available is the
Parisian edition in vol. 9, reedited by K. B. Hase and W. Dindorf, and
published between 1831 and 1865 by A. F. Didot, a publisher and true
Hellenist. The great work of Henri Estienne (Henricus Stephanus) has
inspired the modern project of creating a digital library of Greek literature named *Thesaurus linguae graecae* (TLG).

Thesaurus linguae graecae (TLG E) (Irvine, CA 2000) [CD-ROM].

Prepared by the University of California (Irvine), this electronic
database contains much of the Greek literature from Homer (VIII c.
B.C.) to the fall of Byzantium (A.D. 1453), totaling 76 million words
(February 2000). The software TLG Workplace 10.0 (or previous) of
Silver Mountain Software is the search engine needed for this CD-
ROM. The online version of TLG presently offers access to more than
95 million words:

http://www.tlg.uci.edu

H. G. LIDDELL – R. SCOTT, *A Greek-English Lexicon* (Revised and
    Augmented by H. S. JONES) (Oxford ⁹1925-1940) I-II.

Considered to be the scientific reference dictionary of the Greek
language, this work has many references to the LXX and NT, and
provides the original and etymological meanings of NT lemmas.
E. A. BARBER and others published *A Greek-English Lexicon.* Revised

Supplement (Oxford 1968). The supplement of 153 pages includes new material deriving from inscriptions, papyri and critical editions, as well as corrections of two volumes, beginning in 1940.

G. W. H. LAMPE, *A Patristic Greek Lexicon* (Oxford 1961, 1989).

This is an important complement to the lexicon by Liddell – Scott – Jones. It covers specific occurrences of vocabulary from ancient Christian writers as well as later Byzantine authors.

F. RODRÍGUEZ ADRADOS (ed.), *Diccionario griego-español* (Madrid 1980-) I-VI.

This project is still in the process of publication (volume VI has reached the entry ἐκπελεκάω). The Supplement III, *Repertorio Bibliográfico de la lexicografía griega* (Madrid 1998), has also been published. This dictionary will bring together the vocabulary of the most important works of all Greek authors from Homer to A.D. 600. It will systematically introduce the lemmas from epigraphical and papyrological texts, as well as from different authors, making use of modern editions and assembling a specialized bibliography on Greek lexicography.

J. MATEOS et al., *Diccionario griego-español del Nuevo Testamento.* Análisis semántico de los vocablos (Córdoba 2000-) I-III.

Volume III has reached the entry ἀπώλεια. This semantic analysis of the words occurring in the NT (according to the concordance by K. Aland) is proposed as a prerequisite step for the creation of a lexicon in which other grammatical data, information from antiquity, and the usage in classical Greek will all be utilized. It is essential to consult an introduction that explains the application of the methodology as well as the terminology of the project. See:

> J. PELÁEZ, *Metodología del Diccionario griego-español del Nuevo Testamento* (Córdoba 1996).

P. CHANTRAINE, *Dictionnaire étymologique de la langue grecque*. Histoire des mots (Paris 1968) I-II.

In two volumes (having continuous pagination), the author proposes the etymology of Greek words and reproduces their history, as far as possible.

H. FRISK, *Griechisches etymologisches Wörterbuch* (Indogermanische Bibliothek II. Reihe - Wörterbücher; Heidelberg 1960, 1970, 1972) I-III.

Apart from P. Chantraine's dictionary, it is a fundamental work that allows the user to know the etymology of Greek words. In almost 2,100 pages, volumes I-II contain the articles, and volume III includes supplements, word index, corrigendum and afterword.

L. ROCCI, *Vocabolario greco-italiano* (Città di Castello ³1943).

From its first appearance in 1939 in Rome, it was the main dictionary used in Italian high schools and universities. A third revised edition was published in 1943 in which the author acknowledged a debt to the ninth edition of Liddell – Scott – Jones. This edition was reprinted many times. In 2002, the twenty-fourth printing was made.

F. I. SEBASTIÁN YARZA, *Diccionario griego-español* (Barcelona 1998, 1999) I-II.

Meant mostly for students, the dictionary contains more than 90,000 entries from documents of the archaic, classic and Hellenistic periods, and from biblical and patristic witnesses, together with a large number of proper names.

F. MONTANARI et al., *Vocabolario della lingua greca* (Torino 1995, ²2004).

A tool for students, this work is a scientific dictionary including recent research in the field of Greek philology (particularly newly discovered texts and new editions of critical editions of texts). It includes material from the archaic, classical and Hellenistic periods, as well as biblical and patristic attestations of individual lemmas. There are frequent references to papyri and inscriptions, and a large number of proper names. In the second edition, among other things, verbal paradigms (of ca. 15,000 verbs) and Greek etymologies have been revised and around 5,000 new entries has been added.

A CD-ROM version is also available:

> F. MONTANARI et al., *Vocabolario della lingua greca* (Torino ²2004) [CD-ROM].

3.3 *Other Semitic Languages*

R. Payne SMITH, *Thesaurus syriacus* (Oxonii 1879, 1901) I-II (in one volume Hildesheim 2001).

This highly significant and large-sized work offers the meaning of Syriac words in Latin with numerous examples. An English abridged version of the *Thesaurus* was edited by J. Payne Smith:

> *A Compendious Syriac Dictionary.* Founded upon the Thesaurus syriacus of R. Payne Smith (Oxford 1903, Winona Lake, IN 1998).

C. BROCKELMANN, *Lexicon Syriacum* (Halis Saxonum ²1928, Hildesheim 1995).

This dictionary, recommendable for students of Syriac, gives the meaning of individual lemmas in Latin.

J. FERRER – M. A. NOGUERAS, *Breve Diccionario Siríaco*. Siríaco – Castellano – Catalán (Barcelona 1999).

Designed for beginners, this work contains the complete NT vocabulary of the Peshiṭta. All words are arranged alphabetically, not according to their roots.

M. Pazzini, *Lessico concordanziale del Nuovo Testamento siriaco* (SBFA 64; Jerusalem 2004).

The lexicon is useful for classes and for lexical and grammatical research in the Syriac NT. It registers each form occurring in this literary corpus with lemmas translated into Italian. All words are quoted with their vocalization and their morphological analysis.

C.-F. Jean – J. Hoftijzer, *Dictionnaire des inscriptions sémitiques de l'ouest* (Leiden 1965).

The dictionary (*DISO*) brings together the words from the North-West Semitic inscriptions, written in Old "Canaanite", Phoenician, Punic, Moabite, Hebrew, Yaudic, Old and Official (Imperial) Aramaic, Nabataean, Palmyrean, Hatra and Jewish Aramaic.

J. Hoftijzer – K. Jongeling, *Dictionary of the North-West Semitic Inscriptions* (HO 21/1-2; Leiden – New York – Köln 1995) I-II.

Updating the *DISO*, this work inserted more recent epigraphic material. An appendix (pp. 1249-1266) includes a list of terms from the Amherst papyri: "A Selective Glossary of Northwest Semitic Texts in Egyptian Script", by R. C. Steiner and A. Mosak Moshavi,

G. del Olmo Lete – J. Sanmartín, *Diccionario de la lengua ugarítica* (Aula Orientalis-Supplementa 7-8; Sabadell 1996, 2000) I-II; Eng. tr. *A Dictionary of the Ugaritic Language in the Alphabetic Tradition* (HO 67; Leiden – Boston 2003).

This extensive dictionary of the Ugaritic language was necessary because of the discovery of new archeological finds which have not appeared in previous publications. Its preparation goes back to the 1980s and gathers contributions of archaeologists, epigraphists and philologists, and it tries, as far as it is possible, to harmonize the material. It is based mainly on the alphabetical text published by M. Dietrich – O. Loretz – J. Sanmartín, *The Cuneiform*

Alphabetic Texts from Ugarit, Ras Ibn Hani and Other Places (KTU: Enlarged Edition) (ALASP 8; Münster ²1995). The English translation by W. G. E. Watson appeared in two volumes with continuous pagination.

A. L. OPPENHEIM et al., *The Assyrian Dictionary* (Chicago – Glückstadt 1956-) I-XIX, XXI.

CAD is a very important tool for studying Assyrian and Babylonian texts. It notes cognate and similar words to those of other Semitic languages and offers a secondary selected bibliography. The published volumes cover the letters: A/1-2, B, D, E, G, Ḫ, I-J, K, L, M/1-2, N/1-2, P, Q, R, S, Ṣ, Š/1-3, T, Ṭ, Z.

W. VON SODEN, *Akkadisches Handwörterbuch* (Wiesbaden 1965-1981) I-III.

AHw is an excellent work which presents the vocabulary of important Assyrian and Babylonian texts, often useful for the analysis of the OT.

J. BLACK – A. GEORGE – N. POSTGATE, *A Concise Dictionary of Akkadian* (SANTAG Arbeiten und Untersuchungen zur Keilschriftkunde 5; Wiesbaden ²2000).

Prepared on the basis of *AHw*, the vocabulary includes all existing words, citing only some instances of the use in the literature; it is useful for students.

4. Grammars

4.1 *Hebrew*

H. BAUER – P. LEANDER, *Historische Grammatik der hebräischen Sprache des Alten Testaments* (Halle an d.S. 1922, Hildesheim – Zürich – New York 1991).

This work presents orthography, phonetics and morphology of Biblical Hebrew. In the light of recent Hebrew (and North-West Semitic) studies, many aspects of this grammar are no longer useful, whereas other aspects still preserve their value, in particular verb and noun forms, paradigms, etc.

C. BROCKELMANN, *Hebräische Syntax* (Neukirchen 1956).

The volume is especially informative about Hebrew syntax. It utilizes material from Hebrew inscriptions and Qumran. Some issues are treated carefully and succinctly, while others need verification.

W. GESENIUS, *Hebräische Grammatik* (Leipzig ²⁹1918, 1929) I-II (in one volume Hildesheim – New York 1962).

This revision of the twenty-eighth edition has not been finished. It is the best existing reference Hebrew grammar. At the present time however, complementary, modern studies are necessary.

W. GESENIUS – E. KAUTZSCH, *Gesenius' Hebrew Grammar* (Revised by A. E. COWLEY) (Oxford ²1910).

This English translation of the twenty-eighth German edition is the best Hebrew grammar in English, although it is outdated at times.

P. JOÜON, *Grammaire de l'hébreu biblique* (Rome ²1947).

The first edition was published in 1923; the second edition is practically a corrected reprint. It depends partially on the work of W. Gesenius. The syntax study is the most significant contribution of the grammar by P. Joüon.

P. JOÜON – T. MURAOKA, *A Grammar of Biblical Hebrew* (Revised Edition) (SubBi 27; Roma 2006); Sp. tr. *Gramática del hebreo bíblico* (Instrumentos para el estudio de la Biblia 18; Estella 2007).

The first edition in two volumes (SubBi 14/1-2; Roma 1991; reprinted with corrections in 1993) completed the previous work in French by means of new discoveries of Semitic philology. This new English edition in one volume contains the data from recent research in Biblical Hebrew (up to 2004). The inclusion of bibliographical information and scholarly discussion is placed in abundant footnotes, raising its quality as an advanced grammar.

R. MEYER, *Hebräische Grammatik* (SG 763/763a/763b, 764/764a/ 764b, 5765, 4765; Berlin ³1966-1972) I-IV (in one volume De Gruyter Studienbuch; Berlin – New York ³1992); Sp. tr. *Gramática del hebreo bíblico* (Terrassa 1989).

This grammar is useful chiefly for users with basic knowledge of Biblical Hebrew. It provides a comparative and historical explanation of the nominal and verbal forms, as well as of the syntax and considers data from Ugaritic and Qumran.

This compact grammar was released in small volumes: 1. Introduction, orthography and phonetics; 2. Morphology; 3. Syntax; 4. Index of vols. 1-3. The 1992 reprint adds an updated bibliographical note.

B. K. WALTKE – M. O'CONNOR, *An Introduction to Biblical Hebrew Syntax* (Winona Lake, IN 1990).

This reference grammar is intended for intermediate and advanced users. It illustrates the discussion of syntax by many examples.

4.2 *Aramaic*

H. BAUER – P. LEANDER, *Grammatik des Biblisch-Aramäischen* (Halle an d.S. 1927, Hildesheim – New York 1962).

Even if it requires some corrections, it is the best grammar for studying Biblical Aramaic.

F. ROSENTHAL, *A Grammar of Biblical Aramaic* (PLO 5; Wiesbaden 1961, 1974); Fr. tr. *Grammaire d'araméen biblique* (BeRe 19; Paris 1988).

This small grammar is useful for beginners.

J. RIBERA-FLORIT, *Gramática del Arameo Clásico (Oficial)* (Barcelona 1993).

This work, based on Biblical Aramaic, is intended for college students who know Hebrew.

4.3 *Greek*

F. BLASS – A. DEBRUNNER, *Grammatik des neutestamentlichten Griechisch* (Bearbeitet von F. REHKOPF) (Göttingen [16]1984); Eng. tr. *A Greek Grammar of the New Testament and Other Early Christian Literature* (Chicago 1961); It. tr. *Grammatica del greco del Nuovo Testamento* (ed. G. PISA) (Brescia 1982) = *Grammatica del greco del Nuovo Testamento* (Introduzione allo studio della Bibbia. Supplementi 2; Brescia 1997).

This is a major reference grammar. The sixteenth German edition, which corrected some errors, is a reprint of the fourteenth (1976), the last reworked edition, which was the basis of the Italian translation. The English translation, on the other hand, is a revision of the ninth and tenth German editions, in which the translator, R. W. Funk, incorporated the additional observations of A. Debrunner and his own material.

J. H. MOULTON – F. W. HOWARD, *A Grammar of New Testament Greek* (Edinburgh [3]1949, 1929, 1963, 1976) I-IV.

This is a good grammar of NT Greek, though some updating is necessary.

E. SCHWYZER, *Griechische Grammatik auf der Grundlage von Karl Brugmanns griechischer Grammatik.* I. Allgemeiner Teil. Lautlehre. Wortbildung. Flexion. II. Syntax und syntaktische Stilistik. III. Register. IV. Stellenregister (HAW II/I.1-4; München 1939, 1950, 1953, 1971).

This grammar is very helpful for the study of the Greek language of all periods. After the death of E. Schwyzer, 1943, A. Debrunner finished vol. 2. Prepared by D. J. Georgacas, volume III provides a philological and an analytical index of the previous two volumes. Volume IV includes an index of quotations, composed by F. Radt, as well as corrigenda of the three previous volumes.

M. ZERWICK, *Graecitas biblica Novi Testamenti exemplis illustratur* (SPIB 92; Romae ⁵1966); Eng. tr. *Biblical Greek Illustrated by Examples* (SPIB 114; Rome 1963); Sp. tr. *El griego del Nuevo Testamento* (Instrumentos para el estudio de la Biblia 2; Estella 1997).

Zerwick briefly discusses NT syntax highlighting its differences from classical Greek. The English version is based on the fourth Latin edition (1963).

5. Dictionaries and Encyclopedias

5.1 *Biblical*

P. J. ACHTEMEIER (ed.), *The HarperCollins Bible Dictionary* (San Francisco ³1996); Pol. tr. *Encyklopedia biblijna* (Prymasowska Seria Biblijna 9; Warszawa 1998, 2004); It. tr. *Il dizionario della Bibbia* (Bologna 2003).

In this work, there is a vast number of articles (more than 5,000), which were prepared by many collaborators from different countries. The bibliography of the Italian edition has been updated.

J. B. BAUER (ed.), *Bibeltheologisches Wörterbuch* (Graz 1958, 1962; ³1967) I-II; Sp. tr. *Diccionario de teología bíblica* (Barcelona ²1985).

BThW is an excellent biblico-theological dictionary, prepared for theologians and pastors.

H. CAZELLES – A. FEUILLET (ed.), *Supplément au Dictionnaire de la Bible* (Paris 1928-) I-XIV.

DBS has not been completed yet. Volume XIV, published in fascicles, has reached the letter "T". The work offers many extensive articles, with a rich bibliography. Although some contributions need to be updated, the dictionary retains its importance.

D. N. FREEDMAN et al. (ed.), *The Anchor Bible Dictionary* (New York – London – Toronto – Sydney – Auckland 1992) I-VI = *The Anchor Yale Bible Dictionary* (New Haven, CT – London 2008) I-VI.

This biblical dictionary contains information of varying value. The bibliography is helpful for beginning one's research.

K. GALLING (ed.), *Biblisches Reallexikon* (HAT 1; Tübingen ²1977).

The second edition of the *BRL* is a complete revision of the material of the first edition of 1937, enlarging it with new discoveries presented briefly and precisely.

M. GÖRG – B. LANG (ed.), *Neues Bibel-Lexikon* (Düsseldorf – Zürich 1988-2001) I-III.

This dictionary takes the place of the previous *Bibel-Lexikon* edited by H. Haag (Zürich 1968), and contains many short contributions with an essential bibliography.

R. L. HARRIS – G. L. ARCHER Jr. – B. K. WALTKE, *Theological Wordbook of the Old Testament* (Chicago 1980) I-II.

The work offers descriptions of the important theological terms in the OT. It is intended for pastors and committed Christians. In spite of its usefulness, it does not satisfy the needs of scientific study.

X. LÉON-DUFOUR (ed.), *Vocabulaire de théologie biblique* (Paris 1962); Eng. tr. *Dictionary of Biblical Theology* (New York 1967); It. tr. *Dizionario di teologia biblica* (Torino ⁴1971); Pol. tr. *Słownik teologii biblijnej* (Poznań ²1973); Sp. tr. *Vocabulario de teología bíblica* (Edición revisada y ampliada) (Barcelona 1996).

The work analyzes fundamental biblical terms from the theological point of view.

B. REICKE – L. ROST (ed.), *Biblisch-historisches Handwörterbuch.* Landeskunde, Geschichte, Religion, Kultur, Literatur (Göttingen 1962-1979) I-IV.

BHH offers articles teeming with ideas and provides a well-selected bibliography on themes mentioned in the subtitle.
A CD-ROM version is available as well:

B. REICKE – L. ROST (ed.), *Biblisch-historisches Handwörterbuch.* Landeskunde, Geschichte, Religion, Kultur, Literatur (Digitale Bibliothek 96; Berlin – Göttingen 2003) [CD-ROM].

J. BOTTERWECK – H. RINGGREN (ed.), *Theologisches Wörterbuch zum Alten Testament* (Stuttgart 1970-) I-VIII, X; Eng. tr. *Theological Dictionary of the Old Testament* (Grand Rapids, MI 1977-2006) I-XV; It. tr. *Grande lessico dell'Antico Testamento* (Brescia 1988-) I-VIII; Sp. tr. *Diccionario teológico del Antiguo Testamento* (Madrid 1978-) I.

This is a very good dictionary. The German edition of the Hebrew part is finished, whereas vol. 9, concerning OT Aramaic terms, is still in preparation. The English translation of the Hebrew part is completed. The work contextualizes OT words in their Ancient Near East background (Sumerian, Akkadian, Egyptian, Ugaritic, etc.) and focuses on their theological meaning. Many times, it quotes rabbinic sources and Qumran.

E. JENNI – C. WESTERMANN (ed.), *Theologisches Handwörterbuch zum Alten Testament* (München – Zürich 1971, 1976) I-II; Eng. tr. *Theological Lexicon of the Old Testament* (Peabody, MA 1997) I-III; It. tr. *Dizionario teologico dell'Antico Testamento* (Torino 1978, 1982) I-II; Sp. tr. *Diccionario teológico manual del Antiguo Testamento* (Biblioteca Bíblica Cristiandad; Madrid 1978, 1985) I-II.

This dictionary contributes to a deeper analysis of biblical words in their historical and theological context. It is useful for semantic studies, literary-criticism and tradition-criticism.

G. KITTEL (ed.), *Theologisches Wörterbuch zum Neuen Testament* (Stuttgart 1933-1979) I-X; Eng. tr. *Theological Dictionary of the New Testament* (Grand Rapids, MI 1964-1976) I-X; It. tr. *Grande lessico del Nuovo Testamento* (Brescia 1965-1992) I-XVI.

This monumental work, initiated by G. Kittel and continued by G. Friedrich, represents the most important tool for interpretation of the NT. It offers discussions about the most significant NT words, presenting their etymology, their usage in classical, Hellenistic, and Septuagintal Greek, in Hebrew writings and in the NT. If a word has a corresponding term in OT Hebrew, a discussion about it is offered as well. The semantics and the theological developments in the history of the word are examined with an extensive discussion.

H. BALZ – G. SCHNEIDER (ed.), *Exegetisches Wörterbuch zum Neuen Testament* (Stuttgart 1978, 1981, 1983) I-III; Eng. tr. *Exegetical Dictionary of the New Testament* (Edinburgh 1990, 1991, 1993)

I-III; It. tr. *Dizionario esegetico del Nuovo Testamento* (Brescia 1995, 1998) I-II; Sp. tr. *Diccionario exegético del Nuevo Testamento* (Biblioteca EstB 90-91; Salamanca 1996, 2002) I-II.

EWNT investigates the meaning of Greek words in their NT context.

L. COENEN – E. BEYREUTHER – H. BIETENHARD (ed.), *Theologisches Begriffslexikon zum Neuen Testament* (Wuppertal 1967, 1969, 1971) I-II/1-2; Eng. tr. C. BROWN, *The New International Dictionary of New Testament Theology* (Grand Rapids, MI 1975, 1976, 1978) I-III; It. tr. *Dizionario dei concetti biblici del Nuovo Testamento* (ed. A. TESSAROLO) (Bologna 1976); Sp. tr. *Diccionario teológico del Nuevo Testamento* (Biblioteca EstB 26-29; Salamanca 1983-1985) I-IV.

Designed for theologians and pastors, this work discusses words that express similar ideas, focusing on their theological meaning.

A. DÍEZ-MACHO – S. BARTINA (ed.), *Enciclopedia de la Biblia* (Barcelona 1963) I-VI; It. tr. *Enciclopedia della Bibbia* (ed. A. ROLLA et al.) (Torino 1969-1971) I-VI.

This complete and useful work competently handles questions of proper names, toponymy, linguistics and biblical literature, geography, archaeology, etc. Some issues need updating to include the newest discoveries in biblical science.

5.2 *Non Biblical*

K. GALLING (ed.), *Die Religion in Geschichte und Gegenwart* (Tübingen ³1957-1965) I-VII.

*RGG*³ gathers different materials and has good articles of biblical interest.

A CD-ROM version is available as well:

K. GALLING (ed.), *Die Religion in Geschichte und Gegenwart.*
Handwörterbuch für Theologie und Religionswissenschaft
(Digitale Bibliothek 12; Berlin – Tübingen 2000) [CD-ROM].

H. D. BETZ et al. (ed.), *Die Religion in Geschichte und Gegenwart.*
Handwörterbuch für Theologie und Religionswissenschaft
(Tübingen [4]1998-2005) I-VIII.

Apart from theological entries, this work contains short biblical
articles with, at times, concise bibliography.

J. HÖFER – K. RAHNER (ed.), *Lexikon für Theologie und Kirche* (Freiburg i.B. [2]1957-1967) I-XI.

Produced in a Catholic milieu, this lexicon is designed in particular for pastors, theologians and Church historians. It offers good articles on biblical topics as well.

W. KASPER et al. (ed.), *Lexikon für Theologie und Kirche* (Freiburg –
Basel – Rom – Wien [3]1993-2001) I-XI.

This is one of the most extended encyclopedias, created in
a Catholic milieu. The present lexicon updates the second edition,
taking into consideration the transformations in theological and
ecclesiastical fields after Vatican II.

G. KRAUSE – G. MÜLLER (ed.), *Theologische Realenzyklopädie* (Ber-
lin – New York 1976-2004) I-XXXVI; M. GLOCKNER – A. DÖH-
NERT, *Theologische Realenzyklopädie.* Gesamtregister I: Bibel-
stellen, Orte, Sachen (Berlin – New York 2006); A. DÖHNERT –
K. OTT, *Theologische Realenzyklopädie.* Gesamtregister II:
Namen (Berlin – New York 2007).

Articles in this encyclopedia include almost all theological disci-
plines. The studies of Protestant authors analyze the Christian faith
from an ecumenical perspective, and consider the contributions of
modern research.

With vol. 36, after twenty-eight years of publishing, *TRE* reached the last letter of the alphabet.

T. KLAUSER et al. (ed.), *Reallexikon für Antike und Christentum*. Sachwörterbuch zur Auseinandersetzung des Christentums mit der antiken Welt (Stuttgart 1950-) I-XXI + sup. I.

The lexicon focuses on pre-Christian and Christian antiquity, taking into account their continuity and differences. There are interesting articles for the students of the Bible as well. Volume XXI, 2006, includes the entry "Kreuzzeichen"; volume I of the supplement, 2001, covers the entries "Aaron – Bibliographie II". Volume XXII and volume II of the supplement are being published.

G. WISSOWA (ed.), *Paulys Real-Encyclopädie der classischen Altertumswissenschaft* (Stuttgart 1905-1978).

This encyclopedia of antiquity includes articles very useful for understanding the Bible and the intertestamental period.

K. ZIEGLER – W. SONTHEIMER (ed.), *Der Kleine Pauly*. Lexikon der Antike von Pauly's Realencyclopädie der classischen Altertumswissenschaft (Stuttgart 1964-1975) I-V.

This abbreviated version of the previous encyclopedia provides updated information about Greco-Roman antiquity, helping one to understand both the OT and the NT.

H. CANCIK – H. SCHNEIDER (ed.), *Der Neue Pauly*. Enzyklopädie der Antike (Stuttgart – Weimar 1996-2003) I-XVI; Eng. tr. *Brill's New Pauly*. Encyclopaedia of the Ancient World. Antiquity (Leiden – Boston 2002-) I-XIII.

The interest of the work centers specifically on ancient Greco-Roman culture (language, economics, family, politics, law, religion, literature, arts, society and philosophy), covering the second half of the second millennium B.C. to the early Middle Ages in Europe (A.D.

600/800). C. F. Salazar and other editors translated the work into English, adding a bibliography, updating some articles and providing new ones (at the end of each volume one finds the *Addenda*). The English edition has reached the article "Syloson".

C. ROTH – G. WIGODER (ed.), *Encyclopaedia Judaica* (Jerusalem 1971-1982) I-XVII.

This encyclopedia replaces the previous Jewish encyclopedias and it highlights, in particular, the Jewish contribution to world culture. Many biblical articles provide documentation from the Ancient Near East during the biblical period. The work has many contributions to biblical science such as introductions to biblical books, and the presentation of the thought, religion, society and law of the Jews, as well as many other items.

F. SKOLNIK – M. BERENBAUM (ed.), *Encyclopaedia Judaica* (Detroit ²2007) I-XXII.

The second edition of the *Encyclopaedia Judaica* updates many topics related to Jewish culture. Unlike the first edition, numerous biblical subjects have been omitted.

J. NEUSNER – A. J. AVERY-PECK – W. S. GREEN (ed.), *The Encyclopaedia of Judaism* (Leiden – Boston – Köln 2000) I-III + Supplement One (Leiden – Boston 2003) IV; Supplement Two (Leiden – New York 2004) V.

Sponsored by the Museum of Jewish Heritage in New York, this encyclopedia offers materials on Hebrew religion and Judaism. More than a hundred articles discuss issues in detail. Some articles are more concise, and provide, at times, notes and basic bibliography. Paired to this work is the *Dictionary of Judaism in the Biblical Period, 450 B.C.E. to 600 C.E.* (Peabody, MA 1996), edited by J. Neusner and W. S. Green. This volume makes access to the articles of the encyclopedia easier, providing definitions and useful information. Maintaining the pagination of the *Encyclopaedia*, the editors added new studies in supplement volumes, with 32 new articles in vol. 1, and 21 articles in vol. 2.

An electronic version of this encyclopedia is available:

> J. NEUSNER – A. J. AVERY-PECK – W. S. GREEN (ed.), *The Encyclopaedia of Judaism on CD-ROM* (Leiden 2004) I-V [CD-ROM].

J. MAIER – P. SCHÄFER, *Kleines Lexikon des Judentums* (Stuttgart 1981); Sp. tr. *Diccionario del judaísmo* (Estella 1996).

A brief dictionary containing some selected and important terms. The Spanish translation was made by C. del Valle.

E. STERN et al. (ed.), *The New Encyclopedia of Archaeological Excavations in the Holy Land* (New York – London – Toronto – Sydney – Tokyo – Singapore 1993) I-IV.

The publication of the *New Encyclopedia*, replacing that by M. AVI-YONAH et al. (ed.), *Encyclopedia of Archaeological Excavations in the Holy Land* (London 1975, 1976, 1977, 1978) I-IV, was necessary because of new archaeological discoveries. The articles of the new English edition were updated in 1991. They cover the span of time from pre-history to the Ottoman period.

L. H. SCHIFFMAN – J. C. VANDERKAM (ed.), *Encyclopedia of the Dead Sea Scrolls* (Oxford 2000) I-II.

These two volumes were planned by Oxford University Press, publisher of the DJD. The term *Dead Sea Scrolls* in the title is used in a broad meaning. Though the work privileges the materials from Qumran, it includes also other documents from the Judean Desert. Many internationally renowned scholars offer updated scholarly articles. Their main interest is in geography, archaeology, paleography, biblical studies, history, beliefs, institutions, individuals in ancient history, and on particular research in this field.

E. EBELING – B. MEISSNER et al. (ed.), *Reallexikon der Assyriologie* (Berlin – Leipzig 1932-) I-X.

This is an important work for knowing the background of the biblical Near East. Beginning from vol. 3 (1957-1971) the title of the lexicon was enlarged: ...*und vorderasiatischen Archäologie.* E. Ebeling and B. Meissner were replaced by E. Weidner and W. von Soden; D. O. Edzard joined them for vol. 4 (1972-1975) as the editor. *RLA* especially considers Babylonian and Assyrian materials, and, in a more general way, Hittite, Elamite and Persian documentation. Volume X (2003-2005) finishes with the article "Priesterverkleidung".

F. JOANNÈS et al. (ed.), *Dictionnaire de la civilisation mésopotamienne* (Paris 2001, 2004).

This work was produced by a team of French scholars headed by F. Joannès. The dictionary provides basic knowledge of material, social and cultural conditions of the Mesopotamian region.

6. Introductions to the Bible

6.1 *Introductions to the Old Testament*

B. W. ANDERSON, *Understanding the Old Testament* (Englewood Cliffs, NJ [4]1976) = *The Living World of the Old Testament* (London [4]1986).

This manual emphasizes the history and religion of Israel. The historical background is outlined and archeological data along with the best subsidiary bibliography are furnished with care.

M. Z. BRETTLER, *How to Read the Bible* (Philadelphia 2005).

The work initiates accessibly into the reading of biblical texts in their historical context from the Jewish point of view.

W. BRUEGGEMANN, *An Introduction to the Old Testament*. The Canon and Christian Imagination (Louisville, KY – London 2003); It. tr. *Introduzione all'Antico Testamento*. Il canone e l'immaginazione cristiana (Strumenti 21; Torino 2005).

This well written introduction enables beginners to know the OT books, their main issues, exegetical methods, avoiding discussions on specialist matters.

A. F. CAMPBELL, *The Study Companion to Old Testament Literature*. An Approach to the Writings of the Pre-exilic and Exilic Israel (Old Testament Studies 2; Wilmington, DE 1989).

The study deals mostly with the literary sources of the Old Testament. Therefore it takes into account the present text, the strata and the antecedent literary traditions.

M. D. COOGAN, *The Old Testament*. A Historical and Literary Introduction to the Hebrew Scriptures (New York – Oxford 2006).

By the appellation "Hebrew Scriptures" in the subtitle, the books of the Hebrew Bible and the deuterocanonical books are intended. The presentation is based on the chronology of the Bible and it is not grounded on the dating of its parts. The manual is destined for basic courses. For that reason, scientific discussions are furnished rarely, though bibliographical references are present.

O. EISSFELDT, *Einleitung in das Alte Testament*. Unter Einschluß der Apokryphen und Pseudepigraphen sowie der apokryphen- und pseudepigraphenartigen Qumrān-Schriften (NTG; Tübingen ³1964, ⁴1976) I-IV; Eng. tr. *The Old Testament*. An Introduction Including the Apocrypha and Pseudepigrapha, and also the

Works of Similar Type from Qumran (New York – Evanston, IL 1965); It. tr. *Introduzione all'Antico Testamento* (Brescia 1970-1984) I-IV.

This work is one of the best OT introductions. In the first part, the pre-literary data are discussed and, in the second part, the prehistory of the OT books is presented. In the third part, the individual OT books are described, whereas the forth part deals with the canon, deuterocanonical books, apocrypha and Qumran texts. The fifth part presents some matters linked with the biblical text.

R. FABRIS et al., *Introduzione generale alla Bibbia* (Logos - Corso di studi biblici 1; Leumann ²2006).

The second edition of this substantial introduction differs from the first one (1994), though it maintains its division in four sections: historical, philological, theological and heuristic. Some articles have been reworked (e.g. exegetical methodology), new ones are added (e.g. the history of Israel from the beginning to the Babylonian exile, the debate on NT historiography, Hebrew non-canonical literature, the canon of Hebrew scriptures; inspiration, Bible and computer tools) and the bibliography has been updated.

O. KAISER, *Einleitung in das Alte Testament*. Eine Einführung in ihre Ergebnisse und Probleme (Gütersloh ⁵1984); Eng. tr. *Introduction to the Old Testament*. A Presentation of Its Results and Problems (Oxford 1975).

The introduction addresses accessibly issues associated with the books of the Hebrew Bible (historical tales, prophetical traditions, poetic and wisdom literature, canon), presenting concisely the state of research and some personal solutions of the author.

V. MANNUCCI, *Bibbia come parola di Dio*. Introduzione generale alla Sacra Scrittura (Strumenti 17; Brescia ⁵1985, ¹⁵1997); Sp. tr. *La*

Biblia como Palabra de Dios. Introducción general a la Sagrada Escritura (Temas bíblicos; Bilbao 1985).

The preliminary questions of the Holy Scriptures are presented on the basis of new criteria that have emerged after Vatican II. In this way, the theology of the word of God and the contemporary philosophies of language are the reference frame of this work.

P. MERLO (ed.), *L'Antico Testamento*. Introduzione storico-letteraria (Frecce 60; Roma 2008).

This compendium presents the OT books, along with historical-religious and archeological issues. Describing succinctly the achievements of biblical research, the work is a suitable introduction for students and persons interested in biblical culture.

J. W. ROGERSON – J. M. LIEU (ed.), *The Oxford Handbook of Biblical Studies* (Oxford – New York 2006).

The volume of almost 900 pages includes articles by many authors. They consider the social context of the Old and New Testament, their institutions and literary genres. Methods of research, the transmission of the text, its composition and the interpretation of the Bible are discussed in the light of recent archeological achievements, literary studies on the ancient Near East, Qumran writings, literature of the Greco-Roman and rabbinical period.

J. A. SOGGIN, *Introduzione all'Antico Testamento*. Dalle origini alla chiusura del Canone alessandrino (Biblioteca di cultura religiosa 14; Brescia ⁴1987); Eng. tr. *Introduction to the Old Testament*. From Its Origins to the Closing of the Alexandrian Canon (London – Philadelphia ³1989).

This introduction, which has been well received, describes individual books and issues linked with the Hebrew Bible. Moreover, it presents Palestinian inscriptions from first millennium B.C., manuscripts from the postexilic period and it includes a chronological table with biblical dates.

E. ZENGER (ed.), *Einleitung in das Alte Testament* (Studienbücher Theologie 1,1; Stuttgart ⁶2006); Port. tr. *Introdução ao Antigo Testamento* (Bíblica Loyola 36; São Paulo 2003); It. tr. *Introduzione all'Antico Testamento* (Brescia 2005).

From the first edition of 1995 on, Zenger with other co-authors was rounding out this college textbook with new scientific achievements and bibliography, and he has reworked some previous articles. The description of the biblical books is preceded by the issues on their canonicity, history of the text. A chronological table, geographical maps related to the history of Israel and a vocabulary with technical terms end the work.

6.2 Introductions to the New Testament

R. E. BROWN, *Introduction to the New Testament* (AncBRL; New York 1997); Fr. tr. *Que sait-on du Nouveau Testament?* (Paris 2000); It. tr. *Introduzione al Nuovo Testamento* (Brescia 2001); Sp. tr. *Introducción al Nuevo Testamento* (Biblioteca de ciencias bíblicas y orientales 7; Madrid 2002).

Directed mostly to students, this large work presents in 37 chapters both the introductory issues (chap. 1-5) and the NT books (chap. 6-37). The appendixes are dedicated to the historical Jesus, Jewish and Christian (and Gnostic) writings, which are related to the New Testament.

H. CONZELMANN – A. LINDEMANN, *Arbeitsbuch zum Neuen Testament* (UTB.W 52; Tübingen ¹²1998); It. tr. *Guida allo studio del Nuovo Testamento* (Strumenti 1; Casale Monferrato 1986); Eng. tr. *Interpreting the New Testament*. An Introduction to the Principles and Methods of New Testament Exegesis (Peabody,

MA 1988); Fr. tr. *Guide pour l'étude du Nouveau Testament* (Le Monde de la Bible 39; Genève 1999).

For more than twenty years (first edition in 1975), the authors were elaborating and revising this work, bearing in mind the results of the recent NT research. They use the criteria of historical critical exegesis, applied and shared by other scholars. Methodological fundamentals along with the NT background and individual books are described. Moreover, much attention is paid to the figure of Jesus of Nazareth and to the history of early Christianity.

A. GEORGE – P. GRELOT (ed.), *Introduction critique au Nouveau Testament* (Paris 1976-1991) I-IX; It. tr. *Introduzione al Nuovo Testamento* (Roma 1981-1992) I-IX; Sp. tr. *Introducción crítica al Nuevo Testamento* (BHer 159, 160; Barcelona 1983).

This is a new edition of the *Introduction à la Bible*, edited by A. Robert and A. Feuillet (Paris 1957-1959). The respective volumes inform largely on the following matters: 1. On the Threshold of the Christian Era (J. Carmignac et al., 1976); 2. The Proclamation of the Gospel (X. Léon-Dufour – C. Perrot, 1976); 3. The Apostolic Epistles (J. M. Cambier et al., 1977); 4. The Johannine Tradition (M.-É. Boismard – E. Cothenet, 1977); 5. The Completion of the Scriptures (P. Grelot – C. Bigaré, 1977); 6. Gospels and History (P. Grelot, 1985); 7. The Words of Jesus Christ (P. Grelot, 1986); 8. Homilies on the Scriptures in the Apostolic Age (P. Grelot – M. Dumais, 1989); 9. The Liturgy in the New Testament (P. Grelot et al., 1991).

D. GUTHRIE, *New Testament Introduction* (Leicester – Downers Grove, IL [4]1990).

This is a new revised and augmented version which is addressed mostly to theology students. The main changes concern the Gospels. Furthermore, the bibliography has been updated. At the end of the book, the author has placed appendixes related to the Pauline epistles, chronology of his life, issues on pseudepigraphy and additional reflections on the synoptic problem.

W. G. KÜMMEL, *Einleitung in das Neue Testament* (Heidelberg ²¹1983); Eng. tr. *Introduction to the New Testament* (Nashville ¹⁷1975).

This erudite and popular publication is a classic work that was improved and supplemented many times. It is useful particularly for NT scholars and for advanced students.

W. MICHAELIS, *Einleitung in das Neue Testament*. Die Entstehung, Sammlung und Überlieferung der Schriften des Neuen Testaments (Bern ³1961).

In principle it is a reprint of the second edition (Bern 1954), with the addition of an *Ergänzungsheft* of 48 pages. The state of knowledge was presented with care. The author offers sometimes his rather personal opinions.

C. F. D. MOULE, *The Birth of the New Testament* (London ³1981, San Francisco ³1981); It. tr. *Le origini del Nuovo Testamento* (StBi 15; Brescia 1971).

This revised and corrected edition furnishes solutions of basic issues (dates, authorship etc.) and presents carefully the process that gave origin to the New Testament.

P. VIELHAUER, *Geschichte der urchristlichen Literatur*. Einleitung in das Neue Testament, die Apokryphen und die apostolischen Väter (Berlin – New York 1975).

The work describes the literary history of early Christianity on the basis of documents and different literary forms that appeared in I and II c. A.D.

A. WIKENHAUSER – J. SCHMID, *Einleitung in das Neue Testament* (Freiburg – Basel – Wien ⁶1973); Eng. tr. *New Testament Introduction* (New York 1958); Sp. tr. *Introducción al Nuevo Testamento* (BHer.SE 36; Barcelona ³1978); It. tr. *Introduzione al Nuovo Testamento* (Biblioteca teologica 9; Brescia 1981).

This introduction came into being in the Catholic milieu and it is one of the best works of this kind, though it requires supplementation 25 years after its publication. The provided data are extensive and exact. The issues on the canon and the NT text are described in detail, and the individual writings are presented well.

7. Biblical Theology

7.1 Old Testament Theology

P. BEAUCHAMP, *L'Un et l'Autre Testament*. Essai de lecture (Parole de Dieu; Paris 1976); It. tr. *L'uno e l'altro Testamento*. Saggio di lettura (Biblioteca di cultura religiosa 46; Brescia 1985); IDEM, *L'Un et l'Autre Testament*. II. Accomplir les Écritures (Paris 1990); It. tr. *L'uno e l'altro Testamento*. Compiere le Scritture (Biblica 1; Milano 2001).

The author approaches teleologically the Sacred Scriptures, highlighting the category of "fulfillment". Proposing a "typological" theology in vol. 1, the Old Testament has been described according to its principal parts: Law, Prophets, Writings with apocalyptic literature. Volume II offers a reading of the fundamental OT texts, which illustrate the development of the "figure" until its Christological fulfillment.

B. S. CHILDS, *Old Testament Theology in Canonical Context* (Philadelphia 1986); It. tr. *Teologia dell'Antico Testamento in un contesto canonico* (Cinisello Balsamo 1989).

The work considers the Bible within its canonical context, that is chiefly in its definitive stage and in conformity with the canon of the (Christian) church. Theological issues are presented according to topics (revelation, knowledge of God, goal of the divine revelation, law of God etc.). The last part of the book deals with the human answer to the divine revelation that becomes apparent in obedience and in life marked by thread and promise.

G. VON RAD, *Theologie des Alten Testaments* (München 1957-1960) I-II; Eng. tr. *Old Testament Theology* (Edinburgh 1962-1965, New York 1962) I-II; Fr. tr. *Théologie de l'Ancien Testament* (Genève 1963-1967) I-II; It. tr. *Teologia dell'Antico Testamento* (Biblioteca teologica 6; Brescia 1972-1974); Sp. tr. *Teología del Antiguo Testamento* (Biblioteca de estudios bíblicos 11-12; Salamanca 1982, 1984); Pol. tr. *Teologia Starego Testamentu* (Warszawa 1986).

This monumental work presents a synthesis of modern exegetical research, which has still its followers. The study is based on achievements of the historical critical method and describes the history of tradition that are preserved in the Old Testament. Volume I deals with the theology of Israel's historical traditions, whereas volume II is dedicated to the prophetic traditions of Israel.

C. WESTERMANN, *Theologie des Alten Testaments in Grundzügen* (GAT 6; Göttingen 1978); Eng. tr. *Elements of Old Testament Theology* (Atlanta 1982); It. tr. *Teologia dell'Antico Testamento* (Antico Testamento. Supplementi 6; Brescia 1983); Fr. tr. *Théologie de l'Ancien Testament* (Le monde de la Bible; Genève 1985).

Westermann's work outlines fundamental knowledge of OT theology. The material is arranged in six parts: What does the Old Testament say about God?, The saving God and history, The blessing God and Creation, God's Judgment and God's Compassion, The (human) response, and The Old Testament and Jesus Christ.

W. ZIMMERLI, *Grundriß der alttestamentlichen Theologie* (ThW 3/1; Stuttgart 1972, ⁷1999); Sp. tr. *Manual de teología del Antiguo Testamento* (Academia Christiana 11; Madrid 1980); Eng. tr. *Old Testament in Outline* (Edinburgh 1983); Fr. tr. *Esquisse d'une théologie de l'Ancien Testament* (LeDiv 141; Paris 1990).

The work sums up fundamental notions of OT theology that are disposed on the basis of the identity of God, revealed to Israel in the name of Yhwh. The concise style and the usage of small type characters made it possible to include a great amount of information in this study.

7.2 New Testament Theology

J.-N. ALETTI, *Jésus Christ fait-il l'unité du Nouveau Testament?* (Jésus et Jésus-Christ 61; Paris 1994); It. tr. *Gesù Cristo: unità del Nuovo Testamento?* (Roma 1995); Sp. tr. *Jesu-Cristo ¿factor de unidad del Nuevo Testamento?* (Agape 22; Salamanca 2000).

The monograph deals with the main keynote of the New Testament. The reflections highlight that everything that is told of Jesus has a Christological dimension, so that his person unifies the NT message.

R. K. BULTMANN, *Theologie des Neuen Testaments* (NThG; Tübingen ⁶1968, ⁹1984); Eng. tr. *Theology of the New Testament* (New York 1951); Sp. tr. *Teología del Nuevo Testamento* (Biblioteca EstB 32; Salamanca 1981); It. tr. *Teologia del Nuovo Testamento* (Brescia ⁴1991).

This well-known work has been published many times beginning from 1948. In spite of numerous critics, it continues to be an important point of reference for students and scholars. Bultmann prepared the first six editions. After his death (1977), O. Merk edited and completed the following editions.

98

H. CONZELMANN, *Grundriß der Theologie des Neuen Testament* (Bearbeitet von A. LINDEMANN) (UTB.W 1446; Tübingen ⁶1997); Eng. tr. *An Outline of the Theology of the New Testament* (New York – Evanston, IL 1969); It. tr. *Teologia del Nuovo Testamento* (Biblioteca teologica 5; Brescia ⁴1991).

The work has developed over the course of thirty years (first edition in 1967). As a result, it adds data coming from developments in theological studies and it updates the bibliography. The author follows Bultmann's tradition, completing it or proposing some personal solutions. The author and the coauthor meant this compendium for students, pastors, teachers of religion and engaged Christians. The content of the works exceeds, however, this circle of receivers.

L. GOPPELT, *Theologie des Neuen Testaments* (GTL; Göttingen 1975, 1976) I-II; Eng. tr. *Theology of the New Testament* (Grand Rapids, MI 1981, 1982) I-II; It. tr. *Teologia del Nuovo Testamento* (Brescia 1982, 1983) I-II.

After the author's death (1973), J. Roloff prepared this work for printing. Volume I is dedicated to Jesus' activity from the point of view of its theological meaning (*Jesu Wirken in seiner theologischen Bedeutung*), and volume II contains issues related to multiplicity and the uniqueness of the apostolic witness to Jesus (*Vielfalt und Einheit des apostolischen Christuszeugnisses*). This advanced study deals with all questions of modern NT theology.

F. HAHN, *Theologie des Neuen Testaments* (Tübingen 2002) I-II.

This work of more than 1,700 pages completes worthily the career of the scholar from Munich. Volume I works out diachronically various perspectives of the NT history of theology of early Christianity. Volume II, thematic, discusses arguments in favor of the uniqueness of the New Testament, which are focused on the theme of divine revelation.

J. JEREMIAS, *New Testament Theology.* Proclamation of Jesus (New York 1971); Ger. ed. *Neutestamentiliche Theologie.* I. Die Verkündigung Jesu (Gütersloh 1971); It. tr. *La teologia del Nuovo Testamento* (Brescia ²1976); Fr. tr. *Théologie du Nouveau Testament.* Première partie: La prédication de Jésus (LeDiv 76; Paris 1975).

The German edition appeared simultaneously with the English one. Due to the author's death (1979), the project has not been finished. Taking into account his previous works, the author worked out the subject of the proclamation of Jesus in seven chapters: the reliability of the sayings of Jesus, his mission, the dawn of the time of salvation, the period of grace, the new people of God, Jesus' testimony to his mission, Easter.

W. G. KÜMMEL, *Die Theologie des Neuen Testaments nach seinen Hauptzeugen Jesus, Paulus, Johannes* (GNT 3; Göttingen ³1976); Eng. tr. *The Theology of the New Testament According to Its Major Witnesses: Jesus – Paul – John* (Nashville 1973); It. tr. *La teologia del Nuovo Testamento, Gesù, Paolo, Giovanni* (Brescia 1976).

The work came into being in a Lutheran milieu. It deals with the preaching of Jesus in the synoptic Gospels and with the faith of the early community. The study discusses Pauline theology and the Johannine message of Jesus in the Fourth Gospel and in the epistles.

K.-H. SCHELKLE, *Theologie des Neuen Testaments* (Düsseldorf 1968, 1973, 1970, 1974, 1976 [vol. 4 in two parts]) I-IV; It. tr. *Teologia del Nuovo Testamento* (Bologna 1969, 1980, 1974, 1980) I-IV; Eng. tr. *Theology of the New Testament* (Collegeville, MN 1971, 1973, 1976, 1978) I-IV; Sp. tr. *Teología de Nuevo Testamento* (Barcelona 1975, 1977, 1975, 1978) I-IV; Pol. tr. *Teologia Nowego Testamentu* (Kraków 1985, 1985, 1984) I-III.

This Catholic work presents in four volumes various aspects of NT theology: 1. Creation (world, time, human being); 2. God in Christ; 3. Ethos; 4/1. The fulfillment of the work of creation and salvation; 4/2. the community of disciples and the Church.

8. Biblical Geography (Atlases and Textbooks)

S. MITTMANN – G. SCHMITT (ed.), *Tübinger Bibelatlas*. Auf der Grundlage des Tübinger Atlas des Vorderen Orients (TAVO) / *Tübingen Bible Atlas*. Based on the Tübingen Atlas of the Near and Middle East (Stuttgart 2001).

The atlas contains 27 geographical maps. Twenty-four of them have been taken from the *Tübinger Atlas des Vorderen Orients*. The three additional maps treat of Paul's journeys and his letters, the Christianity of the first four centuries and the archaeology and history of Sinai. The maps of Palestine, the Mediterranean environment, and the Ancient Near East (50 x 72 cm = 19.7" x 28.3") cover the span of time from the third millennium B.C. to 1920.

H. G. MAY et al. (ed.), *Oxford Bible Atlas* (Oxford [2]1974); Sp. tr. *Atlas bíblico Oxford* (Estella [2]1998).

This is a concise historical atlas with 26 maps and pictures of many geographical and archaeological sites. A Spanish edition was undertaken by C. Ruiz Garrido.

E. GALBIATI – F. SERAFINI, *Atlante storico della Bibbia* (Milano 2004); Sp. tr. *Atlas histórico de la Biblia* (Madrid 2004).

This historical atlas spans the time from the fourth millennium B.C. to the Roman period. E. Galbiati, who died in the year of its publication, had already worked on an atlas of this kind with the collaboration of A. Aletti, *Atlante storico della Bibbia e dell'Antico Oriente. Dalla preistoria alla caduta di Gerusalemme nell'anno 70* (Enciclopedie per tutti 7; Milano 1983).

Y. AHARONI, *The Land of the Bible*. A Historical Geography (Revised and Enlarged Edition) (Philadelphia ²1979).

The English version of this classic work was completed after the death of Y. Aharoni (1976) by A. F. Rainey. It deals with all historical periods and discusses data of geographical, political and sociological character, some of which, at times, is absent in some historical works on the Holy Land.

P. A. KASWALDER, *Onomastica biblica*. Fonti scritte e ricerca archeologica (SBF.CMi 40; Jerusalem 2002).

This handbook gives an introduction to the biblical geography of the Old and New Testament, the geography of the Holy Land during the Arabic period and the Crusades, from extra-biblical sources of various periods and presenting many geographical sites.

9. Inscriptions

H. DONNER – W. RÖLLIG, *Kanaanäische und aramäische Inschriften* (Wiesbaden ²1966-1969) I-III.

The three volumes of this anthology contain respectively the text of the inscriptions, comments, and indexes. The 279 inscriptions are divided into six categories: Phoenician, Punic, Neopunic, Moabitic, Hebrew and Aramaic.

H. DONNER – W. RÖLLIG, *Kanaanäische und aramäische Inschriften* (Wiesbaden ⁵2002-) I.

Volume I of the fifth edition provides the revised text of the inscriptions of the previous publication with an addition of some new inscriptions.

J. RENZ – W. RÖLLIG, *Handbuch der althebräischen Epigraphik* (Darmstadt 1995-2003) I-III.

The volumes gather the Hebrew inscriptions from the tenth to the sixth centuries B.C. (all of which were already published), adding a translation, comments and an extensive bibliography. Inscriptions from tombstones, papyri, ostraca, etc. are arranged in chronological ascending order. Volume I is dedicated to seals and paleographical notes.

G. I. DAVIES et al., *Ancient Hebrew Inscriptions*. Corpus and Concordance (Cambridge – New York 1991, 2004) I-II.

This collection provides, in part one, the text of the Hebrew inscriptions of the OT period; the second part offers a concordance that provides access to the corpus of texts and facilitates philological, historical and archaeological research. Volume II contains additions and corrections to the previous study, along with synoptic tables which allow one to compare the content of the entire work with the *Handbuch* by RENZ – RÖLLIG, and with the volume by N. AVIGAD – B. SASS, *Corpus of West Semitic Stamp Seals* (Jerusalem 1997).

F. W. DOBBS-ALLSOPP et al., *Hebrew Inscriptions*. Texts from the Biblical Period of the Monarchy with Concordance (New Haven, CT – London 2005).

All important Hebrew inscriptions, chosen for this new edition, match, to a great degree, those published in the collections of J. Renz and G. I. Davies. However, some texts were excluded because they are too fragmentary or are only with difficulty classifiable as Hebrew inscriptions. F. W. Dobbs-Allsopp, J. J. M. Roberts, C. L. Seow and R. E. Whitaker present each inscription with an introduction, a new transliteration, translation, philological and historical notes along with textual commentary. They provide an up-to-date bibliography and an extended concordance (pp. 657-804).

J. C. L. GIBSON, *Textbook of Syrian Semitic Inscriptions*. I. Hebrew and Moabite Inscriptions. II. Aramaic Inscriptions Including

Inscriptions in the Dialect of Zenjirli. III. Phoenician Inscriptions Including Inscriptions in the Mixed Dialect of Arslan Tash (Oxford 1971, 1975, 1982).

This anthology of Hebrew-Moabite (vol. 1), Aramaic (vol. 2) and Phoenician (vol. 3) inscriptions also provides a translation and philological and historical commentary.

10. Ancient Near East

In this section, some collections of texts translated into modern languages and those containing images from the Ancient Near East will be highlighted.

10.1 *ANET and ANEP*

J. B. PRITCHARD (ed.), *Ancient Near East Texts Relating to the Old Testament* (Princeton, NJ ^{3}1969).

The third edition of *ANET* contains new materials compared to the second edition (1955), and offers a revised translation of the previous texts. The texts are from Egyptian, Sumerian, Akkadian, Hittite, Ugaritic, South Arabian, Canaanite and Aramaic regions, and they are categorized on the basis of their literary form (myths, legends, legislative texts, etc.).

J. B. PRITCHARD (ed.), *The Ancient Near East*. Supplementary Text and Pictures Relating to the Old Testament (Princeton, NJ 1969).

This work is intended as a supplement to the previous version of *ANET* and *ANEP*. It gathers documentation found during recent excavations in Palestine, Syria, Jordan, and Iraq.

J. B. PRITCHARD (ed.), *The Ancient Near East in Pictures Relating to the Old Testament* (With Supplement) (Princeton, NJ ^{2}1969).

This collection of 882 black and white pictures and designs is arranged by different categories: peoples and their clothes, everyday life, etc. Each picture and design is numbered and described.

10.2 *The Context of Scripture*

W. W. HALLO – K. L. YOUNGER Jr. (ed.), *The Context of Scripture*. Canonical Compositions, Monumental Inscriptions, and Archival Documents from the Biblical World (Leiden 1997-2002) I-III.

This is an extended collection of texts from the Ancient Near East, published formerly in other works. It also provides a translation of newly discovered documents. The English version corrects, at times, the existing translations. The anthology offers references to biblical passages, and an updated bibliography. The respective volumes are entitled as follows:

1. Canonical Compositions from the Biblical World (1997);
2. Monumental Inscriptions from the Biblical World (2000);
3. Archival Documents from the Biblical World (2002).

10.3 *SBL Writings from the Ancient World*

This series of the Society of Biblical Literature, from 1990 onward, is edited by B. O. Long. Its goal is to offer the English translation of texts coming from different cultural environments of the Ancient Near East, beginning with Sumerian civilization and extending to the age of Alexander the Great.

Scholars Press in Atlanta has published the following volumes:

E. F. WENTE – E. S. MELTZER (ed.), *Letters from Ancient Egypt* (SBL Writings from the Ancient World 1; 1990).

H. A. HOFFNER Jr. – G. M. BECKMAN (ed.), *Hittite Myths* (SBL Writings from the Ancient World 2; 1990, ²1998).

P. MICHALOWSKI – E. REINER (ed.), *Letters from Early Mesopotamia* (SBL Writings from the Ancient World 3; 1993).

J. M. LINDENBERGER – K. H. RICHARDS (ed.), *Ancient Aramaic and Hebrew Letters* (SBL Writings from the Ancient World 4; 1994).

W. J. MURNANE – E. S. MELTZER (ed.), *Texts from the Amarna Period in Egypt* (SBL Writings from the Ancient World 5; 1995).

M. T. ROTH – H. A. HOFFNER Jr. – P. MICHALOWSKI (ed.), *Law Collections from Mesopotamia and Asia Minor* (SBL Writings from the Ancient World 6; 1995, ²1997).

G. M. BECKMAN – H. A. HOFFNER Jr. (ed.), *Hittite Diplomatic Texts* (SBL Writings from the Ancient World 7; 1996, ²1999).

J. L. FOSTER – S. T. HOLLIS (ed.), *Hymns, Prayers, and Songs.* An Anthology of Ancient Egyptian Lyric Poetry (SBL Writings from the Ancient World 8; 1995).

S. B. PARKER et al. (ed.), *Ugaritic Narrative Poetry* (SBL Writings from the Ancient World 9; 1997).

D. PARDEE – T. J. LEWIS (ed.), *Ritual and Cult at Ugarit* (SBL Writings from the Ancient World 10; 2002).

I. SINGER – H. A. HOFFNER Jr. (ed.), *Hittite Prayers* (SBL Writings from the Ancient World 11; 2002).

M. NISSINEN et al. (ed.), *Prophets and Prophecy in the Ancient Near East* (SBL Writings from the Ancient World 12; 2003).

J. M. LINDENBERGER – K. H. RICHARDS (ed.), *Ancient Aramaic and Hebrew Letters* (SBL Writings from the Ancient World 14; 2003).

N. C. STRUDWICK – R. J. LEPROHON (ed.), *Texts from the Pyramid Age* (SBL Writings from the Ancient World 16; 2005).

J.-J. GLASSNER – B. J. FOSTER (ed.), *Mesopotamian Chronicles* (SBL Writings from the Ancient World 19; 2004).

H. VANSTIPHOUT – J. S. COOPER (ed.), *Epics of Sumerian Kings.* The Matter of Aratta (SBL Writings from the Ancient World 20; 2003).

R. K. RITNER (ed.), *Inscriptions from Egypt's Third Intermediate Period* (SBL Writings from the Ancient World 21; 2005).

J. P. ALLEN – P. DER MANUELIAN (ed.), *The Ancient Egyptian Pyramid Texts* (SBL Writings from the Ancient World 23; 2005).

E. FROOD (ed.), *Biographical Texts from Ramessid Egypt* (SBL Writings from the Ancient World 26; Atlanta 2007).

10.4 *LAPO*

The series *Littératures anciennes du Proche-Orient* began to be published in 1967 by Éditions du Cerf (Paris), under the auspices of the École Biblique et Archéologique Française of Jerusalem. The literary texts are divided into six sections according to geographical area: Egyptian, Sumerian, Akkadian, Hittite, Northwest Semitic, South Arabic.

Thus far, the following volumes are published:

P. BARGUET (ed.), *Le livre des morts des anciens Égyptiens* (LAPO 1; 1967).

G. CARDASCIA (ed.), *Les lois assyriennes* (LAPO 2; 1969).

E. SOLLBERGER – J.-R. KUPPER (ed.), *Inscriptions royales sumériennes et akkadiennes* (LAPO 3; 1971).

J.-C. GOYON (ed.), *Rituels funéraires de l'ancienne Égypte.* Le rituel de l'embaumement, le rituel de l'ouverture de la bouche, les livres de respirations (LAPO 4; 1972, 2000).

P. GRELOT (ed.), *Documents araméens d'Égypte* (LAPO 5; 1972).

A. FINET (ed.), *Le Code de Hammurapi* (LAPO 6; ⁴2002).

A. CAQUOT – M. SZNYCER – A. HERDNER (ed.), *Textes ougaritiques.* Mythes et légendes (LAPO 7; 1974) I.

M.-J. SEUX (ed.), Hymnes et prières aux dieux de Babylonie et d'Assyrie (LAPO 8; 1976).

A. LEMAIRE (ed.), *Inscriptions hébraïques.* Les ostraca (LAPO 9; 1977) I.

A. BARUCQ – F. DAUMAS (ed.), *Hymnes et prières de l'Égypte ancienne* (LAPO 10; 1980).

A. ROCCATI (ed.), La littérature historique sous l'Ancien Empire égyptien (LAPO 11; 1982).

P. BARGUET (ed.), *Les textes des sarcophages égyptiens du Moyen Empire* (LAPO 12; 1986).

W. L. MORAN et al. (ed.), *Les lettres d'El-Amarna*. Correspondance diplomatique du pharaon (LAPO 13; 1987).
A. CAQUOT – J.-L. CUNCHILLOS – J.-M. DE TARRAGON (ed.), *Textes ougaritiques*. Textes religieux et rituels. Correspondance (LAPO 14; 1989) II.
R. J. TOURNAY – A. SHAFFER (ed.), *L'Épopée de Gilgamesh* (LAPO 15; 1994, 2003).
J.-M. DURAND (ed.), *Les documents épistolaires du palais de Mari* (LAPO 16-18; 1997, 1998, 2000) I-III.
C. MICHEL (ed.), Correspondance des marchands de Kanish au début du IIe millénaire avant J.-C. (LAPO 19; 2001).
S. LACKENBACHER (ed.), *Textes akkadiens d'Ugarit*. Textes provenant des vingt-cinq premières campagnes (LAPO 20; 2002).

10.5 *TUAT and TUAT Neue Folge*

O. KAISER et al. (ed.), *Texte aus der Umwelt des Alten Testaments* (Gütersloh 1982-1995) I-III + Ergänzungslieferung (2001).

This extended work provides, in German translation, texts from different areas of the Ancient Near East, updating them on the basis of new discoveries.

The following volumes have been issued:

1. Rechts- und Wirtschaftskunden. Historisch-chronologische Texte (1982-1985); 2/1. Orakel, Rituale. Bau- und Votivinschften. Lieder und Gebete (1986-1991); 2/2. Religiöse Texte. Rituale und Beschwörungen I (1987); 2/3. Religiöse Texte. Rituale und Beschwörungen II (1988); 2/4. Religiöse Texte. Grab-, Sarg-, Votiv- und Bauinschriften (1988); 2/5. Religiöse Texte. Lieder und Gebete I (1989); 2/6. Religiöse Texte. Lieder und Gebete II (1991); 3/1. Weisheitstexte, Mythen und Epen. Weisheitstexte I (1990); 3/2. Weisheitstexte, Mythen und Epen. Weisheitstexte II (1991); 3/3. Weisheitstexte, Mythen und Epen. Mythen und Epen I (1993); 3/4. Weisheitstexte, Mythen und Epen. Mythen und Epen II (1994);

3/5. Weisheitstexte, Mythen und Epen. Mythen und Epen III (1995); Ergänzungslieferung (2001).

An electronic version is also available:

B. BOCK (ed.), *Texte aus der Umwelt des Alten Testaments.* Gesamtedition (Gütersloh 2005) [CD-ROM].

B. JANOWSKI – G. WILHELM (ed.), *Texte aus der Umwelt des Alten Testaments.* Neue Folge (Gütersloh 2004-) I-IV.

This new series completes the previous one. It provides additional texts, which TUAT did not issue. The documents are arranged according to their categories. Furthermore, the editors included material coming from the other cultures as well (Hurrian, Iranian, South Arabic) and from the papyri.
The following volumes are published, at present:

1. *Texte zum Rechts- und Wirtschaftsleben* (2004); 2. *Staatsverträge, Herrscherinschriften und andere Dokumente zur politischen Geschichte* (2005); 3. *Briefe* (2006); 4. *Omina, Orakel, Rituale und Beschwörungen* (2008).

10.6 *Various Anthologies*

In this section some collected translations of texts from the Ancient Near East and Internet sites which can be useful for students are mentioned.

J. BOTTÉRO – S. N. KRAMER (ed.), *Lorsque les dieux faisaient l'homme.* Mythologie mésopotamienne (Bibliothèque des histoires; Paris 1989); It. tr. *Uomini e dèi della Mesopotamia.* Alle origini della mitologia (I millenni; Torino 1992).

E. BRESCIANI (ed.), *Letteratura e poesia dell'antico Egitto* (I millenni; Torino ²1970).

B. R. FOSTER (ed.), *Before the Muses.* An Anthology of Akkadian Literature (Bethesda, MD 1993) I-II.

V. H. MATTHEWS – D. C. BENJAMIN, *Old Testament Parallels*. Laws and Stories from the Ancient Near East (Mahwah, NJ 1997); Sp. tr. *Paralelos del Antiguo Testamento*. Leyes y relatos del Antiguo Oriente Bíblico (Panorama 5; Santander 2004).

G. DEL OLMO LETE (ed.), *Mitos y leyendas de Canaán según la tradición de Ugarit* (FCiBi 1; Madrid 1981).

G. PETTINATO (ed.), *Mitologia sumerica* (CdR Religioni orientali; Torino 2001).

M. QUESNEL – P. GRUSON (ed.), *La Bible et sa culture*. I. Ancien Testament (Paris 2000); Sp. tr. *La Biblia y su cultura*. I. Antiguo Testamento (Santander 2002).

The Electronic Text Corpus of Sumerian Literature

This is a web site of the Oriental Institute of Oxford University. It offers Sumerian literary texts in transcription and translation:

http://www-etcsl.orient.ox.ac.uk

Electronic Tools and Ancient Near Eastern Archives (ETANA)

Developed by various scholarly institutions[5], this Internet site provides valuable data for the study of the Ancient Near East, such as reports on archaeological excavations, editions of ancient and modern texts, foundational monographs, dictionaries, journals and reports in the public domain, etc.:

http://www.etana.org

---

[5] E.g. The American Oriental Society; The American Schools of Oriental Research; Case Western Reserve University Library; The Cobb Institute of Archaeology at Mississippi State University; The Oriental Institute, University of Chicago; The Society of Biblical Literature; The Sonia and Marco Nadler Institute of Archaeology of Tel Aviv University; Vanderbilt Divinity School and the Graduate Department of Religion; Vanderbilt Divinity Library.

11. Qumran and Similar Sites

11.1 *Research Tools*

Two tools are indicated here with which the reader can find other studies and bibliographical collections.

F. GARCÍA MARTÍNEZ – D. W. PARRY, *A Bibliography of the Finds in the Desert of Judah 1970-95*. Arranged by Author with Citation and Subject Indexes (StTDJ 19; Leiden – New York – Köln 1996).

This volume furnishes a comprehensive bibliography on the Dead Sea Scrolls. The subject index is a useful help for accessing entries. This collection integrates two other collections:

> LASOR, W. S., *Bibliography of the Dead Sea Scrolls 1948-1957* (Pasadena, CA 1958).
> JONGELING, B., *A Classified Bibliography of the Finds in the Desert of Judah 1958-1969* (StTDJ 7; Leiden 1971).

A. PINNICK, *The Orion Center Bibliography of the Dead Sea Scrolls (1995-2000)* (StTDJ 41; Leiden – Boston – Köln 2001).

The materials present in this work are available online:

http://orion.mscc.huji.ac.il

The editors of the site The Orion Center for the Study of the Dead Sea Scrolls and Associated Literature (Hebrew University, Jerusalem) intend to provide continuously updated bibliography on the topic.

J. SIEVERS, "Testi di Qumran – alcuni suggerimenti per la ricerca", http://www.biblico.it/doc-vari/sievers_qumran.html [accessed January 9, 2009].

This web site, updated until March 7, 2000, offers a bibliography and useful suggestions for scientific research on Qumran.

11.2 *Discoveries in the Judaean Desert*

Discoveries in the Judaean Desert (*of Jordan*) is an important series, containing the *editio princeps* of texts from the caves of Qumran and from other sites of the Judean Desert. It offers transcriptions, translations of texts, short annotations and photographs. Beginning from 1955, Clarendon Press (Oxford) published the following volumes:

D. BARTHÉLEMY – J. T. MILIK (ed.), *Qumran Cave 1* (DJD 1; 1955).

P. BENOIT – J. T. MILIK – R. DE VAUX (ed.), *Les grottes de Murabba*ʿ*ât. I.* Texte. II. Planches (DJD 2; 1961).

M. BAILLET – J. T. MILIK – R. DE VAUX (ed.), *Les "petites grottes" de Qumrân.* Exploration de la falaise. Les Grottes 2Q, 3Q, 5Q, 6Q, 7Q à 10Q. Le rouleau de cuivre. I. Textes. II. Planches (DJD 3; 1962).

J. A. SANDERS (ed.), *The Psalms Scroll of Qumrân Cave 11* (11QPsª) (DJD 4; 1965).

J. M. ALLEGRO (ed.), *Qumran Cave 4. I* (4Q158–4Q186) (DJD 5; 1968).

R. DE VAUX – J. T. MILIK (ed.), *Qumrân grotte 4. II.* Archéologie. Tefillin, mezuzot et targums (4Q128–4Q157) (DJD 6; 1977).

M. BAILLET (ed.), *Qumrân grotte 4. III* (4Q482–4Q520) (DJD 7; 1982).

E. TOV (ed.), *The Greek Minor Prophets Scroll from Naḥal Ḥever* (8ḤevXIIgr) (The Seiyâl Collection I) (DJD 8; 1990).

P. W. SKEHAN – E. ULRICH – J. E. SANDERSON (ed.), *Qumran Cave 4. IV.* Palaeo-Hebrew and Greek Biblical Manuscripts (DJD 9; 1992).

E. QIMRON – J. STRUGNELL (ed.), *Qumran Cave 4. V.* Miqṣat Maʿaśe ha-Torah (DJD 10; 1994).

E. ESHEL et al. (ed.), *Qumran Cave 4. VI.* Poetical and Liturgical Texts, Part 1 (DJD 11; 1998).

E. ULRICH et al. (ed.), *Qumran Cave 4. VII.* Genesis to Numbers (DJD 12; 1994).

H. W. Attridge et al. (ed.), *Qumran Cave 4. VIII*. Parabiblical Texts, Part 1 (DJD 13; 1994).

E. Ulrich et al. (ed.), *Qumran Cave 4. IX*. Deuteronomy, Joshua, Judges, Kings (DJD 14; 1995).

E. Ulrich et al. (ed.), *Qumran Cave 4. X*. The Prophets (DJD 15; 1997).

E. Ulrich et al. (ed.), *Qumran Cave 4. XI*. Psalms to Chronicles (DJD 16; 2000).

F. M. Cross et al. (ed.), *Qumran Cave 4. XII*. 1–2 Samuel (DJD 17; 2005).

J. M. Baumgarten et al. (ed.), *Qumran Cave 4. XIII*. The Damascus Document (4Q266-273) (DJD 18; 1996).

M. Broshi et al. (ed.), *Qumran Cave 4. XIV*. Parabiblical Texts, Part 2 (DJD 19; 1995).

T. Elgvin et al. (ed.), *Qumran Cave 4. XV*. Sapiential Texts, Part 1 (DJD 20; 1997).

S. Talmon – J. Ben-Dov – U. Glessmer (ed.), *Qumran Cave 4. XVI*. Calendrical Texts (DJD 21; 2001).

G. Brooke et al. (ed.), *Qumran Cave 4. XVII*. Parabiblical Texts, Part 3 (DJD 22; 1996).

F. García Martínez – E. J. C. Tigchelaar – A. S. van der Woude (ed.), *Qumran Cave 11. II* (11Q2–18, 11Q20–30) (DJD 23; 1998).

M. J. W. Leith (ed.), *Wadi Daliyeh I*. The Wadi Daliyeh Seal Impressions (DJD 24; 1997).

É. Puech (ed.), *Qumrân grotte 4. XVIII*. Textes hébreux (4Q521–4Q528, 4Q576–4Q579) (DJD 25; 1998).

P. S. Alexander – G. Vermes (ed.), *Qumran Cave 4. XIX*. Serekh Ha-Yaḥad and Two Related Texts (DJD 26; 1998).

H. M. Cotton – A. Yardeni (ed.), Aramaic, Hebrew, and Greek Documentary Texts from Naḥal Ḥever and Other Sites, with an Appendix Containing Alleged Qumran Texts (The Seiyâl Collection II) (DJD 27; 1997).

D. Gropp et al. (ed.), *Wadi Daliyeh II*. The Samaria Papyri from Wadi Daliyeh – *Qumran Cave 4. XXVIII*. Miscellanea, Part 2 (DJD 28; 2001).

E. CHAZON et al. (ed.), *Qumran Cave 4. XX.* Poetical and Liturgical Texts, Part 2 (DJD 29; 1999).

D. DIMANT (ed.), *Qumran Cave 4. XXI.* Parabiblical Texts, Part 4. Pseudo-Prophetic Texts (Partially Based on Earlier Texts by J. Strugnell) (DJD 30; 2001).

É. PUECH (ed.), *Qumrân grotte 4. XXII.* Textes araméens première partie 4Q529–549, (DJD 31; 2001).

D. M. PIKE et al. (ed.), *Qumran Cave 4. XXIII.* Unidentified Fragments (DJD 33; 2001).

J. STRUGNELL et al. (ed.), *Qumran Cave 4. XXIV.* Sapiential Texts, Part 2. 4QInstruction (Mûsār Lᵉ Mēvîn): 4Q415 ff. with a Re-edition of 1Q26 and an Edition of 4Q423 (DJD 34; 1999).

J. M. BAUMGARTEN et al. (ed.), *Qumran Cave 4. XXV.* Halakhic Texts (DJD 35; 1999).

S. J. PFANN et al. (ed.), *Qumran Cave 4. XXVI.* Cryptic Texts and Miscellanea, Part 1 (DJD 36; 2000).

É. PUECH (ed.), *Qumran Grotte 4. XXVII.* Textes en Araméen, deuxième partie (DJD 37; Oxford 2008).

J. H. CHARLESWORTH et al. (ed.), *Miscellaneous Texts from the Judaean Desert* (DJD 38; 2000).

E. TOV et al. (ed.), *The Text from the Judaean Desert.* Indices and an Introduction to the Discoveries in the Judaean Desert Series (DJD 39; Oxford 2002).

H. STEGEMANN et al. (ed.), *Qumran Cave 1.III: 1QHodayot^a.* With Incorporation of 4QHodayot^{a-f} and 1QHodayot^b (DJD 40; Oxford 2008).

11.3 *The Dead Sea Scrolls Reader*

This series is edited by D. W. Parry and E. Tov, in collaboration with N. Gordon and D. Fry. It presents all non-biblical texts from Qumran and similar sites. The material is grouped in six parts and is arranged by genres and content. On the left-hand page there are passages in Hebrew, Aramaic or Greek (from DJD), whereas the

English translation is located on the right-hand page (from DJD or
M. O. Wise – M. G. Abegg Jr. – E. M. Cook, *The Dead Sea Scrolls.
A New Translation* [San Francisco 1996]). Brill (Leiden – Boston)
has published the following volumes:

> 1. *Texts Concerned with Religious Law* (2004); 2. *Exegetical
> Texts* (2004); 3. *Parabiblical Texts* (2005); 4. *Calendrical and
> Sapiential Texts* (2004); 5. *Poetic and Liturgical Texts* (2005);
> 6. *Additional Genres and Unclassified Texts* (2005).

11.4 *The Dead Sea Scrolls Electronic Reference Library*

In 1993 Brill and Oxford University Press began publishing the
Qumran texts on CD-ROM. *The Dead Sea Scrolls Electronic Reference Library* project supplies microfilms which, thanks to sophisti-
cated software, make possible the visualization of the text in the finest
details. The third CD-ROM incorporates *The Dead Sea Scrolls Reader* series and provides all the texts and images of the non-biblical MSS
in the original languages (with morphological analysis) and in English. The CD-ROMs also contain some modern studies.
Available are:

> Alexander, P. S. – Lim, T. H. (ed.), *The Dead Sea Scrolls Elec-
> tronic Reference Library* (Leiden 1997) I [CD-ROM].
> Tov, E. (ed.), *The Dead Sea Scrolls Electronic Reference Library*
> (Leiden 1999) II [CD-ROM].
> ———, *The Dead Sea Scrolls Electronic Reference Library* (Leiden
> 2006) III [CD-ROM].

12. Rabbinic Texts

This section is addressed to non-specialists in rabbinic studies, especially to students of Holy Scripture. Its main goal is to make it less
difficult for them to access the rabbinic literature cross-referenced to
the Bible.

For the convenience of the reader, abbreviations of this literary collection are provided, followed by a short presentation of some introductory works. In these introductions, the student can find fundamental notions related to rabbinic literature. The exposition itself is a description of works which permit one to go from the Bible to rabbinic texts. For students who do not know Hebrew, modern translations of individual works will be provided afterward (Mishnah, Tosefta, Talmud, etc.) and, for readers who also wish to consult original editions, a list will also be presented[6].

12.1 *Abbreviations*

As for a method of quoting rabbinic texts, see SCHWERTNER, *IATG²*, xl-xli:

Tractates of Mishnah, Tosefta, and Talmud

Ar	ʿArakhin
Av	Avot
AZ	ʿAvoda Zara
BB	Baba Batra
Bekh	Bekhorot
Ber	Berakhot
Bes	Beṣa (Yom Ṭov)
Bik	Bikkurim

---

[6] There are useful concordances for scholarly analysis of the Mishnah, Tosefta and Talmud, such as H. J. KASOVSKY, *Concordantiae totius Mischnae* (Francofurti a.M. 1927) I-II; IDEM, *Thesaurus Mishnae*. Concordantiae verborum quae in sex Mishnae ordinibus reperiuntur (Hierosolymis 1956-1960) I-IV; IDEM, *Thesaurus Thosephthae*. Concordantiae verborum quae in sex Thosephthae ordinibus reperiuntur (Hierosolymis 1932-1961) I-VI; IDEM et al., *Thesaurus Talmudis*. Concordantiae verborum quae in Talmude Babilonico reperiuntur (Hierosolymis 1954-1982) I-XLI + *Index Thesaurus Talmudis*. Concordantiae verborum quae in Talmude Babilonico reperiuntur ad tomos: I-XLI (Hierosolymis 1989).

BM	Baba Meṣiᶜa
BQ	Baba Qamma
Dem	Demai
Ed	ᶜEduyot
Er	ᶜEruvin
Git	Giṭṭin
Hag	Ḥagiga
Hal	Ḥalla
Hor	Horayot
Hul	Ḥullin
Kel	Kelim
Ker	Keritot
Ket	Ketubbot
Kil	Kilʾayim
Maas	Maᶜasrot
Mak	Makkot
Makh	Makhshirin
Meg	Megilla
Meil	Meᶜila
Men	Menaḥot
Mid	Middot
Miq	Miqwaʾot
MQ	Moᶜed Qaṭan
MSh	Maᶜaser Sheni
Naz	Nazir
Ned	Nedarim
Neg	Negaᶜim
Nid	Nidda
Ohal	Ohalot
Orl	ᶜOrla
Par	Para
Pea	Peʾa
Pes	Pesaḥim
Qid	Qiddushin
Qin	Qinnim

RHSh	Rosh HaShana
San	Sanhedrin
Shab	Shabbat
Sheq	Sheqalim
Shevi	Shevi'it
Shevu	Shevu'ot
Sot	Soṭa
Suk	Sukka
Taan	Ta'anit
Tam	Tamid
Tem	Temura
Ter	Terumot
TevY	Ṭevul Yom
Toh	Ṭoharot
Uq	'Uqṣin
Yad	Yadayim
Yev	Yevamot
Yom	Yoma
Yom Ṭov	→ Bes (Beṣa)
Zav	Zavim
Zev	Zevaḥim

Midrashim, Targumim, and Collections

AgAg	Aggadat, Aggadot. Qoveṣ midrashim qeṭanim
AgBer	Aggadat Bereshit
AgEst	Aggadat Ester
AgShir	Aggadat Shir HaShirim
ARN	Avot deRabbi Natan
b	Talmud Bavli
BatM	Bate Midrashot
BemR	Bemidbar Rabba
BerR	Bereshit Rabba
BerRbti	Bereshit Rabbati
BerZ	Bereshit Zuṭa

BHM	Bet HaMidrash
CN	Codex Neofiti
DER	Derekh Ereṣ Rabba
DevR	Devarim Rabba
DEZ	Derekh Ereṣ Zuṭa
EkhaR	Ekha Rabba
EkhaZ	Ekha Zuṭa
EstR	Ester Rabba
Evel Rabbati	→ Sem (Semaḥot)
Kalla	Kalla
LeqT	Leqaḥ Ṭov
m	Mishna
MegTaan	Megillat Taʿanit
MekhSh	Mekhilta deRabbi Shimʿon b. Yoḥai
MekhY	Mekhilta deRabbi Yishmaʾel
MHG Bam	Midrash HaGadol Bamidbar
MHG Ber	Midrash HaGadol Bereshit
MHG Dev	Midrash HaGadol Devarim
MHG Shem	Midrash HaGadol Shemot
MHG Wa	Midrash HaGadol Wayiqra
Midrash Zuṭa	→ EkhaZ, QohZ, RutZ, ShirZ
MMish	Midrash Mishle
MShem	Midrash Shemuʾel
MShir	Midrash Shir HaShirim (ed. L. GRÜNHUT)
MTann	Midrash Tannaʾim (Mekhilta le-Sefer Davarim)
MTeh	Midrash Tehilim (Shoḥer Ṭov)
OsM	Oṣar Midrashim (ed. J. D. EISENSTEIN)
Pesiqta Zuṭarta	→ LeqT (Leqḥ Ṭov)
PesK	Pesiqta deRav Kahana
PesR	Pesiqta Rabbati
PRE	Pirqe deRabbi Eliʾezer
QohR	Qohelet Rabba
QohZ	Qohelet Zuṭa
RutR	Rut Rabba
RutZ	Rut Zuṭa

SAME	Sifre deAggadat Megillat Ester
SekhT	Sekhel Ṭov
Sem	Semaḥot (Evel Rabbati)
SER	Seder Eliyyahu Rabba
SEZ	Seder Eliyyahu Zuṭa
ShemR	Shemot Rabba
ShirR	Shir HaShirim Rabba
ShirZ	Shir HaShirim Zuṭa
Shoḥer Ṭov	→ MTeh (Midrash Tehilim)
SifBam	Sifre Bamidbar
SifDev	Sifre Devarim
Sifra	Sifra
SifZ	Sifre Zuṭa
Sof	Soferim
SOR	Seder ᶜOlam Rabba
SOZ	Seder ᶜOlam Zuṭa
t	Tosefta
Tan	Tanḥuma
TanB	Tanḥuma (ed. S. BUBER)
Tanna deBe Eliyyahu	→ SER, SEZ (Seder Eliyyahu Rabba/Zuṭa)
TFrag	Fragmenten-Targum (Targum Jerusalem II)
TJI	→ TPsJ
TJII	→ TFrag
TJon	Targum Jonathan
TO	Targum Onqelos
TPsJ	Targum Pseudo-Jonathan (Targum Jerusalem I)
WaR	Wayiqra Rabba
y	Talmud Yerushalmi
Yalq	Yalquṭ Shimᶜoni
YalqM	Yalquṭ Makhiri

12.2 *Introductory Works*

G. STEMBERGER, *Einleitung in Talmud und Midrasch* (München
⁸1992); Fr. tr. *Introduction au Talmud et au Midrash* (Paris

1986); Sp. tr. *Introducción a la literatura talmúdica y midrásica* (Biblioteca Midrásica 3; Valencia 1988); Eng. tr. *Introduction to the Talmud and Midrash* (Edinburgh 1991); It. tr. *Introduzione al Talmud e al Midrash* (Tradizione d'Israele 10; Roma 1995).

This is a fundamental reference work. Translations, except for the Italian, are based on the seventh German edition (München 1982), published by H. L. Strack and G. Stemberger. Previous German editions (first to sixth, 1887 to 1976), by H. L. Strack only, still maintain their scholarly significance. The book is divided into three parts: general introduction, Talmudic literature and midrashim. An updated bibliography is also provided.

J. Neusner, *Introduction to Rabbinic Literature* (AncB Reference Library; New York – London – Toronto – Sydney – Auckland 1994).

This is an extensive introduction to rabbinic literature (pp. 720). Apart from its general presentation, each document is described. First the Mishnah, the Tosefta, and the Talmudim, and afterwards different kinds of midrashim and Targumim. The book also provides bibliography with English translations of the selected works. J. Neusner recently published a short (pp. 164) and accessible introduction to rabbinic literature, which partially summarizes this previous work:

> *Rabbinic Literature.* An Essential Guide (Abingdon Essential Guides; Nashville 2005).

M. Pérez Fernández, "Literatura rabínica", *Literatura judía intertestamentaria* (ed. M. Pérez Fernández et al.) (Introducción al estudio de la Biblia 9; Estella 1996) 417-562; It. tr. "Letteratura rabbinica", *Letteratura giudaica intertestamentaria* (Introduzione allo studio della Bibbia 9; Brescia 1998) 367-492.

This brief introduction is a good presentation of rabbinic texts and gives bibliographical recommendations and helpful suggestions for work.

S. Safrai et al. (ed.), *The Literature of the Sages*. First Part: Oral Tora, Halakha, Mishna, Tosefta, Talmud, External Tractates. Second Part: Midrash and Targum, Liturgy, Poetry, Mysticism, Contracts, Inscriptions, Ancient Science and the Languages of Rabbinic Literature (CRI 2/3a-b; Assen – Maastricht – Philadelphia 1987, Assen – Augsburg 2006).

This important collected reference book provides both scientific essays by many collaborators on topics related to rabbinic Judaism and its vicinity, and introductions to various rabbinic works. Moreover, the editors furnish a cumulative bibliography (vol. 1: pp. 415-431; vol. 2: pp. 645-710).

C. Albeck, *Einführung in die Mischna* (SJ 6; Berlin – New York 1971).

This German translation from Hebrew (1960) provides indispensable information for an adequate approach to the Mishnah.

In addition to the works mentioned above, the student can find good articles on basic rabbinic texts in Jewish encyclopedias, such as:

> I. Singer (ed.). *The Jewish Encyclopedia*. A Descriptive Record of the History, Religion, Literature, and Customs of the Jewish People from the Earliest Times to the Present Day (New York – London 1901-1907) I-XII.
>
> C. Roth – G. Wigoder (ed.), *Encyclopaedia Judaica* (Jerusalem 1971-1982) I-XVII. Also on CD-ROM.
>
> F. Skolnik – M. Berenbaum (ed.), *Encyclopaedia Judaica* (Detroit ²2007) I-XXII.

12.3 *From the Bible to Rabbinic Literature*

In this section, the way of searching citations, allusions and rabbinic comments on a particular biblical passage will be described. For this purpose, it is always helpful to consult modern translations of the Talmudim, Mishnah, etc., containing scriptural indexes (see below

§ 12.4-6). Considering that these indexes are not exhaustive, consulting other works is necessary[7].

M. M. KASHER, *Torah Shelemah*. (The Complete Torah) Talmudic-Midrashic Encyclopedia of the Pentateuch (New York 1949-) I-XLIV.

The publication of vol. 44 in Hebrew (1995) completed the book of Numbers[8]. The encyclopedia provides all comments that are included in the rabbinic literature. Biblical passages are indicated along with references to Targum Onqelos and Pseudo-Jonathan; there is also an anthology of all rabbinic sources in which a particular biblical passage is cited. An English translation, based on the previous work, has reached chapter 20 of the book of Exodus:

> M. M. KASHER, *Encyclopedia of Biblical Interpretation*. A Millennial Anthology (New York 1953-) I-IX.

A. HYMAN, *Torah hakethubah vehamessurah*. A Reference Book of the Scriptural Passages Quoted in Talmudic, Midrashic and Early Rabbinic Literature. I. Pentateuch. II. Prophets. III. Hagiographa (Revised and Enlarged by A. B. HYMAN) (Tel Aviv ²1979); IDEM, *Sepher Hahashlamoth*. A Companion Volume to the Second Edition of *Torah Hakethubah Vehamessurah* (Compiled by A. B. HYMAN) (Jerusalem 1986).

Aaron Hyman began this work; it's second edition completed by his son Arthur. This reference book lists, in abbreviated form, all passages from rabbinic sources that discuss particular biblical verses.

---

[7] An annotated bibliography on rabbinic literature was published by D. W. CHAPMAN – A. J. KÖSTENBERGER, "Jewish Intertestamental and Early Rabbinic Literature: An Annotated Bibliographic Resource", *JETS* 43 (2000) 577-618, esp. 606-618.

[8] After volume XXVIII, the subtitle was changed to *A Talmudic-Midrashic Encyclopedia of the Five Books of Moses*.

Each part of the Hebrew Bible has been assigned a volume. The Companion Volume contains corrections and additions to the previous three volumes.

Mishneh Torah [= Repetition of the Law]

In 14 books in Hebrew, Moses Maimonides made an arrangement of Halakhic literature[9]. This basic tool permits one to access legal texts according to a descriptive, thematic or logical presentation of their content through information supplied from the sources (particularly the Talmud, the Mishnah and other rabbinic sources). Almost the entire work has been translated into English, with the title *The Code of Maimonides*. Yale University Press in New Haven, CT, published the following books:

> 2. The Book of Love (ed. M. KELLNER) (YJS 32; 2004) 3. The Book of Seasons (ed. S. GANDZ et al.) (YJS 14; 1961); 3/8. Sanctification of the New Moon (ed. S. GANDZ et al.) (YJS 11; 1956); 4. The Book of Women (ed. I. KLEIN) (YJS 19; 1972); 5. The Book of Holiness (ed. L. I. RABINOWITZ – P. GROSSMAN) (YJS 16; 1965); 6. The Book of Asseverations (ed. B. D. KLEIN) (YJS 15; 1962); 7. The Book of Agriculture (ed. I. KLEIN) (YJS 21; 1979); 8. The Book of Temple Service (ed. M. LEWITTES) (YJS 12; 1957); 9. The Book of Offerings (ed. H. DANBY) (YJS 4; 1950); 10. The Book of Cleanness (ed. H. DANBY) (YJS 8; 1954); 11. The Book of Torts (ed. H. KLEIN) (YJS 9; 1954); 12. The Book of Acquisition (ed. I. KLEIN) (YJS 5; 1951); 13. The Book of Civil Laws (ed. J. J. RABINOWITZ) (YJS 2; 1949); 14. The Book of Judges (ed. A. M. HERSHMAN) (YJS 3; 1949).

W. BACHER, Die Agada

This high quality work, which indicates haggadic interpretations of Holy Scripture, was written originally in German and subsequently

---

[9] For a good introduction, see, I. TWERSKY, *Introduction to the Code of Maimonides (Mishne Torah)* (YJS 22; New Haven, CT – London 1980).

translated into Modern Hebrew. This classic tool does not translate
sources, but describes them. It presents collected material in chronological order according to rabbis and explains why they proposed
a particular translation. Access from the Bible to the Haggadot is fa-
cilitated by a scriptural index.

These are the published volumes:

> *Die Agada der Tannaiten.* I. Von Hillel bis Akiba. Von 30 vor bis 135
> nach der gew. Zeitrechnung. II. Von Akiba's Tod bis zum Ab-
> schluß der Mischna (135 bis 220 nach der gew. Zeitrechnung)
> (Straßburg ²1903, 1890, Berlin 1965-1966).
> *Die Agada der Palästinensischen Amoräer.* I. Vom Abschluß der
> Mischna bis zum Tode Jochanans (220 bis 279 nach der gew.
> Zeitrechnung). II. Die Schüler Jochanans (Ende des dritten
> und Anfang des vierten Jahrhunderts). III. Die letzten Amo-
> räer des heiligen Landes (Vom Anfange des 4. bis zum An-
> fange des 5. Jahrh.) (Straßburg 1892, 1896, 1899, Hildesheim
> 1967).
> *Die Agada der babylonischen Amoräer.* Ein Beitrag zur Geschichte
> der Agada und zur Einleitung in den babylonischen Talmud
> (Frankfurt a.M. ²1913, Hildesheim 1967).
> *Ergänzungen und Berichtigungen zur Agada der babylonischen*
> *Amoräer* (Frankfurt a.M. ²1913, Hildesheim 1967).
> *Die Agada der Tannaiten und Amoräer.* Bibelstellenregister nebst
> einem Anhange: Namen-Register zur Agada der babyloni-
> schen Amoräer (Strassburg 1902).

H. N. BIALIK – Y. H. RAVNITZKY (ed.), *The Book of Legends – Sefer
Ha-Aggadah.* Legends from the Talmud and Midrash (New York
1992).

Positively judged in the introduction by David Stern (pp. xvii-
xxii), this work presents haggadic material according to themes. The
scriptural and thematic indexes make access to haggadic texts less
difficult.

Kommentar zum Neuen Testament aus Talmud und Midrasch

This classic reference series gathers a vast quantity of data from the Jewish background of nascent Christianity. Important material, useful to enrich NT exegesis, is combined with less important quotations. Even though better modern translations of sources exist, this collection as such is still useful and irreplaceable. H. L. Strack and P. Billerbeck, based on previous works, published four volumes with a commentary to the whole NT, beginning from rabbinic texts:

> *Das Evangelium nach Matthäus* (Bill 1; München [2]1956);
> *Das Evangelium nach Markus, Lukas und Johannes und die Apostelgeschichte* (Bill 2; München [2]1956);
> *Die Briefe des Neuen Testaments und die Offenbarung Johannis* (Bill 3; München [2]1954);
> *Exkurse zu einzelnen Stellen des Neuen Testaments.* Abhandlungen zur neutestamentlichen Theologie und Archäologie (Bill 4; München [3]1961).

After the death of the authors, J. Jeremias and K. Adolph completed the work providing two indexes:

> *Rabbinisches Index* (Bill 5; München 1956);
> *Verzeichnis der Schriftgelehrten.* Geographisches Register (Bill 6; München 1961).

The Center for the Study of Christianity of the Hebrew University in Jerusalem is planning a publication of an updated edition of the work by H. L. Strack and P. Billerbeck. For more information, see:

> http://www.csc.huji.ac.il/OldApplication/gold_content.html

12.4 *The Mishnah*

12.4.1 Text and/or Translations

P. BLACKMAN (ed.), *Mishnayoth* (Revised, Corrected, Enlarged) (New
York [2]1964) I-VII.

This edition provides the vocalized Hebrew text with a good English translation and comments. Volume VII contains the indexes,
a short grammar for the Talmud, and a glossary.

H. DANBY (ed.), *The Mishnah*. Translated from the Hebrew with Introduction and Brief Explanatory Notes (Oxford 1933).

This volume offers an introduction to the Mishnah (pp. xiii-xxxii)
along with an annotated and poetic translation based on the Vilna
edition.

C. DEL VALLE (ed.), *La Misná* (Edición revisada y corregida) (Biblioteca EstB 98; Madrid [2]1997).

After the first edition (Madrid 1981), its revision was issued simultaneously with the publication of manuscript A 50 by O. Kauf-
mann; textual variants are indicated. This is a faithful Spanish
translation of the text with a concise commentary in footnotes, and
an excellent series of indexes.

V. CASTIGLIONI (ed.), *Mishnaiot*. Traduzione italiana e note illustrative
(Roma 1962, 1962, 1964) I-III.

This work provides a short introduction to each tractate. It is useful for preliminary consultation. In order to have a more complete
view of the Mishnah's text, it is necessary to consult other modern
translations and/or the Hebrew original.

C. ALBECK (ed.), *Shisha sidre Mishnah* [= *Six Orders of the Mishnah*]
(Jerusalem – Tel Aviv 1952-1959) I-VI.

Albeit not a critical edition, this work is a good tool that satisfies the needs of students and provides the vocalized text of the Mishnah.

12.4.2 Critical editions

The reader interested in critical editions of the Mishnah can consult the following publications which are still incomplete:

G. BEER – O. HOLTZMANN et al. (ed.), *Die Mischna.* Text, Übersetzung und ausführliche Erklärung (Gießen – Berlin 1912-).

This valid edition is named "Gießen Mishnah" and, initially, it was edited by G. Beer and O. Holtzmann, and subsequently, by K. H. Rengstorf, L. Rost and others. The work provides the text, a German translation, an introduction and commentary. Until 1991, 45 tractates have been published. Still to be released are: II/4. *Šeqalim*; II/12. *Haggigah*; III/2. *Ketubbot*; III/3. *Nedarim*; III/7. *Qiddušin*; IV/6. *Šebuᶜot*; IV/7. *ᶜEduyot*; IV/8. *ᶜAbodah Zarah*; V/1. *Zebaḥim*; V/2. *Menaḥot*; V/3. *Ḥullin*; V/4. *Bekorot*; V/6. *Temurah*; V/7. *Keritot*; V/8. *Meᶜilah*; VI/3. *Negaᶜim*; VI/6. *Miqwaot*; VI/8. *Makširin*.

THE INSTITUTE FOR THE COMPLETE ISRAELI TALMUD (ed.), *The Mishnah.* With Variant Readings Collected from Manuscripts, Fragments of the "Genizah" and Early Printed Editions and Collated with Quotations from the Mishnah in Early Rabbinic Literature as well as with Bertinoro's Commentary from Manuscript (Jerusalem 1971-).

To date, this publication makes available the order *Zeraim* edited in two volumes by N. Sacks (1971, 1975). He provides the Hebrew text on the base of the Vilna edition with a critical apparatus, and without any translation.

12.5 *The Tosefta*

The Tosefta editions are based chiefly on the Erfurt or/and Vienna MS. The Erfurt MS (from ca. XII c.) represents the more ancient version; however it preserves only first four orders. The Vienna MS is the only complete MS of the Tosefta, but it is more recent (the beginning of the XIV c.) and it adopts the Halakhah from the Babylonian Talmud.

12.5.1 Text and/or Translations

M. S. ZUCKERMANDEL (ed.), *Tosephta*. Based on the Erfurt and Vienna Codices with Parallels and Variants (Jerusalem ²1937).

This complete single-volume edition of the Tosefta, which does not correspond to present standards, can still be useful. Initially, the editor made use of the Erfurt MS and subsequently took the Vienna MS.

J. NEUSNER (ed.) *The Tosefta*. Translated from the Hebrew. I. Zeraim (The Order of Agriculture). II. Moed (The Order of Appointed Times). III. Nashim (The Order of Women). IV. Neziquin (The Order of Damages). V. Qodoshim (The Order of Holy Things). VI. Tohorot (The Order of Purities) (Hoboken, NJ 1986, New York 1981, 1979, 1981, 1979, 1977).

This complete English translation of the Tosefta does not follow uniform criteria, unlike the MS taken as its basis, which depends on a single tractate. Each volume includes an index of biblical citations, rabbinic quotations and authors.

12.5.2 Critical editions

K. H. RENGSTORF et al. (ed.), *Die Tosefta*. Text (RT; Stuttgart 1953-) I-IV, VI.

This edition is based on the Codex Erfurt and supplements the parts missing in it with those of the Codex Vienna. Volumes III/1.

Jebamot (1953), I/3. *Berakot* (1956), VI. *Ṭoharot* (1967), I. *Zeraim* (1983) contain text (with some translations), whereas other volumes provide only a German translation and commentary.

S. LIEBERMAN (ed.), *The Tosefta*. According to Codex Vienna, with Variants from Codex Erfurt, Genizah Mss. and Editio Princeps (Venice 1521) (New York 1955-) I-V.

This Hebrew edition is based on the Vienna MS. Variants from the Erfurt MS, the Genizah and the *editio princeps* (Venetiis 1521) are included in the critical apparatus. The text, however, is not eclectic. Only exceptionally are readings accepted which differ from those of the Codex Vienna. In vol. 5, the MS Schocken is also used for a part of the order of Nezikin. The orders Qodoshim and Tohorot have not yet been published.

R. NEUDECKER, *Frührabbinisches Ehescheidungsrecht.* Der Tosefta-Traktat Giṭṭin (BibOr 39; Rome 1982).

The origin of this publication is the author's PhD Dissertation presented in 1978 at Hebrew Union College – Jewish Institute of Religion in Cincinnati, OH. The work is the first translation of the Gittin tractate into German (or, indeed, into any modern language). Based on the Erfurt MS, this publication is much better than that of M. S. Zuckermandel. The text is equipped with extensive critical notes; a photographic reproduction of the tractate from the Codex of Erfurt is provided at the end of the book.

12.6 *Talmud*

12.6.1 The Jerusalem Talmud

M. SCHWAB (ed.), *Le Talmud de Jérusalem* (Nouvelle édition) (Paris 1878-1890) I-XI.

This only complete modern translation provides a French text of the Talmud. Each volume contains short analytical and scriptural indexes.

M. HENGEL et al. (ed.), *Übersetzung des Talmud Yerushalmi* (Tübingen 1980-) I/2-3,6-8, II/1,3-8,10-12, III/2,7, IV/1-8.

This good translation is currently being published. Volume I has the title *Der Jerusalemer Talmud in deutscher Übersetzung* (Tübingen 1975); in it, the Institutum Judaicum der Universität Tübingen published the text of *Berakhoth*, translated by C. Horowitz. His two other translations – *Sukkah* (Bonn 1963, Tübingen 1983), *Nedarim* (Düsseldorf-Benrath 1957, Tübingen 1983) – are included in the series *Übersetzung des Talmud Yerushalmi* by the publisher who maintained their original title *Jeruschalmi. Der palästinische Talmud.*

H. W. GUGGENHEIMER (ed.), *The Jerusalem Talmud*. Edition, Translation, and Commentary (SJ; Berlin – New York 2000-).

This edition of the Aramaic text is provided with vocalization, English translation and commentary. The *editio princeps* by D. Bomberg (Venetiis 1523) was a basic text for this work. Until now, de Gruyter has published the following volumes:

First Order: Zeraïm. Tractate *Berakhot* (SJ 18; 2000); First Order: Zeraïm. Tractates *Peah* and *Demay* (SJ 19; 2000); First Order: Zeraïm. Tractates *Kilaim* and *Ševiït* (SJ 20; 2001); First Order: Zeraïm. Tractates *Terumot* and *Maꜥserot* (SJ 21; 2002); First Order: Zeraïm. Tractates *Maꜥaser Šeni, Ḥallah, ꜥOrlah* and *Bikkurim* (SJ 23; 2003); Third Order: Naim. Tractate *Yebamot* (SJ 29; 2004); Third Order: Našim. Tractates. *Soṭah* and *Nedarim* (SJ 31; 2005); Third Order: Našim. Tractate *Ketubot* (SJ 34; 2006); Third Order: Našim. Tractates. *Giṭṭin* and *Nazir* (SJ 39; 2007); Third Order: Našim. Tractate *Qiddušin* (SJ 43; 2008); Fourth Order: Neziqin: Tractates: *Bava Qamma, Bava Meṣiꜥa,* and *Bava*

Batra (SJ 45; 2008); Sixth Order: Tahorot. Tractate *Niddah* (SJ 34; 2006).

Talmud Yerushalmi. According to Ms. Or. 4720 (Scal. 3) of the Leiden University Library with Restorations and Corrections (Jerusalem 2001).

Published by the Academy of the Hebrew Language, this diplomatic and corrected edition is the only complete MS of the Palestinian Talmud.

J. NEUSNER (ed.), *The Talmud of the Land of Israel.* A Preliminary Translation and Explanation (Chicago Studies in the History of Judaism; Chicago 1983-1994) I-XXXV.

This work is the only complete translation into English of the Jerusalem Talmud. A more accurate study requires however the consultation of the other editions[10].

12.6.2 The Babylonian Talmud

This edition of *The Babylonian Talmud* is the publication of The Institute for the Complete Israeli Talmud of Jerusalem from 1972. Its textual basis is the standard Vilna edition (1886), with variants from the Genizah, MSS and medieval quotations, all of which are included in the apparatus. The following volumes have been published:

> *Tractate Ketuboth* (ed. M. HERSHLER) (1972, 1977) I-II; *Tractate Sotah* (ed. A. LISS) (1977, 1979) I-II; *Tractate Yebamoth* (ed. A. LISS) (1983, 1986, 1989) I-III; *Tractate Nedarim* (ed. M. HERSHLER) (1985, 1991) I-II.

---

[10] See critical remarks of S. LIEBERMAN, "A Tragedy or a Comedy?", *JAOS* 104 (1984) 315-319.

I. EPSTEIN (ed.), *The Babylonian Talmud*. Translated into English with
Notes, Glossary and Indices (London 1948-1952) I-XXXV.

This first complete English translation is based on the Vilna text
with variants from MSS and other editions. It does not include the
extensive commentary needed for personal study. Volume XXXV
contains a useful index of scriptural citations.

J. SCHOTTENSTEIN et al. (ed.), *Talmud Bavli* (New York 1990-2004)
I-LXXIII.

This is the second complete translation of the Talmud into
English in 73 vols. It offers, side-by-side, the text of Vilna edition
and its English translations, one literal and the other more liberal, provided to clarify the text's dynamic equivalence. This edition, therefore, makes the Talmud more accessible to all kinds of students. The
English translation is accompanied by extensive explanatory notes at
the foot of the page.

L. GOLDSCHMIDT (ed.), *Der babylonische Talmud* (Berlin 1929-1936)
I-XII.

Often considered as the best, this German translation also offers
explanatory comments in the footnotes. The useful volume of indexes,
entitled *Subject Concordance to the Babylonian Talmud*, was edited
by R. Edelmann (Copenhagen 1959).

M. CALÉS – H. J. WEISS (ed.), *El Talmud de Babilonia* (Buenos Aires
1964-) I-V, VIII-XVII.

In this bilingual work, the editors provide the Spanish translation
of the Babylonian Talmud, based on the Vilna edition.

I. V. BERMAN et al. (ed.), *The Talmud*. The Steinsaltz Edition (New
York 1989-) I-XV, XVIII + Reference Guide (New York 1989).

This edition provides an introduction, vocalized text, literal translation, commented translation (the Hebrew commentary by A. Steinsaltz was translated into English), Rashi's commentary and explanatory notes. Although incomplete, this is a fundamental work to know and understand the treated issues. The Reference Guide is highly recommended because it contains information on the Talmud, its historical background, language, terminology, hermeneutics, Halakhic terms and notions, etc.

J. NEUSNER et al. (ed.), *The Talmud of Babylonia*. An American Translation (BJS 63, 72, 74, 78, 81, 84, 87, 90, 109, 117, 213-223, 227-228, 231, 233-343, 247-254, 256-258, 260-263, 265-268, 272-285; Chico, CA – Atlanta 1984-).

This English translation has been annotated with many remarks. The work supplements the other work by J. NEUSNER, *The Talmud of Babylonia*. Academic Commentary (South Florida Academic Commentary; Atlanta 1994-1999).

12.7 *Midrashim*

12.7.1 Tools

For bibliography, editions of the text and another information on midrashic literature see:

HAAS, L., "Bibliography on Midrash", *The Study of Ancient Judaism*. Mishnah, Midrash, Siddur (ed. J. NEUSNER) (New York 1981 = SFSHJ 49; Atlanta 1992) I, 93-103.

NEUSNER, J., *The Midrash*. An Introduction (Northvale, NJ – London 1990).

NEUSNER, J. – AVERY-PECK, A. J., *Encyclopaedia of Midrash*. Biblical Interpretation in Formative Judaism (Leiden – Boston 2005) I-II.

PÉREZ FERNÁNDEZ, "Literatura rabínica", 469-531; It. tr. "Letteratura rabbinica", 412-466.

STEMBERGER, G., *Midrasch.* Vom Umgang der Rabbinen mit
    der Bibel. Einführung – Texte – Erläuterungen (München
    1989); It. tr. *Il Midrash.* Uso rabbinico della Bibbia. Introdu-
    zione, testi, commenti (Collana di studi religiosi; Bologna
    1992).
STRACK, H. L. – STEMBERGER, G., *Introduction to the Talmud and
    Midrash* (Edinburgh 1991) 254-393.
TARADACH, M., *Le Midrash.* Introduction à la littérature midrashique
    (Drš dans la Bible, les Targumim, les Midrašim) (MoBi 22;
    Genève 1991).

12.7.2 Translations and Editions

After a short presentation of modern versions printed in some collections, a list of other translations and original editions will be provided as well.

a) Collections

H. FREEDMAN – M. SIMON (ed.), *Midrash Rabbah.* Translated into
    English with Notes, Glossary and Indices (London ³1961) I-X.

Soncino Press published this English version of Midrash Rabbah
on Gen, Exod, Lev, Num, Deut, Lam, Ru, Qoh, Esth, Cant. Volume
X, compiled by J. J. Slotki, provides a very useful index of biblical
references.

J. NEUSNER et al. (ed.), *The Components of the Rabbinic Documents.*
    From the Whole to the Parts (South Florida Academic Com-
    mentary 75-84, 89, 94, 98, 100-106; Atlanta 1996-1997).

The South Florida Academic Commentary series in twelve parts
presents the English translation of:

1. *Sifra*; 2. *Ester Rabbah I*; 3. *Rut Rabbah*; 4. *Lamentations Rabbah*;
5. *Song of the Songs Rabbah*; 6. *The Fathers According to Rabbi
Nathan*; 7. *Sifré to Deuteronomy*; 8. *Mekhilta Attributed to Rabbi*

Ishmael; 9. *Genesis Rabbah*; 10. *Leviticus Rabbah*; 11. *Pesiqta deRab Kahana*; 12. *Sifré to Numbers*.

The Yale Judaica Series gathers English translations of Jewish classics, ancient and medieval, making use of Hebrew, Aramaic, Ethiopic and Arabic texts. The translations of midrashim on Psalms and Proverbs, and commentaries on Deuteronomy, on Song of Songs and Pesiqta Rabbati (a collection of sermons for the feasts and special Sabbaths) have been published:

> W. G. BRAUDE (ed.), *The Midrash on Psalms* (YJS 13; New Haven, CT 1959) I-II.
>
> ———, *Pesikta Rabbati*. Discourses for Feasts, Fasts, and Special Sabbaths (YJS 18; New Haven, CT – London 1968).
>
> R. HAMMER (ed.), *Sifre*. A Tannaitic Commentary on the Book of Deuteronomy (YJS 24; New Haven, CT – London 1986).
>
> B. L. VISOTZKY (ed.), *The Midrash on Proverbs* (YJS 27; New Haven, CT – London 1992).
>
> L. BEN GERSHOM, *Commentary on Song of Songs* (ed. M. KELLNER) (YJS 28; New Haven, CT – London 1998).

A. WÜNSCHE (ed.), *Bibliotheca Rabbinica*. Eine Sammlung alter Midraschim (Leipzig 1881) I-V.

This collection of midrashim in German was reprinted twice by Olms Verlag, Hildesheim, in 1967 and 1993, and contains the following volumes:

> 1. *Der Midrasch Kohelet, Der Midrasch Bereschit Rabba*; 2. *Der Midrasch Schir Ha-Schirim, Der Midrasch zum Buche Esther, Der Midrasch Echa Rabbati*; 3. *Der Midrasch Schemot Rabba, Der Midrasch Debarim Rabba, Der Midrasch Ruth Rabba*; 4. *Der Midrasch Bemidbar Rabba, Der Midrasch Mischle*; 5. *Der Midrasch Wajikra Rabba, Die Pesikta des Rab Kahana*.

The Biblioteca Midrásica of the Institución San Jerónimo, directed by M. Pérez Fernández, publishes Spanish translations (in some cases with the original text) of the rabbinic literature. The following midrashim have been published:

> L.-F. GIRÓN BLANC (ed.), *Midrás Éxodo Rabbah I* (Biblioteca Midrásica 8; Valencia 1989).
>
> M. PÉREZ FERNÁNDEZ (ed.), *Midrás Sifré Números*. Versión crítica, introducción y notas (Biblioteca Midrásica 9; Valencia 1989).
>
> L.-F. GIRÓN BLANC (ed.), *Midrás Cantar de los Cantares Rabbá* (Biblioteca Midrásica 11; Estella 1991).
>
> L. VEGAS MONTANER (ed.), *Génesis Rabbah I (Génesis 1–11)*. Comentario midrásico al libro del Génesis (Biblioteca Midrásica 15; Estella 1994).
>
> T. MARTÍNEZ SÁIZ (ed.), *Mekilta de Rabbí Ismael*. Comentario rabínico al libro del Ésodo (Biblioteca Midrásica 16; Estella 1995).
>
> M. PÉREZ FERNÁNDEZ (ed.), *Midrás Sifra*. El comentario rabínico al Levítico I (Biblioteca Midrásica 19; Estella 1997).
>
> M. C. MOTOS LÓPEZ (ed.), *Las vanidades del mundo*. Comentario rabínico al Eclesiastés (Biblioteca Midrásica 22; Estella 2001).

b) Exodus

– Mekilta Attributed to Rabbi Ishmael

This is a commentary on Exod 12,1–23,18; 31,12-17; 35,1-3, by R. Ishmael and his disciples from the III c. A.D. on.

> A. MELLO (ed.), *Il dono della Torah*. Commento al Decalogo di Es. 20 nella Mekilta di R. Ishmael (Commenti ebraici antichi alla Scrittura; Roma 1982).
>
> J. WINTER – A. WÜNSCHE (ed.), *Mechiltha*. Ein tanaitischer Midrasch zu Exodus (Leipzig 1909, Hildesheim 1990).
>
> For the English translation, see above, South Florida Academic Commentary.
>
> For the Spanish translation, see above, Biblioteca Midrásica 16.

H. S. HOROVITZ – I. A. RABIN (ed.), *Mechilta d'Rabbi Ismael cum variis lectionibus* (Corpus Tannaiticum III/3,3,1; Francofurti a.M. 1931, Jerusalem ²1960).

J. Z. LAUTERBACH (ed.), *Mekilta de-Rabbi Ishmael*. A Critical Edition on the Basis of the Manuscripts and Early Editions with an English Translation, Introduction and Notes (Philadelphia 1933-1935) I-III.

– Mekilta of Rabbi Simeon ben Yohai

This is a commentary on Exod 3,2.7-8; 6,2; 12,2–24,10; 30,20–31,15; 34,12.14.18-26; 35,2 from the period of the Tannaim.

J. N. EPSTEIN – E. Z. MELAMED (ed.), *Mekhilta d'Rabbi Šim'on b. Jochai* (Hierosolymis 1955).

c) Leviticus: Sifra

This is a most complete rabbinic commentary on Leviticus. Its materials come from both the school of Rabbi Aqiba and from other tannaitic sources.

J. NEUSNER – R. BROOKS (ed.), *Sifra*. The Rabbinic Commentary on Leviticus. An American Translation (BJSt 102; Atlanta 1985).

J. NEUSNER (ed.), *Sifra*. An Analytical Translation (BJSt 138-140; Atlanta 1988).

For the Spanish translation, see above, Biblioteca Midrásica 19.

J. H. WEISS (ed.), *Sifra*. Commentar zu Leviticus (Wien 1862, New York 1947).

d) Numbers: Sifre to Numbers

This Halakhic commentary on Numbers (5,1–12,16; 15,1-41; 18,1–19,22; 25,1–31,24; 35,9-34) is attributed to the school of Rabbi Ishmael. It contains passages of Rabbi Simeon bar Yohai as well.

J. Neusner (ed.), *Sifré to Numbers*. An American Translation and Explanation (BJSt 118-119; Atlanta 1986).

K. G. Kuhn (ed.), *Sifre zu Numeri* (RT II. Tannaitische Midraschim 3; Stuttgart 1959).

For the Spanish translation, see above, Biblioteca Midrásica 9.

H. S. Horovitz (ed.), *Siphre d'be Rab*. Fasciculus primus: Siphre ad Numeros adjecto Siphre zutta. Cum variis lectionibus et adnotationibus (Corpus Tannaiticum III/3,3,1; Leipzig 1917, Jerusalem 1966).

e) Deuteronomy: Sifre to Deuteronomy

This rabbinic commentary on Deuteronomy (1,1-30; 3,23-29; 6,4-9; 11,10–26,15; 31,14; 32–34) gathers data from different schools; its exegesis has Halakhic, haggadic and philological features.

J. Neusner (ed.), *Sifre to Deuteronomy*. An Analytical Translation (BJSt 98, 101; Atlanta 1987).

E. Cortès – T. Martínez (ed.), *Sifre Deuteronomio*. Comentario tannaítico al libro del Deuteronomio. I. Pisqa 1-160. II. Pisqa 161-357 (CStP 40, 60; Barcelona 1989, 1997).

For the English translation, see above YJS 24.

L. Finkelstein (ed.), *Siphre ad Deuteronomium*. H. S. Horovitzii schedis usus, cum variis lectionibus et adnotationibus (Corpus Tannaiticum III/3,3; Berolini 1933, New York 1969).

D. Hoffmann (ed.), *Midrasch Tannaïm zum Deuteronomium*. II. Deut. 20,10 – Ende (Berlin 1909).

f) Genesis: Genesis Rabbah

This commentary on Genesis (likely from V c. A.D.) is mostly homiletic in nature.

A. Ravenna – T. Federici (ed.), *Commentario alla Genesi (Berešit Rabbâ)* (CdR II. La religione ebraica; Torino 1978).

B. MARUANI – A. COHEN-ARAZI (ed.), *Midrach Rabba I: Genèse Rabba* (Les Dix Paroles; Paris 1987).

J. NEUSNER (ed.), *Genesis Rabbah*. The Judaic Commentary to the Book of Genesis. A New American Translation (BJSt 104-106; Atlanta 1985).

For the Spanish translation, see above, Biblioteca Midrásica 15.

M. A. MIRKIN (ed.), *Bereshit Rabbah* (Tel Aviv 1977, 1971, 1972, 1972) I-IV.

J. THEODOR (ed.), *Bereschit Rabba mit kritischem Apparat und Kommentar*. Parascha I–XLVII (Berlin 1912).

13. Apocrypha

Studies on the apocryphal[11] literature enjoy a new interest these days. Hence, to be of greater use for the students, the basic bibliography will be furnished along with a brief presentation of introductions, critical editions and translations for the OT apocrypha first and then for the NT apocrypha.

13.1 *Old Testament Apocrypha*

13.1.1 Abbreviations

Ahi	Ahiqar
AM	Assumption of Moses
ApAb	Apocalypse of Abraham
ApAdam	Apocalypse of Adam
ApDan	Apocalypse of Daniel
ApEl (Gk.)	Greek Apocalypse of Elijah
ApEl (Heb.)	Hebrew Apocalypse of Elijah
ApEl (Cop.)	Coptic Apocalypse of Elijah
ApEzek	Apocalypse of Ezekiel

---

[11] The adjective "apocryphal" is used here in the Catholic meaning of the word.

ApEzra (Gk.)	Greek Apocalypse of Ezra
ApocrEzek	Apocryphon of Ezekiel
ApocrJer	Coptic Apocryphon of Jeremiah
	(History of the Captivity in Babylon)
ApocrMel	Apocryphon of Melchizedek
ApocrSyrPss	Apocryphal Syriac Psalms
ApSedr	Apocalypse of Sedrach
ApZeph	Apocalypse of Zephaniah
Aris	Letter of Aristeas
AscIsa	MAscIsa 6–11
2 Bar	2 Baruch (Syriac Apocalypse)
3 Bar	3 Baruch (Greek Apocalypse)
4 Bar	4 Baruch (*Paraleipomena Jeremiou*)
BkGi	Book of Giants
BkNoah	Book of Noah
CavTr	Cave of Treasures
ElMod	Eldad and Modad
1 En	1 Enoch (Ethiopic Apocalypse)
BW	Book of the Watchers (1 En 1–36)
PE	Parables (Similitudes) of Enoch (1 En 37–71)
AB	Astronomical Book (1 En 72–82)
BD	Book of Dream-Visions (1 En 83–90)
EE	Epistle of Enoc (1 En 91–107)
2 En	2 Enoch (Slavonic Apocalypse)
3 En	3 Enoch (Hebrew Apocalypse)
Ex	*Exagoge* by Ezekiel the Tragedian
1 (3) Ezra	1/3 Ezra (LXX/Vg)
4 Ezra	4 Ezra
5 Ezra	5 Ezra
6 Ezra	6 Ezra
HistJos	History of Joseph
HistRech	History of the Rechabites
JA	Joseph and Aseneth
JanJam	Jannes and Jambres
Jub	Jubilees

LAB	*Liber antiquitatum biblicarum* (Pseudo-Philo)
LadJac	Ladder of Jacob
LAE	Life of Adam and Eve
LostTr	The Lost Tribes
LP	Lives of the Prophets
3 Macc	3 Maccabees
4 Macc	4 Maccabees
5 Macc	5 Maccabees (Arabic)
MAscIsa	Martyrdom and Ascension of Isaiah
MIsa	MAscIsa 1–5
OS	Odes of Solomon
PenAdam	Penitence of Adam (Arm.)
PrJac	Prayer of Jacob
PrJos	Prayer of Joseph
PrMan	Prayer of Manasseh
PrMos	Prayer of Moses
PrNab	Prayer of Nabonidus (4Q245)
PS	Psalms of Solomon
QuesEzra	Questions of Ezra
RevEzra	Revelation of Ezra
Sib	Sibylline Oracles
SyrMen	Sentences of the Syriac Menander
TAb	Testament of Abraham
TAdam	Testament of Adam
TAmr	Testament of Amram (4Q543,545-548)
THez	Testament of Hezekiah (MA Isa 3,13–4,22)
TIsaac	Testament of Isaac
TJac	Testament of Jacob
TJob	Testament of Job
TKoh	Testament of Kohath
TMos	Testament of Moses
T12Pat	Testaments of the Twelve Patriarchs
TAsh	Testament of Asher
TBenj	Testament of Benjamin
TDan	Testament of Dan

TGad	Testament of Gad
TIss	Testament of Issachar
TJos	Testament of Joseph
TJud	Testament of Judah
TLevi	Testament of Levi
TNaph	Testament of Naphtali
TReu	Testament of Reuben
TSim	Testament of Simeon
TZeb	Testament of Zebulun
TSol	Testament of Solomon
TreatShem	Treatise of Shem
VisEzra	Vision of Ezra
VisLevi	Vision of Levi (Aramaic Levi Document)

Apocryphal fragments (Aristeas the Exegete, Aristobulus, Arta-panus, Cleodemus Malchus, Demetrius, Hellenistic Synagogal Prayers, Pseudo-Orpheus, etc.), which are parts of major works (CLEMENT OF ALEXANDRIA, *Stromata*; EUSEBIUS, *Praeparatio evangelica* or *Historia ecclesiastica*; JOSEPHUS FLAVIUS, *Antiquities* or *Against Apion*, etc.) should be quoted in the following way: the name of the author (or the title) of the fragment; a comma and a space, then the Latin expression "apud" or the English one "in" is placed, followed by a space and the reference to the work in which the fragment is included, e.g.: CLEODEMUS MALCHUS, apud/in JOSEPHUS FLAVIUS, *Antiquities* I, 238-241.

13.1.2 Bibliography

L. DiTOMMASO, *A Bibliography of Pseudepigrapha Research 1850-1999* (JSPE.S 39; Sheffield 2001).

This enormous collection (of more than 1000 pages) is almost complete and integrates the work of J. H. CHARLESWORTH, *The Pseudepigrapha and Modern Research* (SBL.SCSt 7; Missoula, MT 1976; SBL.SCSt 7/1; Chico; CA 1981). The bibliographical survey, which includes even the rare works, is the result of the collaboration of many experts.

J.-C. HAELEWYCK (ed.), *Clavis Apocryphorum Veteris Testamenti* (CChr.SA; Turnhout 1998).

The bibliography has been compiled in a cohesive and thorough manner (critical edition, translations, concordances etc.), incorporating Qumran data as well.

G. DELLING, *Bibliographie zur jüdisch-hellenistischen und intertestamentarischen Literatur 1900-1970* (TU 106; Berlin ²1975).

This collection with 3650 bibliographical entries is arranged according to topics and books.

A. LEHNARDT (ed.), *Bibliographie zu den Jüdischen Schriften aus hellenistisch-römischer Zeit* (Supplementa JSHRZ 6/2; Gütersloh 1999).

This work presents the bibliography of the OT apocrypha and of general issues. It does not include references to the Jewish literature written before 200 A.D.

L. ROSSO UBIGLI, "Gli apocrifi (o pseudoepigrafi) dell'Antico Testamento. Bibliografia 1979-1989", *Henoch* 12 (1990) 259-321.

The author divided her collection into: bibliographies and concordances, translations and anthologies, introductions, preliminary studies, publications relative to individual texts (editions, translations, introductions, studies).

13.1.3 Introductions

A.-M. DENIS et al., *Introduction à la littérature religieuse judéohellénistique* (Pseudépigraphes de l'Ancien Testament) (Turnhout 2000).

In two volumes (having continuous pagination), this excellent introduction describes in detail (in 1420 pages) writings parallel to the Bible from the IV c. B.C. until the first half of the II c. A.D. Along with the content of each writing, various manuscript traditions and their theology and history are described and a rich bibliography is furnished.

G. ARANDA PÉREZ – F. GARCÍA MARTÍNEZ – M. PÉREZ FERNÁNDEZ, *Literatura judía intertestamentaria* (Introducción al estudio de la Biblia 9; Estella 1996); It. tr. *Letteratura giudaica intertestamentaria* (Introduzione allo studio della Bibbia 9; Brescia 1998).

In this textbook, Aranda Pérez presents extensively the OT apocrypha (pp. 207-366), providing basic knowledge and an anthology of selected passages.

M. CIMOSA, *La letteratura intertestamentaria* (La Bibbia nella storia 6; Bologna 1992).

In his introduction to the intertestamental literature, the author deals with Jewish apocalypses, testaments, Qumran data, Judeo-Hellenistic and Judeo-Palestinian writings, and prayers.

R. A. KRAFT – G. W. E. NICKELSBURG (ed.), *Early Judaism and Its Modern Interpreters* (BIMI 2; Philadelphia – Atlanta 1986).

In the third part of this collective work, the Jewish literature has been described according to literary genres: testaments, narratives, historiography, wisdom writings, hymns, odes and prayers.

G. W. E. NICKELSBURG, *Jewish Literature between the Bible and the Mishnah*. A Historical and Literary Introduction (Minneapolis, MN [2]2005).

This well written work brings in the OT apocrypha and the deuteroncanonical books, taking into account literary finds from Qumran, works by Josephus Flavius and Philo.

E. Noffke, *Introduzione alla letteratura mediogiudaica precristiana* (Strumenti 18; Torino 2004).

This study familiarizes one with the history of Judaism from the IV c. B.C. to the II c. A.D. The work describes briefly the literature written in this period: apocrypha, deuterocanonical and Qumran writings.

L. Rost, *Einleitung in die alttestmentlichen Apokryphen und Pseudepigraphen einschließlich der großen Qumran-Handschriften* (Heidelberg 1971); Eng. tr. *Judaism Outside the Hebrew Canon. An Introduction to the Documents* (Nashville 1976).

In the part dedicated to the OT apocrypha (*Die Pseudoepigraphen*), the writings originating in the Greek, Syriac, Palestinian and Qumran milieux are presented. Critical editions, translations, commentaries and other studies are provided as well.

M. E. Stone (ed.), *Jewish Writings of the Second Temple Period.* Apocrypha, Pseudepigrapha, Qumran Sectarian Writings, Philo, Josephus (CRI 2/2; Assen – Philadelphia 1984).

This monograph was carried out due to the collaboration of Jewish and Christian scholars. In almost 700 pages, the apocrypha and the OT deuterocanonical books are described.

Besides the introductions mentioned above, many valid studies on the OT apocrypha are published in the periodical:
Journal for the Study of the Pseudepigrapha (and Related Literature) (Sheffield 1987-)
and in the related series that is growing rapidly:
Journal for the Study of the Pseudepigrapha. Supplement Series (Sheffield – London – New York 1987-), known from vol. 47 (2004) on as Library of the Second Temple Studies.

13.1.4 Critical editions

As for the critical editions, there is no one unique collection. Hence, the user can locate them by means of the bibliographical compilations, and in particular *Clavis Apocryphorum Veteris Testamenti* and *Clavis Apocryphorum Novi Testamenti*, along with modern translations.

13.1.5 Translations

The selective list of the translations of Jewish apocrypha is provided below.

> R. H. CHARLES et al. (ed.), *The Apocrypha and Pseudepigrapha of the Old Testament in English*. I. Apocrypha. II. Pseudepigrapha (Oxford 1913, 1968).
>
> J. H. CHARLESWORTH (ed.), *The Old Testament Pseudepigrapha*. I. Apocalyptic Literature and Testaments. II. Expansions of the "Old Testament" and Legends, Wisdom and Philosophical Literature, Prayers, Psalms, and Odes, Fragments of Lost Judeo-Hellenistic Works (New York 1983, 1985).
>
> A. DÍEZ MACHO et al. (ed.), *Apócrifos del Antiguo Testamento* (Madrid 1982-1987) I-V.
>
> A. DUPONT-SOMMER – M. PHILONENKO (ed.), *La Bible*. Écrites Intertestamentaires (Bibliothèque de la Pléiade 337; Paris 1987).
>
> *Jüdische Schriften aus hellenistisch-römischer Zeit* (JSHRZ) – this is a multivolume series of the Gütersloher Verlagshaus (1973-), that H. Lichtenberger et al. are editing.
>
> E. KAUTZSCH et al. (ed.), *Die Apokryphen und Pseudepigraphen des Alten Testaments*. I. Die Apokryphen des Alten Testaments. II. Die Pseudepigraphen des Alten Testaments (Tübingen 1900).
>
> R. RUBINKIEWICZ (ed.), *Apokryfy Starego Testamentu* (Prymasowska Seria Biblijna 13; Warszawa 1999, 2007).
>
> P. SACCHI et al. (ed.), *Apocrifi dell'Antico Testamento*. I-II. (Classici delle religioni. 2. La religione ebraica; Torino 1981, 1989);

III. (Biblica. Testi e studi 7; Brescia 1999); IV. (Biblica. Testi e studi 8; Brescia 2000); V. Letteratura giudaica di lingua greca (Biblica. Testi e studi 5; Brescia 1997).

H. D. F. SPARKS (ed.), *The Apocryphal Old Testament* (Oxford 1984).

M. WOJCIECHOWSKI, *Apokryfy z Biblii greckiej* (Rozprawy i Studia Biblijne 8; Warszawa 2001).

13.2 *New Testament Apocrypha*

13.2.1 Abbreviations

AcA	Acts of Andrew
AcAM	Acts of Andrew and Matthias
AcAP	Acts of Andrew and Paul
AcB	Acts of Barnabas
AcJas	Acts of James the Great (Legenda maior)
AcJas (Arm.)	Acts of James the Great (Armenian)
AcJas (Gk.)	Acts of James the Great (Greek)
AcJasJn (Arm.)	Acts of James and John (Armenian)
AcJn	Acts of John
AcJn(P)	Acts of John (by Prochorus)
AcJn(R)	Acts of John in Rome
AcP	Acts of Paul
AcPet	Acts of Peter
AcPet (Slav.)	Acts of Peter (Slavonic)
AcPetA	Acts of Peter and Andrew
AcPetP	Acts of Peter and Paul
AcPhil	Acts of Philip
AcPhil (Syr.)	Acts of Philip (Syriac)
AcPil	Acts of Pilate (passage in GosNic)
AcThad	Acts of Thaddaeus
AcThad (Arm.)	Acts of Thaddaeus (Armenian)
AcThom	Acts of Thomas
AcTim	Acts of Timothy

AcTit	Acts of Titus
ApocrJn	Apocryphon of John
ApocrTit	Apocryphal Epistle of Titus
ApPet	Apocalypse of Peter
ApThom	Apocalypse of Thomas
ApV	Apocalypse of the Virgin
ApV (Slav.)	Apocalypse of the Virgin (Slavonic)
ArabInf	Arabic Gospel of the Infancy
ArmInf	Armenian Gospel of the Infancy
AscJas	Ascents of James
AsV	Assumption of the Virgin
BkBart	Book of the Resurrection of Christ by Bartholomew the Apostle
BkElch	Book Elchasai
Cer	Cerinthus
3 Cor	3 Corinthians (part of Acts Paul)
DAddai	The Doctrine of Addai
DApos	The Doctrine of the Apostles
Desc	Christ's Descent into Hell (part of GosNic)
EpAlex	Epistle to the Alexandrians
EpApos	Epistle to the Apostles
EpChrAbg	Epistle of Christ and Abgar
EpChrHea	Epistle of Christ from Heaven
EpDion	Epistle of Dionysius the Areopagite to Timothy
EpLao	Epistle to the Laodiceans
EpLent	Epistle of Lentulus
EpPSen	Epistles of Paul and Seneca
GosB	Gospel of Barnabas
GosBart	Gospel of Bartholomew
GosBas	Gospel of Basilides
GosBirMary	Gospel of the Birth of Mary
GosEb	Gospel of the Ebionites
GosEg	Gospel of the Egyptians (Greek)
GosEve	Gospel of Eve
GosGam	Gospel of Gamaliel

GosHeb	Gospel of the Hebrews
GosJn	Arabic Apocryphal Gospel of John
GosMar	Gospel of Marcion
GosMary	Gospel of Mary (Magdalene)
GosNaass	Gospel of the Naassenes
GosNaz	Gospel of the Nazarenes
GosNic	Gospel of Nicodemus
GosPet	Gospel of Peter
GosPsMt	Gospel of Pseudo-Matthew
GosThom	Gospel of Thomas
GosTradMth	Gospel and Traditions of Matthias
HistJos	History of Joseph the Carpenter
HmDance	Hymn of the Dance (AcJn 94-96)
HmPearl	Hymn of the Pearl (passage of AcThom)
InfGos	Infancy Gospels
InfGosThom	Infancy Gospel of Thomas
LaudBarn	*Laudatio Barnabae* of Alexander Monachus
LegSimTheo	The Legend of Simon and Theonoe, Coptic
LettChrAbg (Eus)	The Letters of Christ and Abgare by Eusebius
LifJn (Gk.)	Life of John the Baptist attributed to St. Mark (Greek)
LifJn (Syr.)	Life of John the Baptist according to Serapion (Syriac)
MartBart	Martyrdom of Bartholomew
MartLk	Martyrdom of Luke
MartMk	Martyrdom of Mark
MartMt	Martyrdom of Matthew
MartP	Martyrdom of Paul
MartPet	Martyrdom of Peter
MartPet (PsLin)	Martyrdom of Peter by Pseudo-Linus
MartPetP	Martyrdom of Peter and Paul by Pseudo-Marcellus
MartPhil	Martyrdom of Philip
MartSteph (Amb)	Martyrdom of Stephen, Ambrosian manuscript
MartSteph (Esc)	Martyrdom of Stephen, Escurial manuscript
MemApos	Memoria of Apostles
PrePet	Preaching of Peter
PreSim	The Preaching of Simon in Ethiopic

ProtJas	Protevangelium of James
PsAbd	Apostolic History of Pseudo-Abdias
PsClem	Pseudo-Clementines
QuestBart	The Questions of Bartholomew
1 RevJn	1Revelation of John the Theologian
2 RevJn	2Revelation of John the Theologian
	attributed to John Chrysostom
RevSteph	Revelation of Stephen
SecGosMk	Secret Gospel of Mark
VisP	Vision of Paul

13.2.2 Bibliography

J. H. CHARLESWORTH et al., *The New Testament Apocrypha and Pseudepigrapha*. A Guide to Publications, with Excursuses on Apocalypses (ATLA Bibliography Series 17; Metuchen, NJ – London 1987).

The work furnishes a bibliography on the Christian apocrypha, explains technical terms of this field of science and presents the apocalypses.

M. GEERARD, *Clavis Apocryphorum Novi Testamenti* (CChr.SA; Turnhout 1992).

It is a selective basic bibliography that includes critical editions, translations and important studies.

13.2.3 Introductions

J. B. BAUER, *Die neutestamentlichen Apokryphen* (WB; Düsseldorf 1968); Fr. tr., *Les apocryphes du Nouveau Testament* (Lire la Bible 37; Paris 1973).

In this introduction, the apocryphal literature of the New Testament is presented concisely (on a hundred pages).

J. H. CHARLESWORTH, *The Old Testament Pseudepigrapha and the New Testament*. Prolegomena for the Study of Christian Origins (MSSNTS 54; Cambridge 1985); It. tr. *Gli pseudepigrafi dell'Antico Testamento e il Nuovo Testamento*. Prolegomena allo studio delle origini cristiane (Studi biblici 91; Brescia 1990).

The monograph tries to answer the question of the manner in which the Jewish apocrypha facilitate the comprehension of the figure of Jesus Christ and his followers.

E. HENNECKE (ed.), *Handbuch zu den neutestamentlichen Apokryphen* (Tübingen 1904).

The author quotes both the critical editions and the basic literature for the NT apocrypha (gospels, apocalypses, acts of the apostles). Moreover, he considers the subapostolic writings (Epistle of Clement, of Barnabas etc.). The work needs an updated supplementation.

F. LAPHAM, *An Introduction to the New Testament Apocrypha* (London – New York 2003).

This guide is destined for pastors, theology and Church history students and for involved laypeople. It presents accessibly Christian documents written in the II and III c. A.D.

W. REBELL, *Neutestamentliche Apokryphen und Apostolische Väter* (München 1992).

This textbook contains an introduction to the gospels, acts of the apostles, apocalypses and writings of apostolic Fathers. Furthermore, the Gnostic Nag Hammadi literature is presented along with its most important writings.

To the aforementioned introductions should be added the annual *Apocrypha*. Revue internationale des littératures apocryphes /

International Journal of Apocryphal Literatures. It is published by
Brepols in Turnhout from 1990 on. The periodical offers valid articles
and discussions on current issues related especially to the NT apocrypha. Occasionally, articles on Gnosis are published as well.

13.2.4 Critical Editions

Corpus Christianorum: Series Apocryphorum (Turnhout 1983-) I-XV.

In the present series, generally the works called the NT apocrypha
are published (the gospels, acts, epistles, apocalypses) and some other
texts.

13.2.5 Translations

A brief selection of modern translations:

> F. BOVON – P. GEOLTRAIN (ed.), *Écrits apocryphes chrétiens* (Paris
> 1977).
> B. D. EHRMAN (ed.), *Lost Scriptures*. Books that Did Not Make It
> into the New Testament (Oxford 2003).
> J. K. ELLIOTT (ed.), *The Apocryphal New Testament*. A Collection of
> Apocryphal Christian Literature in an English Translation
> (Oxford 1993).
> M. ERBETTA (ed.), *Gli Apocrifi del Nuovo Testamento*. I/1. Vangeli.
> Scritti affini ai vangeli canonici. Composizioni gnostiche. Ma-
> teriale illustrativo. I/2. Vangeli. Infanzia e passione di Cristo.
> Assunzione di Maria. II. Atti e leggende. III. Lettere e apoca-
> lissi (Torino 1975, 1981, 1966, 1969).
> E. HENNECKE – W. SCHNEEMELCHER (ed.), *Neutestamentliche Apo-
> kryphen*. I. Evangelien. II. Apostolisches Apokalypsen und
> Verwandtes (Tübingen ⁵1987, ⁶1997); Eng. tr. *New Testament
> Apokrypha*. I. Gospels and Related Writings. II. Writings Re-
> lating to the Apostles. Apocalypses and Related Subjects
> (Cambridge – Louisville, KY ²1991, 1992).
> L. MORALDI (ed.), *Apocrifi del Nuovo Testamento*. I. Vangeli. II. Atti

degli Apostoli. III. Lettere. Dormizione di Maria. Apocalissi (Casale Monferrato 1994).

A. DE SANTOS OTERO (ed.), *Los Evangelios apócrifos*. Colección de textos griegos y latinos, versión crítica, estudios introductorios, comentarios e ilustraciones (BAC; Madrid 1956).

W. SCHNEEMELCHER (ed.), *Neutestamentliche Apokryphen in deutscher Übersetzung* (Tübingen ⁶1997) I-II; Eng. tr. *New Testament Apocrypha* (Cambridge 1991) I-II.

M. STAROWIEYSKI (ed.), *Apokryfy Nowego Testamentu*. I/1. Ewangelie apokryficzne. Fragmenty. Narodzenie i dzieciństwo Maryi i Jezusa. I/2. Ewangelie apokryficzne. Św. Józef i św. Jan Chrzciciel. Męka i zmartwychwstanie Jezusa. Wniebowzięcie Maryi. II/1. Apostołowie. Andrzej. Jan. Paweł. Piotr. Tomasz. II/1. Apostołowie. Bartłomiej. Filip. Jakub Mniejszy. Jakub większy. Judasz. Maciej. Mateusz. Szymon i Juda Tadeusz Ewangeliści. Uczniowie Pańscy. III. Listy i apokalipsy chrześcijańskie (Kraków 2003, 2003, 2007, 2007, 2001).

L. TESCAROLI (ed.), *Letteratura cristiana extracanonica del primo secolo* (Saggi e testi storici 22; L'Aquila – Roma 1996).

14. Exegetical Methods

As for exegetical methods, first a selection of printed text will be presented and after some bibliographical online collections, with many entries useful for research.

J. BARTON, *The Nature of Biblical Criticism* (Louisville, KY – London 2007).

Admitting a debt towards J. Barr, the author describes characteristics and the role of the critical approach to the Holy Scriptures. In addition, he confirms the meaning of both the university and the church. His work is useful for conducting seminars and lectures on hermeneutics.

J. BARTON, *Reading the Old Testament*. Method in Biblical Study (London 1984, ²1996).

In the first edition, reprinted four times, various methods and exegetical approaches are described along with the relationships among them. This second edition was enriched by the presentation of two more recent tendencies: the first of them emphasizes the role of the reader in the text, and the second deals with the link between theory and textuality.

W. EGGER, *Methodenlehre zum Neuen Testament.* Einführung in linguistische und historisch-kritische Methoden (Freiburg 1987); It. tr. *Metodologia del Nuovo Testamento.* Introduzione allo studio scientifico del Nuovo Testamento (CSB 16; Bologna 1989); Sp. tr. *Lecturas del Nuevo Testamento.* Metodología lingüística histórico-crítica (Estella 1990); Port. tr. *Metodologia do Novo Testamento.* Introdução aos métodos lingüísticos e histórico-críticos (Bíblica Loyola 12; São Paulo 1994).

The textbook presents various analytical approaches to the NT texts and offers examples for their practical usage.

P. GUILLEMETTE – M. BRISEBOIS, *Introduction aux méthodes historico-critiques* (Héritage et Projet 35; Montréal 1987); It. tr. *Introduzione ai metodi storico-critici* (Roma 1990).

The present introduction to historical critical methods, apart from their justification and description, includes practical exercises as well.

H. SIMIAN-YOFRE (ed.), *Metodologia dell'Antico Testamento* (Studi biblici 25; Bologna 1994); Port. tr. *Metodologia do Antigo Testamento* (Bíblica Loyola 28; São Paulo 2000).

The work was prepared by H. Simian-Yofre, J. L. Ska, S. Pisano and I. Gargano, professors at the Pontifical Biblical Institute in Rome.

Various research methods are presented and the basic bibliography is furnished.

J. L. SKA, *"Our Fathers Have Told Us"*. Introduction to the Analysis of Hebrew Narratives (SubBib 13; Roma 1990, 2000).

This handbook by the OT exegesis professor at the Pontifical Biblical Institute contains essential elements of the narrative analysis of the Old Testament and suggests hints for their practical application.

O. H. STECK, *Exegese des Alten Testaments: Leitfaden der Methodik*. Ein Arbeitsbuch für Proseminare, Seminare und Vorlesungen (Neukirchen-Vluyn 121989); Eng. tr. *Old Testament Exegesis*. A Guide to the Methodology (SBL Resources for Biblical Study 39; Atlanta 1995, 21998).

This guide aims to prepare the receiver to conduct exegetical analysis of OT passages. For this goal, it presents the tasks of exegesis and indicates application modalities of various methods.

H. ZIMMERMANN, *Neutestamentliche Methodenlehre*. Darstellung der historisch-kritischen Methode (Stuttgart 1967); Sp. tr. *Los métodos histórico-críticos en el Nuevo Testamento* (BAC 295; Madrid 1969); It. tr. *Metodologia del Nuovo Testamento*. Esposizione del metodo storico-critico (Torino 1971).

The present book was born during the seminar on methodology in the Philosophical Theological Academy in Paderborn (Germany). It is a tool that helps students to know and to apply the historical critical method in the exegesis of NT texts.

J. L. SKA, "Bibliografia biblica basilare dell'A.T. / Old Testament Basic Bibliography", http://www.biblico.it/doc-vari/ska_bibl. html [accessed January 9, 2009].

The entries are selected carefully and evaluated for their usefulness to the reader.

M. OEMING, "Bibliographie zur biblischen Hermeneutik", http://www.rzuser.uni-heidelberg.de/~dr6/hermeneutik.html [accessed January 9, 2009].

This bibliographical collection, updated until October 14, 1998, takes philosophical and biblical hermeneutics into consideration, as well as exegetical methods and approaches. Reflecting their diversity, it offers an exhaustive list of contributions, divided into different parts: historical critical method, sociological approach, psychological approach, "new archaeology", structuralist approach, narrative approach, canonical approach, semiotic analysis, approach by the history of reception, psychoanalytical approach, symbolical approach, bibliodrama, liberationist/liberation theology approach, feminist approach, dogmatic reading, fundamentalist reading, existential reading.

J. METZGER, "Vanderbilt Divinity Library Programmatic Bibliography. New Testament", 1-42, http://divinity.library.vanderbilt.edu/bibliographies/new_testament.pdf [accessed January 9, 2009].

In this collection of 42 pages of NT bibliography, about 28 pages are reserved for exegetical methods, grouped in various categories. The entries come from resources of the Divinity Library of Vanderbilt University in Nashville. They are updated up to June 2003.

S. BAZYLIŃSKI, "Bibliografia basilare del N.T. / New Testament Basic Bibliography", http://www.biblico.it/doc-vari/bibl_nt.html [accessed January 9, 2009].

This selective bibliography presents numerous publications in a logical way.

IV. Basic Literary "Types"

In recent decades, the literary sciences have found their place in the exegesis of the Bible which, rightly, is also studied as a literary work. The analysis of the forms of the Sacred Scripture has demonstrated that understanding the form is important for the comprehension of the text, that it belongs to the very nature of the text.

In the title of this chapter, the word "types" is put in quotation marks, since it includes both the stylistic devices (figures of speech) and the methods of argument.

Knowing and learning how to isolate the literary types is the first step of an investigation that cannot prescind from their finality. The goal of the following considerations, however, is more modest, for it intends to make only an introductory presentation of some types. For more complete information, the reader can consult the works cited in the bibliographical selections that follow.

1. Reference Bibliography

1.1 *Classics*

ARISTOTELES, *Ars rhetorica* (ed. W. D. ROSS) (SCBO; Oxonii 1959).
CICERO, *De inventione* (ed. G. ACHARD) (CUFr; Paris 1994).
———, *De oratore* (ed. A. YON) (CUFr; Paris 1964).
———, *De ratione dicendi ad C. Herennium* (ed. G. ACHARD) (CUFr; Paris 1989).
HORATIUS FLACCUS, *Opera: Ars poetica* (ed. E. C. WICKHAM – H. W. GARROD) (SCBO; Oxonii ²1967).
QUINTILIANUS, *Institutionis oratoriae libri duodecim* (ed. M. WINTERBOTTOM) (SCBO; Oxonii 1970) I-II.

1.2 *Studies*

ALONSO SCHÖKEL, L., *Estudios de poética hebrea* (Barcelona 1963).
————, *Manual de poética hebrea* (Madrid 1987); Eng. tr. *A Manual of Hebrew Poetics* (SubBi 11; Roma 1988); It. tr. *Manuale di poetica ebraica* (Biblioteca biblica 1; Brescia 1989).
————, "Poésie hébraïque", *DBS* VIII, 47-90.
ALTER, R., *The Art of Biblical Narrative* (New York 1981).
————, *The Art of Biblical Poetry* (New York 1985).
BÜHLMANN, W. – SCHERER, K., *Stilfiguren der Bibel* (BiBe 10; Fribourg 1973).
BULLINGER, E. W., *Figures of Speech Used in the Bible* (Grand Rapids, MI 1968, 1984); Sp. tr. *Diccionario de figuras de dicción usadas en la Biblia* (Barcelona 1985).
DHORME, É., *La poésie biblique*. Introduction à la poésie biblique et trente chants de circonstance (Vie chrétienne; Paris ⁶1931).
FLOYD, M. H., "Falling Flat on Our Ars Poetica, or Some Problems in Recent Studies of Biblical Poetry", *The Psalms and Other Studies on the Old Testament*. Presented to J. I. Hunt (ed. J. C. KNIGHT – L. SINCLAIR) (Nashotah, WI 1990) 118-131.
FOLLIS, E. R. (ed.), *Directions in Biblical Hebrew Poetry* (JSOT.S 40; Sheffield 1987).
FREEDMAN, D. N., *Pottery, Poetry, and Prophecy*. Studies in Early Hebrew Poetry (Winona Lake, IN 1980).
FRYE, N., *The Great Code*. The Bible and Literature (New York – London 1982); Fr. tr. *Le grand code*. La Bible et la littérature (Paris 1984).
GRAY, G. B., *The Forms of Hebrew Poetry Considered with Special Reference to the Criticism and Interpretation of the Old Testament* (LBS; New York 1915, 1972).
GROSSBERG, D., *Centripetal and Centrifugal Structures in Biblical Poetry* (SBL.MS 39; Atlanta 1989).

VON HERDER, J. G., *Vom Geist der ebräischen Poesie.* Eine Anleitung für die Liebhaber derselben und der ältesten Geschichte des menschlichen Geistes (Leipzig ³1825) I-II.

HORST, F., "Die Kennzeichen der hebräischen Poesie", *ThR* 21 (1953) 91-121.

KENNEDY, G. A., *New Testament Interpretation through Rhetorical Criticism* (Chapel Hill, NC 1984); tr. it. *Nuovo Testamento e critica retorica* (Studi biblici 151; Brescia 2006).

————, *A New History of Classical Rhetoric* (Princeton, NJ 1994).

KÖNIG, E., *Die Poesie des Alten Testaments* (Wissenschaft und Bildung 11; Leipzig 1907).

————, *Stilistik, Rhetorik, Poetik in Bezug auf die biblische Litteratur* (Leipzig 1900).

KUGEL, J., *The Idea of Biblical Poetry.* Parallelism and Its History (New Haven, CT – London 1981, Baltimore – London 1998).

KUNTZ, J. K., "Biblical Hebrew Poetry in Recent Research. Part I. Part II", *CurResB* 6 (1998) 31-64; 7 (1999) 35-79.

LAUSBERG, H., *Elemente der literarischen Rhetorik* (München 1963); It. tr. *Elementi di retorica* (Strumenti; Bologna 1969); Sp. tr. *Elementos de retórica literaria.* Introducción al estudio de la filología clásica románica, inglesa y alemana (Madrid 1983).

————, *Handbuch der literarischen Rhetorik.* Eine Grundlegung der Literaturwissenschaft (München 1960); Sp. tr. *Manual de retórica literaria.* Fundamentos de una ciencia de la literatura (Madrid 1966-1968) I-III; Eng. tr. *Handbook of Literary Rhetoric.* A Foundation for Literary Study (Leiden – Boston – Köln 1998); Pol. tr. *Retoryka literacka.* Podstawy wiedzy o literaturze (Bydgoszcz 2002).

LOWTH, R., *De sacra poësi Hebraeorum praelectiones academicae Oxonii habitae* (Oxonii 1753); Eng. tr. *Lectures on the Sacred Poetry of the Hebrews* (London 1787; AnAm 43; Hildesheim –

New York 1969) I-II; Fr. tr. *Leçons sur la poésie sacrée des Hébreux* (Lyon 1812).

VAN DER LUGT, P., *Strofische structuren in de Bijbels-Hebreeuwse poëzie*. De geschiedenis van het onderzoek en een bijdrage tot de theorievorming omtrent de strofenbouw van de Psalmen (DNL.T; Kampen 1980).

MARTIN, J., *Antike Rhetorik*. Technik und Methode (HAW 2/3; München 1974).

MORTARA GARAVELLI, B., *Manuale di retorica* (Tascabili Bompiani 94; Milano ⁹2005).

MOULTON, R. G., *The Literary Study of the Bible*. An Account of the Leading Forms of Literature Represented in the Sacred Writings (London 1896).

MUILENBURG, J., "A Study in Hebrew Rhetoric: Repetition and Style", *Congress Volume*. Copenhagen 1953 (VT.S 1; Leiden 1953) 97-111.

O'CONNOR, M., *Hebrew Verse Structure* (Winona Lake, IN ²1997).

PAX, E., "Stilistische Beobachtungen an neutralen Redewendungen im Neuen Testament", *SBFLA* 17 (1967) 335-347.

PERELMAN, C. – OBRECHTS-TITECA, L., *The New Rhetoric*. A Treatise on Argumentation (Notre Dame, IN 1971).

PORTEN, S. E. (ed.), *Handbook of Classical Rhetoric in the Hellenistic Period* (330 B.C.-A.D. 400) (Leiden – New York – Köln 1997).

RICHTER, W., *Exegese als Literaturwissenschaft*. Entwurf einer alttestamentlichen Literaturtheorie und Methodologie (Göttingen 1971).

RYKEN, L., *The Literature of the Bible* (Grand Rapids, MI 1974).

SEYBOLD, K., *Poetik der Psalmen* (Poetologische Studien zum Alten Testament 1; Stuttgart 2003); It. tr. *Poetica dei Salmi* (Introduzione allo studio della Bibbia. Supplementi 35; Brescia 2007).

UEDING, G. et al. (ed.), *Historisches Wörterbuch der Rhetorik* (Tübingen 1992-) I-VIII.

VANCE, D. R., *The Question of Meter in Biblical Hebrew Poetry* (SBEC 46; Lewiston – Queenston – Lampeter 2001).
WATSON, W. G. E., *Classical Hebrew Poetry. A Guide to Its Techniques* (JSOT.S 26; Sheffield 1986).
————, *Traditional Techniques in Classical Hebrew Verse* (JSOT.S 170; Sheffield 1994).
WEISS, M., "Wege der neuen Dichtungswissenschaft in ihrer Anwendung auf die Psalmenforschung", *Bib* 42 (1961) 255-305.
WELCH, J. W. – McKINLAY, D. B. (ed.), *Chiasmus Bibliography* (Provo, UT 1999).

2. Parallelism

Parallelism (Gk. παραλληλισμός, "being side-by-side") is perhaps the most characteristic feature of Hebrew poetry. It is a "parallel and symmetrical disposition of words in phrases or in parts of phrases which follow one another, with contemporaneous correspondence of content, to strengthen the expressive effect"[1].

According to the classification of R. Lowth based on the content, there are three types of parallelism: synonymous, antithetic, and synthetic[2].

BERLIN, A., *The Dynamics of Biblical Parallelism* (Revised and Expanded Edition) (The Biblical Resource Series; Grand Rapids, MI – Cambridge 2008).
WAGNER, A. (ed.), *Parallelismus membrorum* (OBO 224; Fribourg – Göttingen 2007).

---

[1] P.-G. MÜLLER, *Lexikon exegetischer Fachbegriffe* (BiBa 1; Stuttgart – Kevelaer 1985) 191.
[2] See, the *Lecture XIX* by LOWTH, *Lectures* II, 24-59.

2.1 *Synonymous Parallelism*

In this figure, the second member of a unit repeats with other words the thought of the first member.

> E.g.   Ps 49,2: "Hear this, all nations, | give ear, all inhabitants of the world";
>
> Ps 51,4: "Wash me clean from my guilt, | purify me from my sin".

2.2 *Antithetic Parallelism*

When the second member of a unit expresses the opposite or contrary thought to that of the first member, the parallelism is antithetic.

> E.g.   Ps 1,6: "The Lord knows the way of the righteous, | but the way of the wicked leads to ruin";
>
> Ps 27,10: "My father and my mother have forsaken me, | but the Lord gathered me up".

2.3 *Synthetic Parallelism*

The construction in which the second member completes the content of the first member is called synthetic parallelism.

> E.g.   Ps 3,5: "I cry to the Lord with my voice | and he answers me from his holy mountain";
>
> Ps 42,2: "As the dear longs for the streams of water, | so my soul longs for you, o God".

2.4 *Climactic (or Comprehensive) Parallelism*

Apart from the above mentioned parallelisms, there is also a climatic one. It occurs when the second member of a unit repeats one or more important words of the first member in order to obtain the effect of a climax or an expressive culmination. In this way, the thought is expressed more completely and efficaciously.

E.g. Gen 12,1: "Go *from* your country, *from* your kindred and *from* your father's house";

Ps 24,8: "The Lord strong and mighty, | the Lord mighty in battle".

3. Rhetorical Devices in Sound

Hebrew authors profited by the combinations of sounds that are not only understood as a poetical or rhetorical device, but which help to highlight the enunciations of a text as well.

3.1 *Alliteration*

Alliteration (Lat. *a*, "to" + *littera*, "letter") is a repetition of the same consonantal sound mainly at the beginning of the subsequent words ("She left the Heaven of Heroes and came down | To make a man to meet the mortal need | A man to match the mountains and the sea | The friendly welcome of the wayside well", E. Markham).

E.g. Isa 31,3: *yhwh yaṭṭeh yādô*, "Yhwh will stretch out his hand";

Ps 127,1: *šāwᵓ šāqad šômēr*, "In vain does the guard keep watch";

Heb 2,18: πέπονθεν... πειρασθείς... πειραζομένοις, "he has suffered... been tested... to those who are tested".

HUGGER, P., "Die Alliteration im Psalter", *Wort, Lied und Gottesspruch*. Beiträge zu Psalmen und Propheten. Festschrift J. Ziegler (ed. J. SCHREINER) (FzB 2; Würzburg 1972) 81-90.

3.2 *Assonance*

This kind of repetition of sound (Lat. *assonans*, "sounding in answer", "harmonizing") derives from the verb and noun inflection, and from some formation of nouns as well.

E.g. Zeph 1,14: *qārôb yôm-yhwh haggādôl | qārôb ûmahēr mᵉᵓōd*, "Near is the great day of the Lord | near and coming very speedily";

Ps 22,17b-18: *kāʾărû yāday wᵉraglāy | ʾăsappēr kol ʿaṣmôtāy*,
"They have pierced my hands and feet, | I can count all my
bones".

SAYDON, P. P., "Assonance in Hebrew as a Means of Expressing Em-
phasis", *Bib* 36 (1955) 36-50, 287-304.

3.3 *Paronomasia (or Pun)*

In general (Gk. παρονομασία, "to alter slightly in naming"), two
words of similar or identical sound are used to highlight the opposition of meanings ("Never in the field of human conflict was so much
owed by so many to so few", W. Churchill).

E.g.   Qoh 7,1: *ṭôb šēm miššemen ṭôb*, "A good name is better than good
        ointment";

        Isa 5,7: "He looked for judgment (*mišpāṭ*) but behold bloodshed
        (*mišpāḥ*); for justice (*ṣᵉdāqâ*) but behold, a cry (*ṣᵉʿāqâ*)".

For some scholars, this rhetorical figure is a playing on words with
regard to a proper name.

E.g.   Zeph 2,4: *ʿazzâ ʿăzûbâ*, "Gaza will be abandoned", *ʿeqrôn tēʿāqēr*,
        "Ekron will be uprooted";

        Zeph 2,9: *ʿammôn kaʿămōrâ*, "Ammon as Gomorrah".

3.4 *Etymological and Pseudo-Etymological Figure*

An etymological figure is a kind of paronomasia that connects
words on the basis of the etymology and, at times, their meaning (e.g.
"joyfully rejoice"). In the Hebrew text of the Bible, it is mostly a sub-
ordination of the direct complement to an intransitive verb.

E.g.   Gen 2,17: *môt tāmût*, "Of death you will die" (= "you shall cer-
        tainly die");

        Gen 47,22: ἐν δόσει γὰρ ἔδωκεν δόμα τοῖς ἱερεῦσιν, "For in giv-
        ing, he [Pharaoh] gave a gift to the priests";

Exod 22,22: *ʾim ʿannēh tᵉʿanneh ʾōtô kî ʾim ṣāʿōq yiṣʿaq ʾēlay šāmōaʿ ʾešmaʿ ṣaʿăqātô*, "If you afflict, afflicting him and if he will cry, crying out to me, I will hear, hearing his cry" (= "If you really afflict him and if he actually cries out to me, I will surely hear his cry");

Jonah 1,10: *wayyîrᵉʾû hāʾănāšîm yirᵉʾâ gᵉdôlâ*, "The men feared with a great fear" (= "The men were exceedingly afraid");

1 John 5,16: ἁμαρτάνοντα ἁμαρτίαν, "sinning a sin" (= "who commits a sin").

A pseudo-etymological figure, on the other hand, occurs when words of similar sound are placed together (e.g. "The minister did not mince his words").

E.g.　Prov 3,29: *ʾal taḥărōš ʿal rēʿăkā rāʿâ*, "do not plot evil against your neighbor";

Gen 2,23: "She shall be called woman (*ʾiššâ*), for from man (*ʾîš*) was she taken".

GOLKA, F. W., "Die *Figura etymologica* im Alten Testament", *"Wünschet Jerusalem Frieden"*. Collected Communications to the XIIth Congress of the International Organization for the Study of the Old Testament, Jerusalem 1986 (ed. M. AUGUSTIN – K.-D. SCHNUCK) (BEAT 13; Frankfurt a.M. – Bern – New York – Paris 1988) 415-424.

3.5 *Rhyme*

This resonant agreement (Gk. ῥυθμός, "rhythm") at the end of a word, of a hemistich or verse is rare in Hebrew poetry.

E.g.　Gen 4,23: "Hear my voice, wives of Lamech, give ear to my utterance (*ʾimrātî*) | because I have slain a man for wounding me, and a boy for bruising me (*lᵉḥabburātî*)";

Isa 41,11-13: "Behold, all shall be ashamed and confounded who rage against you (*bāk*); | they shall be as nothing and perish those who strive against you (*rîbekā*). You will seek, but will not find those who strive against you (*maṣṣutekā*); | they shall be brought to nothing, to naught, those who do battle with you (*milḥamtekā*). For I am Yhwh, your God, who hold your right hand (*yᵉmînekā*) | and I tell you, Fear not, I will help you (*ᶜāzartîkā*)".

4. Other Rhetorical Types

4.1 *Anadiplosis*

The anadiplosis (Gk. ἀναδίπλωσις, "the redouble", "repetition"; Lat. *reduplicatio*) is the repetition of the same word (or words) at the end of one sentence and at the beginning of another. In this way a train of the utterance is elaborated further with major expressive efficacy ("The love of wicked men converts to fear, | That fear to hate, and hate turns one or both | To worthy danger and deserved death", W. Shakespeare, *Richard II*, 5.1.66-68).

> E.g.   Gen 1,1.2: "In the beginning God created the heavens and the earth. And the earth was waste…";
>
> Ps 121,1.2: "I lift up my eyes to the hills, from whence comes my help. My help comes from Yhwh";
>
> Matt 10,40: "He who receives you receives me, and who receives me receives One who send me".

4.2 *Anaphora*

The anaphora (Gk. ἀναφορά, "rising") intensifies expressive efficacy through the repetition of one or more words at the beginning of successive sentences, clauses, phrases, or parts thereof. ("Through me the way is to the city dolent; | Through me the way is to eternal dole; | Through me the way among the people lost", Dante Alighieri, *Hell*, III, 1-3).

E.g.   Jer 51,20-23: *"With you I shatter (w^{e}nippaṣtî b^{e}kā)* nations, | with you I destroyed kingdoms, | *with you I shatter* the horse and the rider, | *with you I shatter* chariot and driver, | *with you I shatter* man and woman, | *with you I shatter* old and young, | *with you I shatter* young man and girl, | *with you I shatter* the shepherd and his flock, | *with you I shatter* the ploughman and his team, | *with you I shatter* governors and prefects";

Ps 29,1-2: *"Give to the Lord*, sons of God, | *give to the Lord* glory and might. *Give to the Lord* the glory of his name".

4.3 *Anastrophe*

As a figure of word (Gk. ἀναστροφή, "a turning back"; Lat. *reversio*, "return"), anastrophe repeats the same words or phrases in reverse order ("One for all, all for one", A. Dumas; cf. Hyperbaton, § 4.18; Hysteron-proteron, § 4.20; Chiasm, § 4.6). These words or ideas belong often to two different literary units.

E.g.   Exod 9,31: "The flax (a) and the barley (b) were smitten, for the barley (b') was in the ear and the flax (a') was in bud";

2 Cor 1,3: "Blessed be the God (a) and Father (b) of our Lord Jesus Christ, the Father (b') of mercies and God (a') of all comfort".

4.4 *Asyndeton*

This stylistic figure omits conjunctions (Gk. ἀσύνδετον, "unbound", "disconnected") between the parts of a sentence or between a series of (phrases) which are coordinated between them ("veni, vidi, vici", "I came, I saw, I conquered", Julius Caesar).

E.g.   Judg 5,27: "Between her feet he crumpled, he fell, he laid; between her feet he crumpled, he fell; where he crumpled, there he fell dead";

Luke 17,28: "Likewise as it was in the days of Lot: they ate, they drank, they bought, they sold, they planted, they build".

4.5 *Brachylogy (or Conciseness)*

Brachylogy (Gk. βραχύς, "short" + λόγος, "speech") is a condensed expression or laconic speech to express a thought.

> E.g.   Prov 10,1: "A wise son makes his father glad; a foolish son is a grief of his mother";
>
> Matt 21,22: "Whatever you ask in prayer with faith, you will receive".

4.6 *Chiasm (Inverted Parallelism)*

The chiasm (χιασμός from Greek letter χ) is a literary device which repeats corresponding or opposite words in inverted order, following the pattern A, B | B', A',

> e.g.   Isa 5,20: "Woe to those who call evil good and good evil, | who put darkness in place of light and light in place of darkness, | who put bitter in place of what is sweet and sweet in place of what is bitter"

or A, B, C | C', B', A'

> e.g.   Isa 22,22: "He will open and none will shut, | he will shut and none will open".

Di Marco, A., *Il chiasmo nella Bibbia*. Contributi di stilistica strutturale (Ricerche e proposte; Torino 1980).

4.7 *Climax*

This figure of word (Gk. κλῖμαξ, "ladder") repeats certain important words in a series of connected phrases. The chain of phrases, which coincide, is arranged in a growing (or diminishing) order of quality, importance, expression etc. ("We from the greatest body | Have issued to the heaven that is pure *light*; | *Light* intellectual replete with *love*, | *Love* of true good replete with *ecstasy*, | *Ecstasy* that transcendeth every sweetness", Dante Alighieri, *Paradise*, XXX, 38-42).

E.g.   Joel 1,3-4: "Tell your children of it, | and let your children tell
       their children, | and their children another generation! | What the
       cutter has left, the locust has devoured, | what the locust has left,
       the grub has devoured | and what the grub has left, the hopper has
       devoured";

       John 1,1-2: "In the beginning was the Word, and the Word was
       with God, and the Word was God. He [Word] was in the beginning
       with God".

4.8 *Anticlimax*

The anticlimax disposes a series of ideas or words in a decreasing
order of vigor and intensity. It contrasts sometimes the effect that the
climax has provoked. The transitions can be very sharp ("En tierra, en
humo, en polvo, en sombra, en nada", "Become but ash, smoke,
shadow, dust and night", L. de Góngora, *Mientras por competir...*, last
line).

E.g.   1 John 3,17 after 3,16: "[16]Hereby we have known love, that he
       laid down his life for us; and we ought to lay down our lives for
       the brethren. [17]If anyone has the world's goods and sees his
       brother in need, and closes his heart to him, how can the love of
       God abide in him?";

       Matt 25,14-30: The parable of the talents – the servants receive re-
       spectively five, two and one talent; and the settling accounts takes
       place in a decreasing order.

4.9 *Comparison (or Simile)*

A concept is clarified by comparing it with another one. The comparison (Gk. παραβολή, "comparison", "juxtaposition"; Lat. *simili-
tudo*) is frequently recognizable due to a conjunction "as, like" or by
the sequence of words "so... as", "like... like", "just as... so", etc. At
times, however, these expressions disappear completely. In these
cases, when a term is not identified by another one, an analogy occurs.

E.g.   Ps 1,3: "He will be like a tree planted near streams of water";

Ps 144,12: "May our sons be like plants, grown up in their youth; our daughters like corner pillars, for the construction of the temple".

4.10 *Enthymeme*

An enthymeme (Gk. ἐνθύμημα, "thought", "argument") is an elliptical (truncated) syllogism, in which one of two premises is implied (but unexpressed).

E.g.   Matt 27,19: "Have nothing to do with that righteous man".

In this syllogism the major premise: "It is wrong to punish the just and innocent man", is given only *in spirit* (ἐν θυμῷ). It is tacitly understood. In her petition, Pilate's wife annunciates the minor premise: "Jesus is a righteous man" and the conclusion of the syllogism: "Have nothing to do with him".

4.11 *Epanadiplosis (Encircling)*

This figure of word (Gk. ἐπαναδίπλωσις, "the redouble", "a doubling upon again"; Lat. *epanadiposis*) is a kind of inclusion which repeats the same word (words) at the beginning and at the end of a sentence or of a verse ("never we will do it for a friend, never").

E.g.   Exod 32,16: "The tables were work of God, and the writing was the writing of God, incised upon the tables";

Ps 122,7-8: "Peace be within your walls, | quietness in your palaces. | For my brothers and companions' sake, | I desire say: 'Peace be within you!'";

Phil 4,4: "Rejoice in the Lord always. Again I will say: Rejoice".

4.12 *Epanorthosis*

An epanorthosis (Gk. ἐπανόρθωσις, "correcting") rephrases the preceding word, which expresses primarily a judgment, and substitutes or corrects it by another more precise or adequate word or words.

E.g.   Mark 9,24: "I belief, help my unbelief";

John 12,27: "Father, save me from this hour? But for this purpose I have come to this hour!".

4.13 *Epimerismos*

This figure of thought (Gk. ἐπιμερισμός, "distribution"; Lat. *enumeratio*), called also enumeratio or list, arranges in a series the parts of a whole, which is not mentioned. Often, synonyms and/or antonyms are coordinated syndetically or asyndetically ("I did this, that and other thing").

E.g.   Isa 1,11.13: "What to me is the multitude of your sacrifices?, says Yhwh. I am sated with burnt offerings of rams and the fat of fed beasts. And I do not delight in the blood of bulls and of lambs and of he-goats [...] Bring no more vain oblations, incense is an abomination unto me";

1 Pet 4,3: "For the time that has passed is sufficient for doing what the Gentiles like to do: living in licentiousness, passions, drunkenness, orgies, carousing, and lawless idolatry".

4.14 *Epimone*

This figure of thought (Gk. ἐπιμονή, "a staying on", "dwelling upon"; Lat. *commoratio*, "delay", "lag") is a form of repetition which consists in dwelling upon an important point in which is the heart of the matter. Discussing a topic, one returns on this core element using words which arouse impression.

E.g.　Matt 7,21-23: "Not everyone who says: Lord, Lord, will enter the kingdom of heaven, but he who does the will of my Father who is in heaven. Many will say to me in that day: Lord, Lord, did we not prophesy in your name and drive out demons in your name, and work many miracles in your name? And then I will declare to them: I never knew you; depart from me, you that work iniquity";

John 21,15-17: "Jesus said to Simon Peter: 'Simon, son of John, do you love me more than these?'. He said to him: 'Yes, Lord, you know that I love you'. He said to him: 'Feed my lambs». He said to him a second time: 'Simon, son of John, do you love me?'. He said to him: 'Yes, Lord, you know that I love you'. He said to him: 'Tend my sheep'. He said to him the third time: 'Simon, son of John, do you love me?'. Peter was grieved that he said to him the third time: Do you love me?, and he said to him: 'Lord, you know everything; you know that I love you'. Jesus said to him: 'Feed my sheep'".

4.15 *Epiphora (or Epistorphe)*

An epiphora (Gk. ἐπιφορά, "addition", "repetition") repeats the same word (or words) at the end of two or more successive verses, hemistiches, strophes.

E.g.　Gen 13,6: "The land could not support both of them *dwelling together (lāšebet yaḥdāw)*, because their possessions were so great that they could not *dwell together (lāšebet yaḥdāw)*";

Ps 115,9-11: "The house of Israel trusts in the Lord: *he is their help and their shield*. O house of Aaron, trust in the Lord: *he is their help and their shield*. You who fear the Lord, trust in the Lord: *he is their help and their shield*".

4.16 *Expolitio*

The *expolitio* (Lat. "adorning", "embellishing"; Gk. ἐξεργασία, "a working out") is a form of the *commoratio* (cf. § 4.14). This figure of thought is a repetition which refines the meaning of a word – embellishes and reinforces – and not only clarifies or interprets.

> E.g. Ps 17,1: "Hear, Yhwh, the righteousness, | pay attention to my cry, | give ear to my prayer";
>
> Ps 18,1-2: "I will love you, Yhwh, my strength. | Yhwh my crag and my fortress and my liberation. My God, my rock, I will trust in him. | My shield and the horn of my salvation, my tower".

4.17 *Hendiadys*

A hendiadys is a figure in which an idea is expressed by two coordinated terms (Gk. ἔν διὰ δυοῖν, "one through two"), usually two nouns in place of one noun modified by an adjective or a specifying complement.

> E.g. Gen 1,26: "Let us make man in our image, after our likeness";
>
> 1 Chr 22,5: "My son Solomon is young and inexperienced, but the house to be built for the Lord must be exceedingly magnificent, of fame and of glory in any country".

4.18 *Hyperbaton*

This syntactic figure inverts some elements in a sentence in comparison with their normal order (Gk. ὑπέρβατον, "transposition"). As a rhetorical trope, the hyperbaton reversing the word order highlights their meaning or overtone ("Why should their liberty than ours be more?", W. Shakespeare, *Comedy of Errors*, II.1.11).

> E.g. Jer 14,1: "Which was the word of Yhwh to Jeremiah, on the occasion of the drought", ʾăšer hāyâ dᵉbar-yhwh ʾel-yirmᵉyāhû ʿal dibrê habbaṣṣārôt;
>
> John 6,60: "Hard is this word".

4.19 *Hyperbole*

A hyperbole (Gk. ὑπερβολή, "excess", "exaggeration") consists of the exaggeration of a quality or an action until it is incredible (*to split one's sides laughing*).

E.g.   Gen 11,4: "Come, let us build for ourselves a city and a tower, whose top will reach to heaven";

Matt 11,23: "And you, Capernaum, will you be exalted to heaven? You will go down to the netherworld!".

4.20 *Hysteron Proteron*

Its name derives from the transliteration of Greek ὕστερον πρότερον, "posterior anterior", "the latter as first". The figure reverses the logical order of words in comparison with the natural order of actions ("He died in the Vatican, he was born in Wadowice").

E.g.   Ps 2,7: "You are my son (*b*ᵉ*nî*), today I have begotten you (*y*ᵉ*lidtîkā*)";

Ps 44,2: "O God, we have heard with our ears, our fathers have told us";

Rev 5,2: "Who is worthy to open the scroll and break its seals?".

ZURRO RODRÍGUEZ, E., "El hysteron-proteron en la poesía bíblica hebrea", *EstB* 58 (2000) 399-415.

4.21 *Isocolon*

This syntactical figure (Gk. ἰσόκωλον, "formed of even members") consists in the juxtaposition of two or more members of a whole (of a sentence or verse), which are equal in number of words or in syntactical structure ("Buy two, pay one"; "The bigger they are, the harder they fall").

E.g.   Heb 7,26 – three parallel phrases: ὅσιος, ἄκακος, ἀμίαντος | κεχωρισμένος ἀπὸ τῶν ἁμαρτωλῶν | ὑψηλότερος τῶν οὐρανῶν γεόμενος, "Holy, innocent, undefiled; separated from sinners; exalted above the heavens";

1 Cor 8,6, lit.: "but for us one God, the Father, from whom all things, and we into him; and one Lord, Jesus Christ, for him all things, and we through him".

4.22 *Litotes*

A litotes (Gk. λιτότης, "plainness", "simplicity") consists in a formal attenuation of the expression of judgment or predicate by denying the opposite idea, offering either an understatement or reinforcing it substantially.

E.g.   Mark 12,34: "Your are not far from the kingdom of God", the relationship of the scribe toward the kingdom is not yet perfect;

1 Cor 9,17: "For if I do it willingly, I have a reward", Paul thinks "without payment", but omitting this word, he reinforces its meaning.

4.23 *Merismus*

A merismus (Gk. ὁ μερισμός, "division", "distribution") expresses a whole or a totality which is reduced into two members (which are never extremes, see below Polar Expression, § 4.27), chosen either from a complete set or by dividing this totality into two halves.

E.g.   Deut 4,6: "heaven and earth" = the universe;

Ps 36,7: "O Lord, you sustain man and beast";

Ps 49,3: "Both low and high, rich and poor together".

HONEYMAN, A. M., "Merismus in Biblical Hebrew", *JBL* 71 (1952) 11-18.

KRAŠOVEC, J., *Der Merismus im Biblisch-hebräischen und Nordwestsemitischen* (BibOr 33; Rome 1977).

4.24 *Metaphor*

A metaphor (Gk. μεταφορά, "a transfer") is based on an implied similitude, having an analogical relationship and is used to express a different concept.

> E.g. Ps 55,22: "His mouth is smoother than butter, but war is in his heart; softer than oil are his words, but they are drawn swords", deceitful speech of the wicked;
>
> John 10,9: "I am the gate".

4.25 *Metonymy*

A metonymy (Gk. μετωνυμία, "change of name") transfers the meaning of a word to another one. This figure is not based on similitude, but on the relationship of the spatial, temporal or causal affinity. For instance, the container is used for the contained ("the stadium was applauding"), the cause for the effect ("he gave death in a vial"), the place for the event ("Watergate changed American politics"), the symbol for the represented object ("the land belongs to the crown"), the author's name for his work ("to admire Picasso"), the abstract for a concrete concept ("love forgives all"), the part of the body for its function ("a level head"), etc. For some authors the limits between the metonymy and the synecdoche are not very clear, so that some cases may be classified differently.

> E.g. Lev 26,6: "The sword [the war] will not pass through your land";
>
> Prov 12,19: "The lip [namely, the enunciation] of truth endures for ever";
>
> Luke 16,29: "They have Moses [namely, his writings] and the prophets [namely, their writings]; let them listen to them!".

4.26 *Personification*

A personification (Lat. *persona*, "persona" + *facere*, "to do") attributes human characteristics most of all to an abstract quality that acts as a subject in a social relationship.

> E.g. Isa 59,14-15: "And judgment is driven back and justice stands aloof; truth stumbles in the public square, and righteousness cannot enter. So truth is lacking, and he who turns from evil is despoiled. The Lord saw this and it displeased him, that there is no more judgment";
>
> Ps 85,10.11.12.14: "His salvation is near for those who fear him and his glory will dwell in our land. Mercy and truth will meet, justice and peace will kiss. Truth will sprout out of the earth and justice will look down from heaven. Justice will walk before him and make his footsteps a way".

4.27 *Polar Expression*

A polar expression is close to the antithesis or counter-position. A couple of members of a set, which occupy extreme poles, are selected as representatives of the totality.

> E.g. Isa 1,6: "From the sole of the foot to the head there is no soundness in it";
>
> Rev 1,8; 21,6; 22,13: "I am the Alpha and the Omega".

BOCCACCIO, P., "I termini contrari come espressioni della totalità in ebraico", *Bib* 33 (1952) 173-190.

LAMBERT, G., "Lier-délier. L'expression de la totalité par l'opposition de deux contraires", *VivPen* [= *RB*] 3 [= 52] (1943-1944) 91-103.

4.28 *Prosopopoeia*

This is a figure of thought (Gk. προσωποποιία, "dramatization") in which absent or deceased persons, or inanimate, abstract objects, may speak as if they were present, living and animate.

> E.g.   Gen 4,10: "The voice of your brother's blood is crying to me from the soil";
>
> Ps 35,10: "All my bones say: 'O Lord, who is like you...'".

4.29 *Symploche*

A symploche is an interweaving (Gk. συμπλοκή, "intertwining", "combination") of two different words in a similar order: one time at the beginning and the other time at the end of the phrase.

> E.g.   Isa 65,13-14: "Thus says the Lord God: '*Behold, my servants* shall eat *and you* shall hunger; *behold, my servants* shall drink *and you* shall be thirsty; *behold, my servants* shall rejoice *and you* shall be put to shame; *behold, my servants* shall shout for joy of heart, *and you* shall cry out for grief of heart and shall howl in anguish of spirit'";
>
> 1 Cor 15,42-44: "*What is sown* is perishable, *what is raised* is imperishable; *what is sown* is contemptible, *what is raised* is glorious, *what is sown* is weak *what is raised* is powerful; *what is sown* is a natural body, *what is raised* is a spiritual body".

4.30 *Synecdoche*

A synecdoche (Gk. συνεκδοχή, "understanding one thing with another") is a trope in which a word receives something from the meaning of the other word with which it is internally associated. For instance, a part is used for the whole or vice versa, the general for the special or vice versa, or the singular for the plural or vice versa.

E.g.   Exod 1,7: "Children" is used for descendants; Isa 53,12: "He bore the sins of many", many stands for all (cf. v. 6; Heb 9,28; Matt 1,21);

Ps 87,2: "The gates of Zion", in which the name of the gates indicates either the temple in Zion or the entire city;

1 Cor 3,6: "Apollos" stands for any minister.

4.31 Topos

The topos (Gk. τόπος, "place") is a recurring literary theme in a work, in the subject of an author or of a period, and of a tradition.

E.g.   The phrase "Pangs and agony will seize them, they will be in pain as a woman in travail" comes out with variants in many texts (cf. Isa 13,8; 21,3; 42,14; Jer 6,24; 22,23; 30,6; 49,24; 50,43; Mic 4,9-10) so that it becomes a *topos*[3].

BRADLEY, D. G., "The Topos as Form in the Pauline Paraenesis", *JBL* 72 (1953) 238-246.

MULLINS, T. Y., "Topos as a New Testament Form", *JBL* 99 (1980) 541-547.

5. Middôt

Among many *middôt* (Hebr. lit. "measures") which appear in the rabbinic and biblical literature three rabbinic rules, fairly frequently used, will be discussed: *qal waḥômer*, *gᵉzērᵃʾ šāwâ* and *ʾal tiqrê*.

The following bibliography informs about these and other norms.

BODENDORFER, G., "Die Tora ist nicht im Himmel. Rabbinische Exegese und Hermeneutik", *Sinnvermittlung*. Studien zur Geschichte von Exegese und Hermeneutik I (ed. P. MICHEL – H. WEDER) (Zürich 2000) 115-140.

---

[3] For a discussion on this topos, see ALONSO, *A Manual*, 185.

CARUCCI VITERBI, B., "Le regole ermeneutiche per l'interpreta-
    zione del testo biblico: Torah scritta e Torah orale", *La lettura
    ebraica delle Scritture* (ed. S. J. SIERRA) (Bologna ²1996) 75-
    101.
JACOBS, L., "Hermeneutics", *EJ* VIII, 366-372.
LUZÁRRAGA, J., "Principios hermenéuticos de exégesis bíblica en el
    rabinismo primitivo", *EstB* 30 (1971) 177-193.
PERANI, M., "L'interpretazione della Bibbia presso i Rabbi. Aspetti
    dell'ermeneutica rabbinica", *RivBib* 45 (1997) 329-346.
STEMBERGER, G., "Hermeneutik der Jüdischen Bibel", *Hermeneu-
    tik der Jüdischen Bibel und des Alten Testaments* (ed. C. DOH-
    MEN – G. STEMBERGER) (KStTh 1/2; Stuttgart – Berlin – Köln
    1996) 23-132, esp. 83-109.
TOWNER, W. S., "Hermeneutical Systems of Hillel and the Tannaim.
    A Fresh Look", *HUCA* 53 (1982) 101-135.

5.1 *Qal waḥômer*

The *qal waḥômer* is an *a fortiori* method of reasoning which intends to prove that a particular thesis has an even stronger rationale
to be admitted as valid than another thesis which has already been
recognized as correct.

> E.g.   Gen 44,8: "Behold, we even brought back to you from the land of
> Canaan the money that we found in the mouths of our bags, and
> how, then, could we steal silver or gold from your master's
> house?";
>
> Heb 9,13-14: "For if the blood of goats and bulls and the sprin-
> kling of a heifer's ashes can sanctify those who are defiled so that
> their flesh is cleansed, how much more will the blood of Christ,
> who through the eternal Spirit offered himself unblemished
> to God, cleanse our consciences from dead works to worship the
> living God!".

5.2 Gᵉzērāʾ šāwâ

The *gᵉzērāʾ šāwâ* is reasoning by analogy (or identity). It can be used when, in the biblical text, two identical or similar expressions appear, even in distant passages. By means of one expression, the context and the application of the other is explained.

E.g.   1 Cor 3,19-20: "([18]Let no one deceive himself. If any one among you thinks that he is wise in this age, let him become a fool that he may become wise;) [19]for the wisdom of this world is folly with God. For it is written: "He catches the wise in their craftiness," [Job 5,13]. [20]And again: "The Lord knows that the thoughts of the wise are vain" [Ps 93,11 LXX]".

The reference to wise men (σοφοί), present in the OT texts, shows that Paul is making an analogy of Job 5,13 with Ps 93,11 LXX so as to conclude his considerations about the wisdom of preaching; in this way Paul's criterion, which prefers proclaiming the cross to rhetorical preaching, was confirmed once again (cf. 1 Cor 1,10–3,17).

BASTA, P., *Gezerah Shawah*. Storia, forme e metodi dell'analogia biblica (SubBi 26; Roma 2006).

CHERNICK, M., "Internal Restrains on Gezerah Shawah's Application", *JQR* 80 (1990) 253-282.

LORENZIN, T., "Il Salterio: torah di Davide", *Torah e kerygma: dinamiche della tradizione nella Bibbia*. XXXVII Settimana Biblica nazionale (Roma, 9-13 Settembre 2002) (ed. I. CAREDELLINI – E. MANICARDI) (RStB 16; Bologna 2004) 67-86.

————, "L'uso delle regole ermeneutiche al tiqré e gezerah shawah nel Sal 18", *Initium Sapientiae*. Scritti in onore di F. Festorazzi nel suo 70° compleanno (ed. R. FABRIS) (SRivBib 36; Bologna 2000) 83-93.

PLAG, C., "Paulus und die Gezera schawa. Zur Übernahme rabbinischer Auslegungskunst", *Jud.* 50 (1994) 135-140.

5.3 *ʾal tiqrê*

The *ʾal tiqrê* (Aram. "do not read this, but that")[4] consists in interpreting or in introducing a different meaning through changes of vocalization, transposition of consonants, substitution of one consonant for another, introduction of a different division of a word or a sentence. The goal of this interpretative proceeding was to update and indicate that an ancient biblical passage was related to historical events, when it was analyzed exegetically.

E.g.   2 Sam 17,25 (TM): "Amasa was a son of a man called Ithra the Ishmaelite (*yitrāʾ hayyiśrᵉʾēlî*)" (cf. "Israelite" in 2 Sam 17,25 [LXX]). 1 Chr 2,17 refers to this sentence: "Abigail bore Amasa and the father of Amasa was Jether the Ishmaelite (*yeter hayyišmᵉʿēʾlî*)". On the basis of the changing of a consonant, Amasa from "Israelite" became "Ishmaelite". The reason of this procedure was probably the tendency of the Chronicler to insert among the descendents of Ram, ancestors of king David, foreign people as well. Owning to this insertion, the reign of David assumes universal marks;

Ps 72,5: the masoretic phrase "they will fear you" (*yîrāʾûkā*), is translated by the LXX συμπαραμενεῖ, "he will remain", "he will endure", "he will extend" (with the retranslation *yaʾărîk* or *yaʾărôk*). The Greek translator made us of the *ʾal tiqrê* proceeding most likely to make the text liturgically more intelligible, and perhaps to avoid the anthropomorphic vocabulary with regard to God.

Isa 54,13: the masoretic expression *bānayik* "your sons", differs from its qumranic variant בוניכ, "your builders" (*bônêkî* with *waw* added above *bet*; cf. 1QIsaᵃ), identifying them with wise man (Talmud offers this reading as an example of *ʾal tiqrê*; cf. bBer 64a).

---

[4] The full formula *ʾal tiqrê... ʾellāʾ* occurs more often next to the other: *ʾal tiqrê* (*kēn*), *ʾal tᵉhî qôreʾ* or *ʾal tōʾmar*.

LE DÉAUT, R., "Usage implicite de l'ʾal tiqré dans le Targum de Job de Qumrân?", *Salvación en la Palabra. Targum – Derash – Berith. En memoria del profesor A. Díez Macho* (ed. D. MUÑOZ LEÓN) (Madrid 1986) 419-432.

LORENZIN, T., "L'uso di un procedimento esegetico analogo all'al tiqré in 1 e 2Cronache", *RivBib* 40 (1992) 67-76.

TORCZYNER, H., "Al tikre", *EJ(D)* II, 74-87.

V. Writing an Exegetical Work

In this chapter, some practical guidance will be offered to the reader to help him organize a written work on exegetical topics more effectively. Afterwards, two preparatory stages of literary composition will be described: formulating a thesis and drawing it up. Finally, the main elements of a text's arrangement will be outlined[1].

1. Formulating a Thesis

In this initial phase, it is important to acquire a good understanding of the text and to gather bibliographical entries pertinent to the biblical passage.

1.1 *Research*

1.1.1 Working with Critical Editions

The student gradually comes to know the text through attentive reading in the original language, using *BHS*, NA[27] or other editions of

---

[1] The following works were consulted for this chapter: U. Eco, *Come si fa una tesi di laurea*. Le materie umanistiche (Tascabili Bompiani 441; Milano 1977, 2002); Sp. tr. *Cómo se hace una tesis doctoral* (Barcelona [10]1991); J. Janssens, *Note di metodologia*. Elenco bibliografico – Nota bibliografica – Stesura del testo (Ad uso degli studenti) (Roma [5]1996); J. Langan, *College Writing Skills* (Boston [5]2000); R. Lesina, *Il nuovo manuale di stile*. Guida alla redazione di documenti, relazioni, articoli, manuali, tesi di laurea (Bologna [2]1994, 1998). Useful for English writers are works by J. Gibaldi, *MLA Handbook for Writers of Research Papers* (New York [6]2003); A. A. Lunsford – F. E. Horowitz, *The Everyday Writer* (Boston – New York [2]2001); K. L. Turabian, *A Manual for Writers of Term Papers, Theses and Dissertations* (Chicago [6]1996).

the Bible (cf. chap. I, § 1). Translation into one's own language (or into that of the paper) with the help of a good lexicon (cf. chap. III, § 3) and a good grammar (cf. chap. III, § 4)[2] permits one to resolve any difficulties inherent in the text. The goal of the study of textual variants, which follow the translation, is to comprehend how the text has been transmitted. For the very first selection of variants, the critical apparatus of the printed edition is sufficient. However, sometimes it is important to have recourse to larger collections and other valuable tools[3].

For the Hebrew Old Testament, it is possible to make use of these works:

B. KENNICOTT, *Vetus Testamentum Hebraicum cum variis lectionibus* (Oxonii 1776, 1780, Hildesheim 2003) I-II;

---

[2] Apart from the works quoted in chap. III, for Hebrew verbal system, see A. NIC-CACCI, *Sintassi del verbo ebraico nella prosa biblica classica* (SBFA 23; Jerusalem 1986); Eng. tr. *The Syntax of the Verb in Classical Hebrew Prose* (JSOT.S 86; Sheffield 1990); IDEM, *Lettura sintattica della prosa ebraico-biblica*. Principi e applicazioni (SBFA 31; Jerusalem 1991); E. VAN WOLDE (ed.), *Narrative Syntax and the Hebrew Bible*. Papers of the Tilburg Conference 1996 (BiblInterp 29; Leiden – New York – Köln 1997); W. T. VAN PEURSEN, *The Verbal System in the Hebrew Text of Ben Sira* (SStLL 41; Leiden– Boston 2004).

[3] For example, the work by D. BARTHÉLEMY, *Critique textuelle de l'Ancien Testament*. 1. Josué, Juges, Ruth, Samuel, Rois, Chroniques, Esdras, Néhémie, Esther. 2. Isaïe, Jérémie, Lamentations. 3. Ézéchiel, Daniel et les 12 Prophètes. 4. Psaumes (OBO 50/1-4; Fribourg – Göttingen 1982, 1986, 1992, 2005). To use the masora of *BHS* one can consult the volume of P. H. KELLEY – D. S. MYNATT – T. G. CRAWFORD, *The Masorah of Biblia Hebraica Stuttgartensia*. Introduction and Annotated Glossary (Grand Rapids, MI – Cambridge 1998) or other works given in chap. I, § 1. For the reconstruction of the original OT text, a comparison with the data from Qumran is useful. To this end, consult the volumes of the series DJD (cf. chap. III, § 11.2), *Revue de Qumran* and the translation of F. GARCÍA MARTÍNEZ (ed.), *Textos de Qumrán* (Madrid 1992); Eng. tr. *The Dead Sea Scrolls Translated* (Leiden 1994); It. tr. *Testi di Qumran* (Biblica. Testi e studi 4; Brescia 1996).

G. B. DE ROSSI, *Variae lectiones Veteris Testamenti* (Parmae 1784, 1785, 1786, 1788; reprint in two volumes: Bibliotheca Rossiana 7; Amsterdam 1969-1970) I-IV.

As for the New Testament in Greek, there is no such complete repertoire. Therefore, one can use the series *Arbeiten zur neutestamentlichen Textforschung* (Berlin 1963-) and printed editions with a critical apparatus more ample than that of NA[27], as, for instance:

H. VON SODEN, *Die Schriften des Neuen Testaments in ihrer ältesten erreichbaren Textgestallt hergestellt auf Grund ihrer Textgeschichte* (Göttingen 1911, 1913) I-II;

C. VON TISCHENDORF (ed.), *Novum Testamentum graece* (Lipsiae [8]1869, [8]1872) I-II.

After analysis of the variants, one ought to compare the Hebrew text with the Greek[4], Aramaic, Syriac and Latin versions, and the Greek text of the New Testament with the Syriac, Latin and Coptic translations. For such a comparison, critical editions are indispensable (cf. chap. I, § 1.2, § 2); for rapid consultation, polyglot Bibles are very helpful, e.g.:

B. WALTON, *Biblia Sacra Polyglotta* (Londini 1654, 1655, 1656, 1657, 1657, Graz 1963, 1964, 1964, 1964, 1964) I-V.

For the Pentateuch, this work also quotes the Samaritan Pentateuch, whereas, for the New Testament, the versions in Syriac, Latin, Ethiopic, Arabic, and, for the four Gospels, the Persian version, are cited.

---

[4] To trace the variants of the OT text in Greek, it is possible to use R. HOLMES, *Veteris Testamenti Graeci, versionis Septuaginta-viralis, cum variis lectionibus denuo edendi, specimen* (Oxonii 1795) I; IDEM – J. PARSONS, *Vetus Testamentum Graecum cum variis lectionibus* (Oxonii 1818, 1823) II-III or A. E. BROOKE – N. MCLEAN (ed.), *The Old Testament in Greek* (Cambridge 1906-1917) I; IIDEM – H. S. J. THACKERAY (ed.), *The Old Testament in Greek* (Cambridge 1927-1935, 1940) II-III.

Biblia Polyglotta Matritensia (Matriti 1957-).

The Consejo Superior de Investigaciones Científicas (Madrid), plans to publish the following series: I. Antiguo Testamento en hebreo; II. Nuevo Testamento en griego; III. Antiguo Testamento en griego; IV-V. Antiguo Testamento en arameo (Targumim); VI. Antiguo y Nuevo Testamento en siríaco; VII. Vetus Latina; VIII. Vulgata Hispana; IX. Nuevo Testamento en copto; X. Versión castellana. The following volumes have already been published:

> I. *Prooemium* (1957); IV. *Targum Palaestinense in Pentateuchum.* Additur Targum Pseudojonatan ejusque hispanica versio (1. Genesis, ed. A. Díez Macho, 1988; 2. Exodus, ed. A. Díez Macho, 1980; 3. Leviticus, ed. A. Díez Macho, 1980; 4. Numeri, ed. A. Díez Macho, 1977; 5. Deuteronomium, ed. A. Díez Macho, 1980); VI. *Vetus Evangelium Syrorum.* Diatessaron Tatiani (ed. I. Ortiz de Urbina, 1967); VII. *Vetus Latina* (21. Psalterium uisigothicum-mozarabicum, ed. T. Ayuso Marazuela, 1957); VIII. *Vulgata Hispana* (21. Psalterium S. Hieronymi de Hebraica Ueritate interpretandum, ed. T. Ayuso Marazuela, 1960).

The textual investigation described above is completed through exegetical examinations; among them, the study of individual lexemes, particularly those that are important for discovering the meaning of the analyzed passage. For this purpose, the use of concordances (cf. chap. III, § 1) and synopses (cf. chap. III, § 2) is crucial, along with comparative philology of Semitic languages (cf. chap. III, § 3.3)[5].

---

[5] English speaking students can find additional advice on how to do exegetical research in the introduction of D. Stuart, *Old Testament Exegesis*. A Handbook for Students and Pastors (Louisville – London [3]2001), its companion volume by G. D. Fee, *New Testament Exegesis*. A Handbook for Students and Pastors (Louisville – London [3]2002), and M. J. Gorman, *Elements of Biblical Exegesis*. A Basic Guide for Students and Ministers (Peabody, MA 2001).

1.1.2 Choosing a Subject

The subject or goal of a written work should not be too ambitious, too narrow or too technical. Formulating a question whose answer is obvious has no place in a scientific work. In the same way, the writer should not go over already established issues or propose a hypothesis which omits important data or contains errors in the analysis of the text. For this reason, it is necessary to become adequately acquainted with the topic by means of fundamental reference works: important commentaries, exegetical and theological dictionaries, encyclopedias, etc.

Preliminary reading and research are possible today not only in the library, but also on the Internet. This tool allows verification of bibliographical resources for the studied theme. The first step is a subject research in *BILDI*, in *BiBIL*, in *RAMBI* or in other databases containing biblical bibliography. It is possible to ascertain if there are articles available online by consulting the site *Biblical Studies on the Web* (http://www.bsw.org), which offers a list of periodicals which are at least partially accessible[6].

During an attentive reading of the documentation which is gathered slowly but surely, the researcher should not forget the content and the arrangement of his composition. First decisions are made concerning the concrete information which he wishes to present and those regarding their arrangement. It is opportune to draw up an outline of the work, which comprehensively visualizes the thesis with some supporting features. Formulating some reasons has many advantages, even though these may be successively changed a number of times; writing down a working hypothesis helps to define the area of the written work and aids in making useful notes.

---

[6] See the list of Internet sites in chap. II, § 3.

1.2 *Making Notes / Index Cards*

Having the outline in mind, the researcher may make notes concerning items to include in his paper. For gathering records, he may use index cards of size A5 or A6 (3" x 5"; 4" x 6"; 9" x 8"). It is also possible make use of database software; the cards will be printed at some point of the work.

Index cards are arranged by topic (biblical text and verses; theme to be studied) or by authors (alphabetical order). Direct quotations may be written, the thought of an author may be summed up in personal way, or quotations with summaries may be combined together. At times, the writer may paraphrase, using his own words instead of those of the cited authors. Since research implies condensed information, it will be opportune to make more use of the summaries than of paraphrases.

A direct quotation must be transcribed exactly as it appears in the original work and enclosed in quotation marks. If the meaning is not altered, it is admissible to omit some words in the quotation, which are not pertinent for point to be analyzed. This omission should be indicated by an ellipsis, placed in square brackets [...].

In summary, the original material is condensed by writing it in personal words. Summaries have the shape of a list and/or a short paragraph.

In including exact quotations or personal summaries, the source and the pages from which each piece of information comes must be indicated accurately. In a scholarly composition, documentary evidence about all factual data from technical works, which are not common knowledge[7], should be furnished.

---

[7] Moreover, when the quotation serves as a motto in a written composition, the footnote is not added; instead, the name of the author and the title of cited work is usually furnished.

To what should the researcher pay attention during his biblical investigation?

First of all, one should take into consideration all elements which explain in some way the difficulties related to a particular biblical passage: different manuscript witnesses, ancient versions, difficulties related to the rendering of some phrase and/or expressions, tensions within the passage and literary critical attempts to solve them. Furthermore, one should examine both the way in which authors divide the text and the criteria they provide for their division. Moreover, the researcher may quote suggestions proposed by scholars to interpret the text and make annotations of elements concerning thematic, historical or theological conclusions deriving from their analysis of the text.

1.3 *Organization of the Gathered Material*

This step follows the gathering of the documentation and precedes the writing. The goal is to refine a detailed summary from which the composition itself will be developed.

There are at least five ways to set out a theme: a) an outline; b) questions; c) a list; d) a graph; e) a summary-hypothesis.

1.3.1 Outline

The step which follows the writing of index cards is an outline, that is a preliminary synthesis, articulated and extended. The starting point is the interaction between the biblical text and the scientific purpose of the researcher, who writes down in simple phrases or propositions all that passes through his mind in relation to the topic.

This kind of exercise helps to familiarize one with the project itself. Ideas and initial impressions often become clearer after drawing them up, and they may guide other reflections and research. An outline helps to plan the whole work, to arrange and to develop sections and thoughts. In a particular way, it is possible to determine the most important arguments and demonstrative passages which each presentation requires. The preparation of the outline facilitates deciding how to arrange the documentation that has been collected: chronologically, in categories, or in another logical way.

1.3.2 Questions

While questioning the biblical text, new ideas arise which may be written in an interrogative form. Among them, obvious questions should be included, like: "Who is speaking?", "What is he saying?", "Who is he addressing?", "Why does he say it?", "In what way does he do it?" and "In which period and in which circumstances is the text placed?".

1.3.3 Compilation of a List

Reflections which come from the reading of the sources may be put one after another without a preestablished order; in that way, less significant details can be derived from the most important ones. The goal of this procedure is simply to do an inventory, a list of all considerations.

1.3.4 Compilation of a Graph

A diagram in the form of a cluster or a map helps at times to transform the gathered documentation into a summary. This procedure is particularly useful for people who think predominantly in a visual way. In a graph, dots, lines, bars, arrows, circles, etc., indicate connections and interrelations among concepts.

1.3.5 Preparation of a Summary-Hypothesis

Although one's intended plan for the paper often develops by using the four above-mentioned procedures – namely, outlining, questioning, compiling a list and a graph – it can also emerge gradually from an attentive reading of the gathered documentation. An attempt to articulate a summary permits one to see if the written work needs more annotations. If the drafting of a solid plan is impossible, it would be important to reinvestigate the matter in order to clarify the most important points of the thesis, and the arguments in favor of it.

Elaboration of a summary-hypothesis requires great attention to the exact expression of words for a particular point in the presentation, the arguments and the order as well. The outline is a detailed project which helps a composition to become unified, furnished with proofs, and arranged well.

In practice, one writes down a provisional thesis statement in a few words which become the frame on which the whole composition depends.

2. Drawing up the Composition

After many readings and making note-cards, the researcher should reach his summary-hypothesis, which presents a clear idea of how he wishes to elaborate the written work. It serves as a framework for the first draft. At that point, a title should be proposed that sums up the project, and an introduction composed that gives an analytical summary of the proposed work. If an introduction and summary is impossible, then it is clear that a scholar ought to choose another subject.

2.1 *First Draft*

In the course of the first draft, it is necessary to be ready to add thoughts and supplementary notes, which did not emerge during the initial annotations. In the case of running into an obstacle, it is sufficient to leave a blank space or a comment "Investigate" or "Do later", and finish the draft. It is impractical to take time to correct words and phrases that may later be eliminated. Rather, in this phase, it is important to focus on making the thesis clear and on providing careful argumentation with many supporting elements.

Throughout the first draft, attention centers on the content and its arrangement; grammar, construction and spelling can be corrected later. Nothing of substance should be left outside of this draft; it is easier to shorten a composition than to add new components.

2.2 *Steps of Revision*

The written work not only has a subject, but also a thesis. The author's personal reflections and conclusions, and not those of others, constitute the core of the work.

One draft alone is not usually sufficient. Often, two or three drafts are necessary. They are the heart of every literary composition. Revising means to rewrite the work, going through all previous steps in order to make the thesis more convincing. The revision is not a simple cosmetic correction of the text. The writer should be ready to shift his material and to include new points and rewrite previous ones in order to create a truly scholarly composition.

How does the author make this revising process less difficult? In the first place, the initial draft should be put aside for a certain amount of time, for some hours, or, better, for a couple of days. This interval and a fresh reading permit more objectivity. A valuable procedure is to write corrections on the printed text and then to read the draft aloud. Hearing how the composition sounds helps to identify problems connected with the meaning and style of the text. Eventually, personal reflections and changes will be added at the margins of the written work. These comments will assist in subsequent drafts.

While revising, the author's attention should focus on the content, on the exposition, and on the form of the composition.

2.2.1 Revision of the Content

Improving the content focuses on three elements: the sequence of the composition, explanatory passages, and the internal arrangement of the written work.

As for the unity of the written work, it is essential to ensure that the thesis is enunciated clearly at the beginning or at least plainly suggested. Next, the writer should take time on the exposition of the thesis, making sure that each paragraph contributes to the proof of the thesis.

The second stage concerns supporting arguments in favor of the initial thesis. In particular, the writer ought to establish that there are at least some points in support of his thesis, as well as to ascertain the incisiveness of the specific demonstrations for each point and to evaluate their variety.

The third stage scrutinizes the internal arrangement of the written work. It is necessary to ensure that the introduction engages the reader's attention and that the conclusion be truly conclusive, as well as to ascertain whether the title is accurate. It is also important to verify if the text of the composition follows a clear method of organization; if the purpose of each section is explained by its own thesis statement or phrase; and, finally, if transitions are smooth and whether other connecting need be inserted.

2.2.2 Revision of the Exposition

Improving sentences involves the examination of the balance of words and expressed concepts. The whole work needs to be checked for the consistency of perspective. In particular, one should verify if the language used calls everything by its proper name. When introducing a new term for the first time, it must be defined. Obviously it is better to avoid terms which the writer is unable to define. It is particularly important that quotations do not produce misunderstandings, and that concepts are expressed in appropriate words, and that the vocabulary utilized prescinds from jargon, pomposity, clichés, or from self-referential language which manifests itself by an abuse of the first singular person (I, my, etc.).

Even though the writer should try to maintain the consistency of his point of view (the level of formality, factual objectivity, being polemical or impartial), an occasional variation of style and periodic usage of figurative language is not bad.

2.2.3 Revision of the Form

After the revision of content and style, comes the editing. In other words, the writer checks and corrects the arrangement, the coherence of the redactional style, the use of capitals, italics and quotation marks, punctuation errors, orthographic or grammatical mistakes, accuracy of quotations, footnotes and bibliographical references. This editing should be applied uniformly to the entire composition.

3. Elements of Text Arrangement

Building upon these reflections, the particular components of the written work will be presented in this section.

3.1 *Title*

The title ought to be short and simple. It should describe the subject in a precise way and it should arouse interest. It can be supplemented with a subtitle and does not need to be followed by a period.

3.2 *Preface*

The preface is always positioned at the very beginning of a work, before (the table of contents and) the introduction.

This optional component is written by the author or by someone else. The preface calls attention to the treated theme, and underlines the reasons that induced the author to write the text, highlighting its qualities, validity and scholarly contribution.

If the work lacks an introduction, the preface can describe the work's arrangement and the adopted method.

Brief acknowledgments of people who offered material or moral support in the writing of the work or who furnished permissions for using previously published material, can be included directly after the preface.

3.3 *Introduction*

Brief (2-3 pages, for books sometimes longer) and clear, the introduction is supposed to indicate the issue treated (what the author wishes to say) and to describe the methodology adopted. An introduction ought to offer at least the following elements: a presentation of subject, a review of the present state of scholarly research, an explanation of the method of the work, its division and arrangement, and acknowledgments (above all in books).

An article can begin more simply with a short sentence, a clarifying statement, a question or a setting up of an issue.

3.4 *Body*

The central part of the work is the actual exposition of the fruit of the research and reflection of the author.

The body may be divided in parts, chapters, articles, paragraphs, etc. It is possible to use different systems of numbering, e.g.: 1., 1.1, 1.1.1, a); Chapter I, Article 1, § 1; etc. After the numbers one puts the titles, which should correspond to the content included within the respective section.

Before analyzing a biblical passage, it is necessary to fix its limits on the basis of content and form. In other words, the question must be answered as to where the passage starts (*terminus a quo*) and where it ends (*terminus ad quem*). Further, it is necessary to pay attention to the passage's proximate and remote context.

After determining the passage, one proceeds with textual criticism, whose goal is to establish the critical text used in subsequent analysis. Based on the witnesses of codices, *external* criticism permits one to come to a decision about which reading is more certain. In the case of differences between codices, it is crucial to apply *internal* criticism on the basis of context, author's style, words, terminology, and idiosyncratic expressions.

Other text-related problems are then considered and briefly treated, such as the way of translating some phrases and expressions. In particular, only those elements which are important or significant for the discussed topic are considered. They are approached technically (through versions, lexicons, and grammars). At this point, it is also possible to insert some considerations on literary criticism.

Following this, the organization of the text and its division are taken into consideration. It would suffice to present a structure of the text and to explain the structure synthetically.

The exegetical analysis of the passage occupies the principal part of the work. It is a matter of engaging the text analytically at great depth and treating the most important issues raised. This investigation is performed in accordance with one or more methods: form criticism, redaction criticism, structural criticism, semiotics, rhetorical criticism, etc.

At the end of this investigation, the interpretation of the passage ought to propose a thematic, historical, and theological synthesis.

3.5 *Conclusion*

There can be two types of conclusions: a) recapitulation; b) essay.

As for recapitulation (summary), a synthesis of outcomes should be offered, without leaving pending unsolved issues. This kind of conclusion is preferable for shorter works.

In the case of books or of extensive works, an essay can be more suitable. However, it is an intensive process, for it simultaneously demands the capacity to present a literary synthesis which offers the reader a bird's eye view of the thesis, prospectives, and other possibilities.

3.6 *List of Symbols and Abbreviations*

It is preferable to draw up, in alphabetical order, a single list of symbols and abbreviations, citing in full the name or the title of the work or of the periodical, followed, after a comma, by the place of publication (optional).

3.7 *Bibliography*

The bibliography, arranged alphabetically, contains references to the sources and to all studies quoted in the process of work[8]. Such a list can be inserted at the end of the publication, before the table of contents, or at the beginning of the work, after the table of contents. Each bibliographical entry should end with a period.

3.8 *Table of Contents*

Each work is provided with a table of contents (or index), which lists the headings with the corresponding page numbers (no punctuation after the headings). Its function permits one to find the themes treated in the text. The table of contents also gives an immediate structure to the contents and to the disposition of the text.

3.9 *Indexes*

Alphabetical lists of names and places, technical terms and topics, biblical quotations, etc. are as a rule included in more extensive

---

[8] As for the manner of making citations, see suggestions in chap. VI.

works (dissertation, monographs). Indexes make finding necessary data easier.

3.10 *Quotations*

It is recommended to cite contributions in their original language. It is indispensable to do this with critical editions. In fact, a translation limits the reliability of the source.

3.10.1 Literal Quotations

Quotations, taken directly from another context and put into one's own work, can be inserted into the text in different ways.

Within the running text, in quotation marks, short citations may be inserted, namely, those of less than four typed lines, cited in the language used for the whole composition. If in the quoted fragment there are words or expressions in proper quotation marks, these marks have to be changed in second level marks (e.g. single quotation marks ' ').

Outside of the body of the text, literal citations of more than four typed lines are inserted in the form of an indented paragraph with a blank spacing above and below, and at the left (or at the right), without quotations marks, often written in smaller font size and with reduced spacing.

If a piece of the original text is omitted, an ellipsis in brackets [...] should indicate the omission.

If some words are added to clarify the literal quotation, to supply lacking words or letters in the original text or to assign the authorship of supplementary special typeface in the quotation (e.g. italics, bold), these additions are placed in square brackets.

As it was with the case of preparing index cards, it is essential to reproduce the original text faithfully, preserving even the punctuation marks. A possible error in the original text is indicated by the sign [!] or by the term [*sic*].

3.10.2 Paraphrastic Quotations

This is a matter of adapting and explaining the original text in one's own words or in a simpler way. The original is often translated, developed or further amplified. In any case, at the foot of the page it should be indicated that one is adapting or translating. In case of personal translation, it is not necessary to make such a note. If the translation comes from the work in the language in which the composition is written, this work should be specified. In both cases, the original text is quoted, if relevant, in the footnote in quotation marks.

When the exact words or specific thought of a point in a written work has been gathered from sources, supplying documentary evidence is absolutely necessary.

The lack of documentation on information cited from specialized works, or the literal quotation, of any length whatsoever, of a published text without explicit indication of the source of their provenance is called plagiarism[9]. It represents a very grave error, since it violates the rights of another author and, in presenting another author's work as one's own, constitutes a lie.

"Self-plagiarism" happens when the author publishes anew his own work (or its parts) under another title or he translates it without any mention of this.

3.10.3 Quotation and Language

It is good to write the body of the text in one language in order to offer a smooth composition. So as to keep one's work from being dull, quotations in many foreign languages should preferably be short paraphrases, abstracts and translations. They should be provided with precise bibliographical documentation in footnotes.

---

[9] On this topic, see GIBALDI, *Handbook*, 65-75.

As for philological studies and issues, citing passages in the original language (Hebrew, Greek, Syriac, Arabic, Latin, etc.) is recommended.

3.10.4 Biblical Quotations

For the abbreviations, see: "Instructions for Contributors", *Bib* 79 (1998) 595-596
or online edition: "Editorial Instructions for Contributors", http://www.bsw.org/?l=711.

– Manner of Citation

Num 20,6-10 – The hyphen ("-") is used to indicate the verses which follow one another.
Jer 29,7.11.20 – The period (".") is used to indicate more verses which do not follow one another.
Mark 8,34–9,1 – The en dash ("–") is used to indicate more verses which follow one another and belong to two different chapters.

– Other References

The quotation of one or more verses should be done in the following way: v. 1; vv. 2-4 (in German V. and VV. are also used). The signs V., VV., v. or vv. are always followed by a space before the verse number. The abbreviations f., ff. or s., ss., or n., nn., to indicate "following", "folgende(n)", "siguiente(s)", "suivant(s)", "seguente(i)", "następny(e)", should not be used.

3.10 *Transliteration and Transcription*

Transliteration transposes one or more words written in a language into the equivalent character of another language.
Transcription is a graphical transposition of the characters of one alphabet in an other alphabet on the basis of the pronunciation.

3.11.1 Hebrew

a) Academic Style I

T. O. LAMBDIN, *Introduction to Biblical Hebrew* (London 1971, 1982) xxi-xxvii, proposed the following transliteration, which considers the *bəḡaḏkəp̄aṯ*:

Consonants

Character		Transliteration	Character		Transliteration
א	*ʾālep̄*	ʾ	ל	*lāmeḏ*	*l*
ב	*bêṯ*	*b*	מ ם	*mēm*	*m*
ב		*ḇ*	נ ן	*nûn*	*n*
ג	*gimel*	*g*	ס	*sāmek̲*	*s*
ג		*ḡ*	ע	*ʿayin*	ʿ
ד	*dāleṯ*	*d*	פ	*pēʾ*	*p*
ד		*ḏ*	פ ף		*p̄*
ה	*hēʾ*	*h*	צ ץ	*ṣāḏê*	*ṣ*
ו	*wāw*	*w*	ק	*qôp̄*	*q*
ז	*zayin*	*z*	ר	*rêš*	*r*
ח	*ḥêṯ*	*ḥ*	שׂ	*śîn*	*ś*
ט	*ṭêṯ*	*ṭ*	שׁ	*šîn*	*š*
י	*yôḏ*	*y*	ת	*tāw*	*t*
כ	*kap̄*	*k*	ת		*ṯ*
כ ך		*k̲*			

Vowels

Character			Transliteration	Character		Transliteration
qāmeṣ	—		*ā*	*paṭaḥ*	—	*a*
ṣērê	—	ʾ—	*ē, ê*	*səḡôl*	—	*e*
ḥîreq	ʾ—		*î*	*ḥîreq*	—	*i (ī)*
ḥôlem	— ו		*ō, ô*	*qāmeṣ ḥāṭûp̄*	—	*o*
šûreq	ו		*û*	*qibbûṣ*	—	*u*

Reduced vowels

šəwāʾ	—ְ	*ə*	*ḥāṭēp̄ səḡôl*	—ֱ	*ĕ*
ḥāṭēp̄ paṯaḥ	—ֲ	*ă*	*ḥāṭēp̄ qāmeṣ*	—ֳ	*ŏ*

Other combinations

בָּה = *bāh*, בָה = *bāh*, בָי = *bâ* (raro), בֶּה = *bēh*, בֶּה = *beh*, בֵי = *bê*, בֹּה = *bōh*,
רוּחַ = *rûᵃḥ* (*paṯaḥ furtivum*).

b) Academic Style II

"Instructions for Contributors", *Bib* 70 (1989) 579-580, offer this style, which transliterates the *bᵉgadkᵉpat* always in the same way:

Consonants

Character		Transliteration	Character		Transliteration
א	*ʾālep*	ʾ	מ ם	*mēm*	*m*
ב	*bêt*	*b*	נ ן	*nûn*	*n*
ג	*gimel*	*g*	ס	*sāmek*	*s*
ד	*dālet*	*d*	ע	*ʿayin*	*ʿ*
ה	*hēʾ*	*h*	פ ף	*pēʾ*	*p*
ו	*wāw*	*w*	צ ץ	*ṣādê*	*ṣ*
ז	*zayin*	*z*	ק	*qôp*	*q*
ח	*ḥêt*	*ḥ*	ר	*rêš*	*r*
ט	*ṭêt*	*ṭ*	שׂ	*śîn*	*ś*
י	*yôd*	*y*	שׁ	*šîn*	*š*
כ ך	*kap*	*k*	ת	*tāw*	*t*
ל	*lāmed*	*l*			

Vowels

Character		Transliteration	Character		Transliteration
qāmeṣ	—ָ	*ā*	*paṯaḥ*	—ַ	*a*
ṣērê	—ֵ ֵי	*ē, ê*	*sᵉḡôl*	—ֶ	*e*
ḥîreq	ִי	*î*	*ḥîreq*	—ִ	*i (ī)*

| *ḥôlem* | — ו | *ō, ô* | *qāmeṣ ḥāṭûp* | — | *o* |
| *šûreq* | ו | *û* | *qibbûṣ* | — | *u* |

Reduced vowels

| *šᵉwāʾ* | — | *e* | *ḥāṭēp sᵉgôl* | — | *ĕ* |
| *ḥāṭēp pataḥ* | — | *ă* | *ḥāṭēp qāmeṣ* | — | *ŏ* |

Other combinations

בָּה = *bāh*, בָּה = *bâ*, בָּא = *bāʾ*, בֶּה = *bēh*, בֶּה = *beh*, בֶּי = *bè*, רוּחַ = *rûaḥ* (*pataḥ furtivum*).

c) Transcription

The following transcription is inspired by the proposal of P. H. ALEXANDER et al. (ed.), *The SBL Handbook of Style for Ancient Near Eastern, Biblical, and Early Christian Studies* (Peabody, MA 1999) 28:

Consonants

Character		Transcription	Character		Transcription
א	*alef*	ʾ or omit	מ ם	*mem*	*m*
ב	*bet*	*b*; *v* (spirant)	נ ן	*nun*	*n*
ג	*gimel*	*g*; *gh* (spirant)	ס	*samek*	*s*
ד	*dalet*	*d*; *dh* (spirant)	ע	*ayin*	ʿ or omit
ה	*he*	*h*	פ ף	*pe*	*p*; *f* (spirant)
ו	*vav*	*v* or *w*	צ ץ	*tsade*	*ts*
ז	*zayin*	*z*	ק	*qof*	*q*
ח	*khet*	*h* or *kh*	ר	*resh*	*r*
ט	*tet*	*t*	שׂ	*sin*	*s*
'	*yod*	*y*	שׁ	*shin*	*sh*
כ ך	*kaf*	*k*; *kh* (spirant)	ת	*tav*	*t*; *th* (spirant)
ל	*lamed*	*l*			

Vowels

Character			Transcription	Character		Transcription
qamets	—ָ		*a*	*patakh (furtivum)* —ַ		*a*
tsere	—ֵ	ֱ—	*e*	*segol*	—ֶ	*e*
hireq	ֵ—		*i*	*hireq*	—ִ	*i*
holem	—ֹ	ו	*o*	*qamets khatuf*	—ָ	*o*
shureq	ו		*u*	*qibbuts*	—ֻ	*u*

Reduced vowels

Character		Transcription	Character		Transcription
shwa mobile	—ְ	*e*	*khatef segol*	—ֱ	*e*
khatef patakh	—ֲ	*a*	*khatef qamets*	—ֳ	*o*

3.11.2 Aramaic

The Hebrew transliteration style is used.

3.11.3 Greek

In scholarly publications, it is recommended to leave Greek characters. For other publications, the transliteration of the Greek text is permissible. The distinctions between epsilon and eta, omicron and omega have to be maintained, whereas the accents, smooth breathing, dieresis, etc., can be omitted.

Character	Transliteration	Character	Transliteration
α	*a*	ξ	*x*
β	*b*	ο	*o*
γ	*g*	π	*p*
δ	*d*	ρ	*r*
ε	*e*	σ ς	*s*
ζ	*z*	τ	*t*
η	*ē*	υ	*y*
θ	*th*	υ	*u* (in diphthongs: *au, eu, ēu, ou, ui*)
ι	*i*	φ	*ph*

κ	*k*	χ	*ch*
λ	*l*	ψ	*ps*
μ	*m*	ω	*ō*
ν	*n*	ʽ	*h*
ᾳ	*a(i)*	ῃ	*ē(i)*
ῳ	*ō(i)*		

3.11.4 Phoenician and Punic

J. Friedrich – W. Röllig – M. G. Amadasi Guzzo, *Phönizisch-punische Grammatik* (unter Mitarbeit von W. R. Mayer) (AnOr 55; Roma ³1999) 7, offer the following style:

Character	Transliteration	Character	Transliteration
א	ʾ	ל	*l*
ב	*b*	מ	*m*
ג	*g*	נ	*n*
ד	*d*	ס	*s*
ה	*h*	ע	ʿ
ו	*u̯*	פ	*p*
ז	*z*	צ	*ṣ*
ח	*ḥ*	ק	*q*
ט	*ṭ*	ר	*r*
י	*i̯*	שׁ	*š*
כ	*k*	ת	*t*

3.11.5 Akkadian

For the transliteration of Akkadian characters, the systems of *AHw* or *CAD* can be used, which employ the following alphabetical order: *a, b, d, e, g, ḫ, i, j* (*y* in *CAD*), *k, l, m, n, p, q, r, s, ṣ, š, t, ṭ, u, w, z*.

Sumerian logograms are quoted in small caps. Determinatives are put in superscript in minuscule; in a similar way, logogram numbers are also put in superscript.

3.11.6 Coptic

B. LAYTON, *A Coptic Grammar with Chrestomathy and Glossary.*
Sahidic Dialect (PLO 20; Wiesbaden 2000) 13:

Character	Transliteration	Character	Transliteration
ⲗ	*a*	ⲡ	*p*
ⲃ	*b*	ⲣ	*r*
ⲅ	*g*	ⲥ	*s*
ⲇ	*d*	ⲧ	*t*
ⲉ	*e*	ⲩ	*w*
ⲍ	*z*	ⲫ	*ph*
ⲏ	*ē*	ⲭ	*kh*
ⲑ	*th*	ⲯ	*ps*
ⲓ	*y*	ⲱ	*ō*
ⲕ	*k*	ⲙ	*š*
ⲗ	*l*	ϥ	*f*
ⲙ	*m*	ϩ	*h*
ⲛ	*n*	ⲭ	*č*
ⲝ	*ks*	ϭ	*kʸ*
ⲟ	*o*	ⲧ	*ty*

Achmimic adds

ꙁ   *ẖ*

Bohairic adds

ꙃ, ḥ   *ẖ*

For linguistic issues on Coptic, see different contributions quoted
in the appendix *Linguistics* by A. S. ATIYA (ed.), *The Coptic Ency-*
clopedia (New York – Toronto 1991) VIII, 13-227.

3.11.7 Syriac

W. McIntosh THACKSTON, *Introduction to Syriac*. An Elementary Grammar with Readings from Syriac Literature (Bethesda, MD 1999) offers the following transliteration method.

Consonant		Transliteration	Consonant		Transliteration
Serto	Estrangelo		Serto	Estrangelo	
ܐ	ܐ	ʾ	ܠ	ܠ	*l*
ܒ	ܒ	*b, b̲*	ܡ	ܡ	*m*
ܓ	ܓ	*g, g̲*	ܢ	ܢ	*n*
ܕ	ܕ	*d, d̲*	ܣ	ܣ	*s*
ܗ	ܗ	*h*	ܥ	ܥ	ʿ
ܘ	ܘ	*w*	ܦ	ܦ	*p, p̲*
ܙ	ܙ	*z*	ܨ	ܨ	*ṣ*
ܚ	ܚ	*ḥ*	ܩ	ܩ	*q*
ܛ	ܛ	*ṭ*	ܪ	ܪ	*r*
ܝ	ܝ	*y*	ܫ	ܫ	*š*
ܟ	ܟ	*k, k̲*	ܬ	ܬ	*t, t̲*

Vowel diacritics (Serto)

◌ܲ	*a*		◌ܼ	*i*
◌ܵ	*ā*		◌ܼ	*u*
◌ܸ	*e*			

Vowel diacritics (Estrangelo)

◌̣	*a*	◌̇ / ◌̈ (cf. ܗ, ܗܝ)	*ê*	
◌̤	*ā*	◌̣	*i*	
◌̈ (cf. ܗ)	*e*	◌ܘ	*u*	
◌̇ / ◌̈ (cf. ܗܝ)	*ē, ey*	◌ܘ	*o/ō*	

3.11.8 Ugaritic

For the transliteration of the Ugaritic, Gordon's proposal may be used. See: C. H. GORDON, *Ugaritic Textbook*. Grammar, Texts in Transliteration, Cuneiform Selections, Glossary, Indices (AnOr 38; Roma 1965, 1967) 13-15. For another style see: M. DIETRICH – O. LORETZ – J. SANMARTÍN, *The Cuneiform Alphabetic Texts from Ugarit, Ras Ibn Hani and Other Places* (KTU: Enlarged Edition) (ALASP 8; Münster ²1995).

Character	Transliteration	Character	Transliteration
	a		*k*
	i		*l*
	u		*m*
	b		*n*
	g		*s*
	d		*ṡ, ś* [KTU]
	ḏ		*ʿ*
	h		*ġ, ǵ* [KTU]
	w		*p*
	z		*ṣ*
	ḥ		*q*
	ḫ		*r*
	ṭ		*š*
	ẓ		*t*
	y		*ṯ*

3.11.9 Egyptian

For the transliteration of elementary graphemes, see R. HANNIG, *Großes Handwörterbuch Ägyptisch-Deutsch*. Die Sprache der

Pharaonen (2800-950 v. Chr.) (Kulturgeschichte der antiken Welt 64; Mainz 1995) xxxvii-xxxviii and A. GARDINER, *Egyptian Grammar. An Introduction to the Study of Hieroglyphs* (Oxford ³1957, 1976) 27:

Sign	Transliteration	Sign	Transliteration
🦅	ꜣ		ḥ
ꓭ	j, i [Gardiner]		ḫ
ꓭꓭ \\	y		ḫ
	ꜥ	― ꓲ	z/s, s [Gardiner]
	w		š
	b	◿	q, ḳ [Gardiner]
□	p		k
	f		g
	m		t
	n		ṯ
	r		d
	h		ḏ

In his work, R. Hannig also discusses other systems of transcription and transliteration of Egyptian texts (pp. xxiii-lix).

3.11.10 Arabic

There are different ways of transliterating the Arabic alphabet. In the scientific world, the style provided by the periodical *Arabica* is recognized. The Journal of Arabic and Islamic Studies / Revue d'études arabes et islamiques (Leiden 1954-).

Character	Transliteration	Character	Transliteration
ا	ʾ	ض	ḍ
ب	b	ط	ṭ
ت	t	ظ	ẓ
ث	ṯ	ع	ʿ
ج	ǧ	غ	ġ
ح	ḥ	ف	f
خ	ḫ	ق	q
د	d	ى	k
ذ	ḏ	ل	l
ر	r	م	m
ز	z	ن	n
س	s	ه	h
ش	š	و	w
ص	ṣ	ي	y

Vowels

أى	ā	◌َ	a
و	ū	◌ُ	u
ي	ī	◌ِ	i

Diphthongs

وَ	aw	يَ	ay

tā marbūṭa = *a*, *at* (construct state)

Article

أل   *al-* and *l-* (also before "solar" consonants)

3.11.11 Other Alphabets

Usage of fundamental grammars and reference tools is recommended.

3.12 *Layout*

If one uses a word processor, it is highly recommended to prepare the file on the basis of styles which determine parameters of the page: size, margins, indentations, font style and size of the main text, of the quotations which form separate paragraphs and of the footnotes (or endnotes), headers and footers. Moreover, it is worthwhile to provide model documents for symbols and abbreviations, a bibliography, and the table of contents (or index).

To standardize the text, typographical rules (a "style sheet") proposed, for instance, by R. Meynet, *Norme tipografiche per la composizione dei testi con il computer* (Roma [7]2007) may be used or those which are followed by a biblical series. The suggestions of one's director may be useful as well.

Since the periodicals and the publishers often request that the work be submitted according to their own criteria, it is appropriate to use a format which allows one to easily change the layout of the page. In any case, it is impossible to entirely avoid the "manual" work which will be needed to complete the final arrangement of the text.

VI. DOCUMENTATION IN EXEGETICAL WORKS

In this chapter, the manner of citation in footnotes (or endnotes) and in bibliographic entries will be highlighted. Some important rules for compiling an alphabetical list will also be furnished.

1. References

"Instructions for Contributors", *Bib* 70 (1989) 557-594; 79 (1998) 591-596; online edition: "Editorial Instructions for Contributors", http://www.bsw.org/?l=711

This is a basic text to learn how to make a citation.

SCHWERTNER, S. M., *Internationales Abkürzungsverzeichnis für Theologie und Grenzgebiete / International Glossary of Abbreviations for Theology and Related Subjects* (*IATG²*) (Berlin – New York ²1992).

This work is fundamental for abbreviations and symbols.

Moreover, it is possible to consult:

> ALEXANDER, P. H. et al. (ed.), *The SBL Handbook of Style for Ancient Near Eastern, Biblical, and Early Christian Studies* (Peabody, MA 1999).
> *The Chicago Manual of Style* (Chicago – London ¹⁵2003).
> FARINA, R., *Metodologia*. Avviamento alla tecnica del lavoro scientifico (BSRel 6; Zürich ²1974).
> GIBALDI, J., *MLA Style Manual and Guide to Scholarly Publishing* (New York ²1999).
> JANSSENS, J., *Note di metodologia*. Elenco bibliografico – Nota bibliografica – Stesura del testo (Ad uso degli studenti) (Roma ⁵1996).

LESINA, R., *Il nuovo manuale di stile*. Guida alla redazione di documenti, relazioni, articoli, manuali, tesi di laurea (Bologna ²1994, 1998).

PRELLEZO, J. M. – GARCÍA, J. M. (ed.), *Invito alla ricerca*. Metodologia del lavoro scientifico (Roma 1998).

2. Abbreviations

ALTHANN, *Elenchus of Biblica 2005*, 7-13 can partially supplement the abbreviations lacking in the work by SCHWERTNER, *IATG²*. On the basis of this volume and of volumes 1995-2004, the following list was prepared.

ABiG	Arbeiten zur Bibel und ihrer Geschichte
ACCS	*Ancient Christian Commentary on Scripture*
ACPQ	*American Catholic Philological Quarterly*
AcSum	Acta Sumerica
ActBib	*Actualidad Bibliográfica*
AcTh(B)	*Acta Theologica*, Bloemfontein
AETSC	*Annales de l'École Théologique Saint-Cyprien*
AfR	*Archiv für Religionsgeschichte*
AGWB	Arbeiten zur Geschichte und Wirkung der Bibel
AHIg	*Anuario de historia de la iglesia*
AJBS	*African Journal of Biblical Studies*
AJEC	Ancient Judaism & Early Christianity
AJPS	*Asian Journal of Pentecostal Studies*
AJSR	*Association for Jewish Studies Review*
Ä&L	*Ägypten und Levante*
AltOrF	*Altorientalische Forschungen*
AnBru	*Analecta Bruxellensia*
AncBD	D. N. FREEDMAN et al. (ed.), *The Anchor Bible Dictionary* (New York – London – Toronto – Sydney – Auckland 1992) I-VI
AncHB	*Ancient History Bulletin*

ANESt	*Ancient Near Eastern Studies*
ANilM	*Archéologie du Nil Moyen*
AnnTh	*Annales Theologici*
AnScR	*Annali di Scienze Religiose*
AnStR	*Annali di studi religiosi*, Trento
APB	*Acta Patristica et Byzantina*
Apocr	Apocrypha
AramSt	Aramaic Studies
Archaeom	Archaeometry
ARET	Archivi reali di Ebla, testi
ARGU	Arbeiten zur Religion und Geschichte des Urchristentums
ARJ	*The Annual of Rabbinic Judaism*
AsbJ	*The Asbury Journal*
ASJ	*Acta Sumerologica*
ATM	Altes Testament und Moderne, Münster
ATT	*Archivio teologico torinese*
AtT	*Atualidade teológica*
AuOr	*Aula Orientalis*
AuOr.S	Aula Orientalis Suplement
AUPO	*Acta Universitatis Palackianae Olomucensis*
AWE	Ancient West & East
B&B	*Babel und Bibel*
BAChr	The Bible and Ancient Christianity
BAIAS	*Bulletin of the Anglo-Israel Archaeological Society*
BBR	*Bulletin for Biblical Research*
BCSMS	*Bulletin of the Canadian Society for Mesopotamian Studies*
BEgS	*Bulletin of the Egyptiological Seminar*
BHQ	A. SCHENKER et al. (ed.), *Biblia Hebraica Quinta* (Stuttgart 2004-)
Bib(L)	*Bíblica*, Lisboa
BiblInterp	*Biblical Interpretation*
BiblInterp	Biblical Interpretation Series
Biblioteca EstB	Biblioteca de Estudios Bíblicos

BiCT	*The Bible and Critical Theory* [electronic journal]
BnS	La Bibbia nella storia
BolT	*Boletín teológico*
Bor	*Boreas*
BoSm	*Bogoslovska Smorta*
BOTSA	*Bulletin for Old Testament Studies in Africa*
BPVU	Biblische Perspektiven für Verkündung und Unterricht
BRT	*The Baptist Review of Theology /*
	La Revue Baptiste de Théologie
BSÉG	*Bulletin de la Société d'Égyptologie*
BSGJ	*Bulletin der schweizerischen Gesellschaft*
	für judaistische Forschung
BSLP	*Bulletin de la Société de Linguistique de Paris*
BuBB	*Bulletin de bibliographie biblique*
BurH	*Buried History*
BWM	Bibelwissenschaftliche Monographien
CahPhRel	*Cahiers de l'École des Sciences philosophiques*
	et religieuses
CAL.N	*Comprehensive Aramaic Lexicon, Newsletter*
CamArchJ	*Cambridge Archaeological Journal*
Carmel(T)	*Carmel*, Toulouse
Carmel(V)	*Carmel*, Venasque
CBET	*Contributions to Biblical Exegesis and Theology*
CBRL	*Newsletter of the Council for British Research*
	in the Levant
CCO	*Collectanea Christiana Orientalia*
CHANE	Culture and History of the Ancient Near East
ChDial	*Chemins de Dialogue*
CICat	*Caietele Institutului Catolic*
CLEC	*Common Life in the Early Church*
CLehre	*Die Christenlehre*
CMAO	*Contributi e Materiali di Archeologia Orientale*
CoMa	*Codices Manuscripti*
ConAss	*Convivium Assisiense*
ConnPE	Connaissances des Pères de l'Église

CoSe	*Consacrazione e Servizio*
CQuS	Companion to the Qumran Scrolls
CredOg	*CredereOggi*
CritRR	*Critical Review of Books in Religion*
CR&T	*Conversations in Religion and Theology*
CSMSJ	*The Canadian Society for Mesopotamian Studies Journal*
CTrB	*Cahiers de traduction biblique*
CuBR	*Currents in Biblical Research*
CuesTF	*Cuestiones Teológicas y Filosóficas*
CurResB	*Currents in Research*: *Biblical Studies*
DiscEg	*Discussions in Egyptology*
DosArch	*Les Dossiers de l'Archéologie*
DosB	*Les Dossiers de la Bible*
DQ	Documenta Q
DSBP	S. A. PANIMOLLE (ed.), *Dizionario di spiritualità biblico-patristica. I grandi temi della S. Scrittura per la "lectio divina"* (Roma 1992-)
DSD	Dead Sea Discoveries
DT(B)	*Divus Thomas*, Bologna
EBM	*Estudios Bíblicos Mexicanos*
EfMex	*Efemérides Mexicana*
EgArch	*Egyptian Archaeology, Bulletin of the Egypt Exploration Society*
ERSY	*Erasmus of Rotterdam Society Yearbook*
EThF	*Ephemerides Theologicae Fluminenses*
ETJ	*Ephrem's Theological Journal*
EurJT	*European Journal of Theology*
EyV	*Evangelio y Vida*
FCNT	*The Feminist Companion to the New Testament and Early Christian Writings*
FgNT	*Filología Neotestamentaria*
FIOTL	*Formation and Interpretation of Old Testament Literature*
FolTh	*Folia theologica*
FoSub	Fontes et subsidia ad Bibliam pertinentes

HBM	Hebrew Bible Monographs
HBO	*Hallesche Beiträge zur Orientwissenschaft*
HorWi	*Horyzonty Wiary*
HPolS	*Hebraic Political Studies*
HTSTS	*HTS Teologiese Studies / Theological Studies*
IAJS	*Index of Articles on Jewish Studies*
ICMR	*Islam and Christian-Muslim Relations*
ICSTJ	*ICST Journal*
IHR	*International History Review*
IJCT	*International Journal of the Classical Tradition*
IJSCC	*International Journal for the Study*
	of the Christian Church
IJST	*International Journal of Systematic Theology*
IncW	*The Incarnate Word*
INTAMS.R	*International Academy for Marital Spirituality Review*
IRBS	*International Review of Biblical Studies*, formerly *IZBG*
IslChr	*Islamochirstiana*
ITBT	*Interpretatie*
ITE	*Informationes Theologiae Europae*
Itin(L)	*Itinerarium*, Lisboa
Itin(M)	*Itinerarium*, Messina
JAAT	*Journal of Asian and Asian American Theology*
JAB	*Journal for the Aramaic Bible*
JAGNES	*Journal of the Association of Graduates*
	in Near Eastern Studies
JANER	*Journal of Ancient Near Eastern Religions*
JAnS	*Journal of Anglican Studies*
JATS	*Journal of the Adventist Theological Society*
JBMW	*Journal for Biblical Manhood and Womanhood*
JBSt	*Journal of Biblical Studies* [electronic journal]
JBTSA	*Journal of Black Theology of South Africa*
JCoS	*Journal of Coptic Studies*
JECS	*Journal of Early Christian Studies*
JEGTFF	*Jahrbuch der europäischen Gesellschaft*
	für theologische Forschung von Frauen

JEMH	*Journal of Early Modern History*
JGRChJ	*Journal of Graeco-Roman Christianity and Judaism*
JHiC	*Journal of Higher Criticism*
JHScr	*Journal of Hebrew Scriptures* [electronic journal]
JIntH	*Journal of Interdisciplinary History*
JISt	*Journal of Interdisciplinary Studies*
JJSS	*Jnanatirtha (Journal of Sacred Scripture)*
JJTP	*Journal of Jewish Thought & Philosophy*
JKTh	Jahrbuch für kontextuelle Theologien
JMEMS	*Journal of Medieval and Early Modern Studies*
JPentec	*Journal of Pentecostal Theology*
JPentec.S	Journal of Pentecostal Theology. Supplement
JPersp	*Jerusalem Perspective*
JPJRS	*Jnanadeepa, Pune Journal of Religious Studies*
JProgJud	*Journal of Progressive Judaism*
JRadRef	*Journal from the Radical Reformation*
JRTI	*Journal of Religious and Theological Information*
JRTR	*Jahrbuch für Religionswissenschaft und Theologie der Religionen*
JSem	*Journal for Semitics*
JSHS	*Journal for the Study of the Historical Jesus*
JSHS.S	Journal for the Study of the Historical Jesus Supplementary Series
JSQ	*Jewish Studies Quarterly*
JSSEA	*Journal of the Society for the Study of Egyptian Antiquities*
JStAI	*Jerusalem Studies in Arabic and Islam*
JTrTL	*Journal of Translation and Textlinguistics*
KUSATU	*Kleine Untersuchungen zur Sprache des Alten Testaments und seiner Umwelt*
LecDif	*Lectio Difficilior* [electronic journal]
LeD	*Lire et Dire*
LHBOTS	Library of Hebrew Bible / Old Testament Studies
LingAeg	*Lingua Aegyptia*
LNST	Library New Testament Studies

LSDC	*La Sapienza della Croce*
L&S	*Letter and Spirit*
MAI	*Masters Abstracts International*
MastJ	*Master's Seminary Journal*
MEAH.A	*Miscelánea de estudios árabes y hebraicos. Arabe-Islam*
MEAH.H	*Miscelánea de estudios árabes y hebraicos. Hebreo*
MESA.B	*Middle East Studies Association Bulletin*
MethT	*Method and Theory in the Study of Religion*
MillSt	*Milltown Studies*
MissTod	*Mission Today*
MoBe	*Modern Believing*
MSJ	*Master's Seminary Journal*
MTSR	*Method and Theory in the Study of Religion*
NABU	*Nouvelles Assyriologiques Brèves et Utilitaires*
NAC	New American Commentary
NAC(SBT)	New American Commentary Studies in Bible and Theology
NAOTS	*Newsletter on African Old Testament Scholarship*
NEA	*Near Eastern Archaeology*
NET	Neutestamentliche Entwürfe zur Theologie
NewTR	*New Theology Review*
NHMS	*Nag Hammadi and Manichaean Studies*
NIBC	New International Biblical Commentary
NICNT	New International Commentary on the New Testament
NIDB	K. D. SAKENFELD et al. (ed.), *The New Interpreter's Dictionary of the Bible* (Nashville 2006-) I-III
NIGTC	New International Greek Testament Commentary
NIntB	L. E. KECK et al. (ed.), *The New Interpreter's Bible* (Nashville 1994-1998) I-XII
NotesTrans	*Notes on Translation*
NSK.AT	Neuer Stuttgarter Kommentar: Altes Testament
NTGu	New Testament Guides
NTMon	New Testament Monographs
NTTRU	*New Testament Textual Research Update*
NV(Eng)	*Nova at Vetera* (English edition)

ÖARR	*Österreichisches Archiv für Recht und Religion*
OecCiv	*Oecumenica Civitas*
OrBibChr	Orbis biblicus et christianus
OrExp	*Orient-Express, Notes et Nouvelles d'Archéologie Orientale*
PaiC	*Paideia Cristiana*
PaRe	*The Pastoral Review*
PJBR	*Polish Journal of Biblical Research*
PKNT	Papyrologische Kommentare zum Neuen Testament
PoeT	*Poetics Today*
PredOT	Prediking van het Oude Testament
PresPast	*Presenza pastorale*
ProcGLM	*Proceedings of the Eastern Great Lakes and Midwest Bible Societies*
ProEc	*Pro ecclesia*
ProySal	*Proyecto Centro Salesiano de Estudios*
PzB	*Protokolle zur Bibel*
Qol(I)	*Qol*, Novellara
QVC	*Qüestions de Vida Cristiana*
RANL	*Rendiconti dell'Accademia Nazionale dei Lincei*
RANL.mor	*Rendiconti dell'Accademia Nazionale dei Lincei, Classe di scienze morali*
RANT	*Res Antiquae*
RASM	*Revue africaine des sciences de la mission*
RBBras	*Revista Bíblica Brasileira*
RBLit	*Review of Biblical Literature*
REAC	*Ricerche di egittologia e di antichità copta*
REAug	*Revue d'études augustiniennes et patristiques*
RelT	*Religion and Theology*
RenSt	*Renaissance Studies*
ResB	*Reseña Bíblica*
RevCT	*Revista de cultura teológica*
RF(CR)	*Revista de filosofía*, Costa Rica
RF(UI)	*Revista de filosofía*, México
RGRW	Religions in the Graeco-Roman World

Ribla	*Revista de interpretação bíblica latino-americana*
RICAO	*Revue de l'Institut Catholique de l'Afrique de l'Ouest*
RiSCr	*Rivista di storia del cristianesimo*
RRJ	*Review of Rabbinic Judaism*
RRT	*Reviews in Religion and Theology*
R&T	*Religion and Theology = Religie en teologie*
RTE	*Rivista di teologia dell'evangelizzazione*
RTLit	*Review of Theological Literature*
RTLu	*Rivista Teologica di Lugano*
SAA Bulletin	State Archives of Assyria Bulletin
SAAA	Studies on the Apocryphal Acts of the Apostles
SAAS	State Archives of Assyria Studies
SaThZ	*Salzburger theologische Zeitschrift*
SBL.SCSt	SBL Septuagint and Cognate Studies
SBSl	*Studia Biblica Slovaca*, Svit
SdT	*Studi di teologia*
SEAP	*Studi di Egittologia e di Antichità Puniche*
SECA	Studies on Early Christian Apocrypha
SeK	*Skrif en Kerk*
Sen.	*Sendros*
SetRel	*Sette e Religioni*
SiChSt	*Sino-Christian Studies*
SIDIC	*Service International de Documentation Judéo-Chrétienne*
SLJTR	*Sri Lanka Journal of Theological Reflection*
SMEA	*Studi micenei ed egeo-anatolici*
SMEBT	Serie Monográfica de Estudios Bíblicos y Teológicos de la Universidad Adventista del Plata
Spiritus(B)	*Spiritus*, Baltimore
SPJMS	*South Pacific Journal of Mission Studies*
SRATK	*Studia nad Rodziną*, Akademia Teologii Katolickiej
STAC	Studien und Texte zu Antike und Christentum
StBob	*Studia Bobolanum*
StEeL	*Studi epigrafici e linguistici*
StPhiloA	*Studia Philonica Annual*

StSp(K)	*Studies in Spirituality*, Kampen
StSp(N)	*Studies in Spirituality*, Nijmegen
StWC	*Studies in World Christianity*
SUBB	*Studia Universitatis Babeş-Bolyai*
TBAC	The Bible in Ancient Christianity
TC.JBTC	*TC: A Journal of Biblical Textual Criticism* [electronic journal]
TCNN	*Theological College of Northern Nigeria*
TENTS	Texts and Editions for New Testament Studies
TEuph	*Transeuphratène*
TFE	*Theologische Frauenforschung in Europa*
TGr.T	Tesi Gregoriana, Serie Teologia
ThEv(VS)	*Théologie évangélique*, Vaux-sur-Seine
ThirdM	*Third Millennium*
ThLi	*Theology & Life*
T&K	*Texte und Kontexte*, Stuttgart
TKNT	Theologischer Kommentar zum Neuen Testament
TMA	*The Merton Annual*
TrinJ	*Trinity Journal*
TTE	*The Theological Educator*
VeE	*Verbum et Ecclesia*
VeVi	*Verbum Vitae*
Vivar(C)	*Vivarium*, Catanzaro
Vivar(L)	*Vivarium*, Leiden
VivH	*Vivens Homo*
VO	*Vicino Oriente*
VoxScr	*Vox Sripturae*
VTW	*Voices from the Third World*, Bangalore
WAS	Wiener alttestamentliche Studien
WaW	*Word and World*
WBC	Word Biblical Commentary
WGRW	*Writings from the Greek and Roman World*
WUB	*Welt und Umwelt der Bibel*
YESW	*Yearbook of the European Society of Women in Theological Research*

ZAC	*Zeitschrift für antikes Christentum*
ZAR	*Zeitschrift für altorientalische*
	und biblische Rechtgeschichte
ZME	*Zeitschrift für medizinische Ethik*
ZNT	*Zeitschrift für Neues Testament*
ZNTG	*Zeitschrift für neuere Theologiegeschichte*
ZPT	*Zeitschrift für Pädagogik und Theologie*
ZThG	*Zeitschrift für Theologie und Gemeinde*

3. Footnotes

In this section, some suggestions will be made regarding the correct citation of bibliographic elements in footnotes. Since there are different ways of quoting, a review of information for the most frequent cases will firstly be provided and then other styles will be presented.

3.1 *Sequence of Information*

a) *Book*: author (or editor), title, subtitle, series, its number, place, edition (if not the first one), date, (individual number if single volume of multivolume work is cited), (pages).

b) *Article in a periodical*: author, title, subtitle, abbreviated name of the periodical, volume number, date, pages.

c) *Article in a collected work*: author, title of the article, subtitle, title of the work, subtitle, editor, series, its number, place, date, pages.

The data for bibliographical entries should be obtained from the title page or its equivalent. If they are absent, the use of the cover or of the packing is admissible. For the description of an article, the data placed immediately before and after it should be used. Moreover, one checks the numbers of pages (or columns).

It is not necessary to adopt each element of writing from the source (capital letters, punctuation, etc.). However, in all of the bibliographical entries, the same sequence of information and the same punctuation consistently should be applied.

3.2 *Rules for Books*

AUTHOR – The initial letters of the First and Middle Name + Surname (or the name of the collective body); SMALL CAPITALS are used.

First name and middle name: after the first name a period (full stop) and a space are placed; then the first letter of the middle name should be written followed by a period and a space; in case of names separated by a hyphen "-", after the inicial of the first name are placed: a period, a hyphen, the initial of the middle name and a period.

Double surnames are separated by a hyphen "-", if the rules of a particular language require this.

Two surnames are separated by an en dash "–", preceded and followed by a space.

When the work is written by several authors, usually surnames of all the authors are quoted, if their number doesn't exceed three. However, when the surnames are more than three, after the first surname, instead of other ones, the abbreviation "et al." (et alii, "and others") is placed.

In case of the EDITOR, after the (last) surname, followed by a space, "ed.", "éd.", "Hrsg.", "a cura di", "red.", etc., is used in parentheses "()", followed by a comma and a space.

If it is necessary to quote an entire work by several authors which does not have an editor, its title alone is to be used.

Names of the collective body should be quoted according to the original spelling. When in a document there are names of two institutions, only the name of the first one should be provided.

Title. Subtitle – *Italics* and Roman type.

[For works by an author, published by an editor, the latter is indicated by the opening of a parenthesis "(", then "ed.", and a space, which is followed by the initial of the first name + surname in SMALL CAPITALS, and closing of the parenthesis ")"]

Name and number of series – After the parenthesis "(", abbreviation is used; after the number, if there is one, a semicolon ";" is used.

When the editor indicates the year of the lecture or seminar instead of the volume number, such indication should be recorded. If a volume of a series gathers different lectures in various issues, immediately after the year of the lecture a slash "/" is placed and, without a space, the issue number.

[Dissertation, which has been not published – in place of the name and number of series, one writes the abbreviation "Diss." and puts the name of the academic institution in which the defense took place]

Place of publication – It is written according to the original spelling of the name at the time of publication.

For a city with double name, the names are separated by a hyphen "-", if the rules of a particular language require it.
More than one city of publication is separated by an en dash "–", preceded and followed by a space.
In case of the name of the place in Latin, the *genitivus locativus* or the *ablativus loci* should be maintained, e.g., Romae for Roma, Londini for Londinum, Parisiis for Parisii.

Date – It is put after the name of the city, followed by a space; after the date the parenthesis ")" is closed.

The number of the edition is placed in superscript, before the date, if the edition cited is not the first one.

Volume number – in Roman numerals, in capitals, without vol., Bd., T., and is followed by a comma.

Page number(s) – They are cited without p., pp., S., SS., pag., etc.; and are followed by a period or a semicolon.

If the quoted pages are paginated in Roman numerals, they should be written in lower case.

For forthcoming books, the page number is omitted and the expression "(forthcoming)" should be used.

[Footnote number, if there is one – After the page number, a comma is used, followed by a space, and the abbreviation "n.", {German: "Anm."}, followed by a space and a footnote number; then a period or a semicolon is placed].

NB No publisher's name is mentioned. If the place of publication is unknown, "[s.l.]" (*sine loco*) should be written; the unknown date is quoted as "[s.a.]" (*sine anno*)[1]. If a work is released in a place or on a date that are omitted, but are otherwise known with certainty, these elements are put in square brackets; if they are deduced with near certainty: in square brackets, after the place or the date a question mark should be inserted.

Even though the insertion of abbreviations of names of US States and territories is not obligatory, for homonymous cities, their usage is recommended (e.g. Cambridge, MA). Their insertion can be useful for less known cities (e.g. Montclair, NJ). The abbreviation of a State or a territory is written in capitals, and it is located after the name of the city, followed by a comma and a space.

---

[1] Abbreviations from modern languages can also be used.

The following abbreviations are used by *US Postal Service*:

AK	Alaska	AL	Alabama	AR	Arkansas
AS	American Samoa	AZ	Arizona	CA	California
CO	Colorado	CT	Connecticut	DC	District of Columbia
DE	Delaware	FL	Florida	GA	Georgia
GU	Guam	HI	Hawaii	IA	Iowa
ID	Idaho	IL	Illinois	IN	Indiana
KS	Kansas	KY	Kentucky	LA	Louisiana
MA	Massachusetts	MD	Maryland	ME	Maine
MI	Michigan	MN	Minnesota	MO	Missouri
MS	Mississippi	MT	Montana	NC	North Carolina
ND	North Dakota	NE	Nebraska	NH	New Hampshire
NJ	New Jersey	NM	New Mexico	NV	Nevada
NY	New York	OH	Ohio	OK	Oklahoma
OR	Oregon	PA	Pennsylvania	PR	Puerto Rico
RI	Rhode Island	SC	South Carolina	SD	South Dakota
TN	Tennessee	TX	Texas	UT	Utah
VA	Virginia	VI	Virgin Islands	VT	Vermont
WA	Washington	WI	Wisconsin	WV	West Virginia
WY	Wyoming				

E.g.

T. R. HENN, *The Bible as Literature* (London – New York 1970) 9-15.

H. SIMIAN-YOFRE, *El desierto de los dioses*. Teología e Historia en el libro de Oseas (Córdoba 1993) 83.

S. MOWINCKEL, *Psalmenstudien*. I. Āwän und die Individuellen Klagepsalmen. II. Das Thronbesteigungsfest Jahwäs und der Ursprung der Eschatologie. III. Kultprophetie und prophetische Psalmen. IV. Die technischen Termini in den Psalmenüberschriften. V. Segen und Fluch in Israels Kult und Psalmendichtung. VI. Die Psalmdichter (Kristiania 1921, 1922, 1923, 1923, 1924, 1924).

F. M. ABEL, *Histoire de la Palestine depuis la conquête d'Alexandre jusqu'à l'invasion arabe* (EB; Paris 1952) II, 105-129.

W. MARCHEL, *Abba, Père!* La prière du Christ et des chrétiens (AnBib 19; Rome 1963) 50, n. 189.

H. W. WOLFF, *Dodekapropheton I: Hosea* (BK 14/1; Neukirchen-Vluyn ²1965) xiv-xvii.

A. SÁENZ-BADILLOS, *Historia de la lengua hebrea* (Estudios orientales 2; Sabadell s.a.²) 201-209.

L. F. HARTMAN – A. A. DI LELLA, *The Book of Daniel* (AncB 23; Garden City, NY 1978) 55-56.

S. Z. LEIMAN (ed.), *The Canon and Masorah of the Hebrew Bible.* An Introductory Reader (LBS; New York 1974).

L'Antico Testamento e le culture del tempo. Testi scelti (Roma 1990).

M. BEN UZZIEL, *Kitāb al-Khilaf.* Treatise on the Differences between Ben Asher and Ben Naphtali (ed. L. LIPSCHÜTZ) (The Hebrew University Bible Project Monograph Series 2; Jerusalem 1965) 9-15.

A. PINTO LEÓN, *Lamed y sus relaciones.* Indicaciones para su traducción (Diss. PIB; Roma 1990) 54.

E. WOUNGLY-MASSAGA, *Une délivrance et ses relectures.* Étude de la perception de Dieu dans le Psaume 34 (Mémoire de l'Institut des Sciences bibliques de l'Université de Lausanne; Lausanne 1983) 28-72.

P. KAHLE, *Der hebräische Bibeltext seit Franz Delitzsch* (FDV 1958; Stuttgart 1961).

W. SCHLACHTER, *Passivstudien* (NAWG 1984/3; Göttingen 1984) 117-173.

F. COCCO, *Il sorriso di Dio.* Studio esegetico della "benedizione di San Francesco" (Nm 6,24-26) (Collana biblica; Bologna 2009) (forthcoming).

---

² Writing "[1988]" instead of "s.a." would be better, for the date of the publication is known.

3.3 *Articles*

These written studies are published in periodicals or journals, in edited volumes and in volumes in honor of someone (homenaje, mélanges, Festschrift, miscellanea, in onore di qualcuno, księga pamiątkowa), and as independent sections of dictionaries and encyclopedias.

3.3.1 Rules for Periodicals

AUTHOR – cf. books.

"Title. Subtitle" – Roman type and in quotation marks " ".

For texts in French and Italian, guillemets « » may be used – followed by a comma and a space.

Name of the periodical – Italics. The name should be abbreviated if possible; a space follows.

Volume number – In Arabic numerals.

If the article is published in a volume paginated by fascicle (issue), after the volume number a slash "/" is placed and, immediately after, the fascicle or issue number is written.

If the issue is divided into parts that do not use continuous numbering, after the issue number, a comma is placed which is followed by the number of the part; a space follows.

Year – In parentheses "()"; a space follows.

For *La Civiltà Cattolica*, which is published in biweekly fascicles in four volumes with an independent pagination, after the year a slash "/" is placed and, without placing a space, the volume number is written in Roman numerals, in capitals.

Page number(s) – cf. books.

E.g.

E. VOGT, "Das Wachstum des alten Stadtgebietes von Jerusalem", *Bib* 48 (1967) 337, 339.

J. FLEISHMAN, "Why Did Simeon and Levi Rebuke Their Father in Genesis 34:31?", *JNSL* 26/2 (2000) 101-116.

A. A. BRUX, "Arabic-English Transliteration for Library Purposes", *AJSL* 47/1,2 (1930) 1-30.

M. GILBERT, "Qoelet o la difficoltà di vivere", *CivCatt* 154 (2003/II) 450-459.

3.3.2 Rules for an Article in an Encyclopedia or a Dictionary

AUTHOR – cf. books[3].

"Title. Subtitle" – cf. article; it is cited without "in"

Title of the work – *Italics* with possible abbreviation.

Volume number – In Roman numerals, in capitals.

Page number(s).

E.g.

A. BAUMANN, "מוט", *ThWAT* IV, 728-734.

Y. BLAU, "Menahem ben Jacob ibn Saruq", *EJ* XI, 1305-1306.

H. CAZELLES, "Royauté sacrale et la Bible. I. Royauté sacrale et dé-sacralisation de l'État dans l'Ancien Testament", *DBS* X, 1056-1077.

E. JENNI, "עָנָן ʿānān, Wolke", *THAT* II, 351-353.

---

[3] Sometimes, encyclopedias, lexicons and dictionaries put the initials of the author only, after the article or the entry. In this case, the surname should be written in full form.

3.3.3 Rules for a Journal Article with Multiple Page Locations and Volumes

AUTHOR – cf. books.

"Title. Subtitle" – cf. article.

Name of the periodical – cf. article.

Volume number – cf. article.

Year – cf. article.

Page numbers of the first part of the article are followed by a comma and a space if the article is continued in the same volume; page numbers are followed by a semicolon, by volume number, by year and by page numbers if the article is continued in a different volume.

E.g.

M. HARAN, "Studies in the Account of the Levitical Cities. I. Preliminary Considerations. II. Utopia and Historical Reality", *JBL* 80 (1961) 45-54, 156-165.

J. L'HOUR, "L'Impur et le Saint dans le Premier Testament à partir du livre du Lévitique", *ZAW* 115 (2003) 524-537; 116 (2004) 33-54.

3.3.4 Rules for an Article in an Edited Volume and in a Festschrift

AUTHOR – cf. books.

"Title. Subtitle" – cf. article; "in" is not used.

Title. Subtitle of the work – cf. books.

EDITOR – in parentheses "()", "ed." ("éd.", "Hrsg.", "a cura di", "red.", etc.) followed by a space, the initial of the name, a period, a space and the SURNAME.

Name and series number – cf. books.

Place of publication – cf. books.

Date – cf. books.

Volume number – cf. books.

Page number(s) – cf. books.

E.g.

F. F. BRUCE, "The Theology and Interpretation of the Old Testament", *Tradition and Interpretation*. Essays by Members of the Society for Old Testament Studies (ed. G. W. ANDERSON) (Oxford 1979) 385-416.

H. GESE, "Natus ex virgine", *Probleme biblischer Theologie*. Festschrift G. von Rad (Hrsg. H. W. WOLFF) (München 1971) 75.

S. P. BROCK, "Genesis 22 in Syriac Tradition", *Mélanges Dominique Barthélemy*. Études bibliques offertes à l'occasion de son 60ᵉ anniversaire (éd. P. CASETTI – O. KEEL – A. SCHENKER) (OBO 38; Fribourg – Göttingen 1981) 1-30.

3.3.5 Rules for a Chapter or a Section within a Separately-Titled Volume (in a Multivolume, Edited Work)

AUTHOR – cf. books.

"Title. Subtitle" – cf. article. The title of the chapter or paragraph is written; "in" is not used.

Title of the work, etc.

Page number(s).

E.g.

I. MEYER, "Die Klagelieder", *Einleitung in das Alte Testament* (ed. E. ZENGER et al.) (KStTh 1/1; Stuttgart – Berlin ³1998) 430-435.

S. PISANO, "Il testo dell'Antico Testamento", *Metodologia dell'Antico Testamento* (ed. H. SIMIAN-YOFRE) (CSB 25; Bologna 1995) 39-78.

3.4 *Rules for a Review*

AUTHOR of the review – initial of the name + surname (cf. books) followed by a comma and a space; then "review of" is used, followed by a space.

The reviewed work – cf. books (as a rule) and articles.

The publication that contains the review – if it is a periodical, rules for articles should be applied.

E.g.

K. A. FOX, review of A. J. MALHERBE, *The Letters to the Thessalonians. A New Translation with Introduction and Commentary* (AncB 32B; New York 2000), *NT* 44 (2002) 395-397.

J.-M. AUWERS, review of M. MILLARD, *Die Komposition des Psalters. Ein formgeschichtlicher Ansatz* (FAT 9; Tübingen 1994), *RTL* 26 (1995) 496-501.

T. COLLINS, review of G. H. WILSON, *The Editing of the Hebrew Psalter* (SBL.DS 76; Chicago [*sic*] 1985), *JSSt* 32 (1987) 193-196.

P. BRIKS, review of R. NEU, "Die Bedeutung der Ethnologie für die alttestamentliche Forschung", *Ethnologische Texte zum Alten Testament. Vor- und Frühgeschichte Israels* (ed. C. SIGRIST – R. NEU) (Neukirchen-Vluyn 1989) I, 11-26, *Szczecińskie Studia Kościelne* 2 (1991) 97-100.

3.5 *Rules for an Introduction, Preface, Foreword or Afterword Written by Someone Other than by Author*

AUTHOR of the introduction… (initial of the name + surname) – followed by a comma and a space; then, in Roman type, and without quotation marks "introduction to / preface to / presentazione to", etc., followed by a space, is used.

Work which includes the introduction... – cf. books.
Page number(s).

E.g.

L. MORALDI, introduzione to GIUSEPPE FLAVIO, *Antichità giudaiche* (CdR; Torino 1998) 26-27.

J. DORÉ, présentation to P. GRELOT, *Le Mystère du Christ dans les psaumes* (CJJC 74; Paris 1998) 7-10.

N. LOHFINK, prefazione to J. Y.-S. PAHK, *Il canto della gioia in Dio. L'itinerario sapienziale espresso dall'unità letteraria in Qohelet 8,16–9,10 e il parallelo di Gilgameš Me. iii* (SMDSA 52; Napoli 1996) ix-xi.

D. N. FREEDMAN, prolegomenon to G. B. GRAY, *The Forms of Hebrew Poetry Considered with Special Reference to the Criticism and Interpretation of the Old Testament* (LBS; New York 1915, 1972) vii-lvi.

H. KÜNG, foreword to *The Rivers of Paradise*. Moses, Buddha, Confucius, Jesus, and Muhammad as Religious Founders (ed. D. N. FREEDMAN – M. J. McCLYMOND) (Grand Rapids, MI 2001) vii-ix.

D. M. TUROLDO, postfazione to G. RAVASI, *Cantico dei Cantici* (Oscar Saggi; Milano 1996) 235-241.

3.6 Reprint

The model for books is used. After the date of the original edition, followed by a comma and a space, the name of the city is written if it is different from that in the previous publication, and the date of the reprint; the rest of information is given as usual.

E.g.

J. L. SKA, *Introduzione alla lettura del Pentateuco*. Chiavi per l'interpretazione dei primi cinque libri della Bibbia (Collana biblica; Roma 1998, Bologna 2000) 135-138.

P. JOÜON, *Grammaire de l'hébreu biblique* (Rome ²1947, 1987) § 121a.

H. GUNKEL – J. BEGRICH, *Einleitung in die Psalmen*. Die Gattungen der religiösen Lyrik Israels (Göttingen ⁴1933, 1985).

C. F. KEIL, *Leviticus, Numeri und Deuteronomium* (BC 1/2; Leipzig ³1870, Gießen – Basel 1987).

3.7 *A New or a Revised Edition*

The model used for books is applied. In case of a revision or a revised and enlarged edition, relative information is quoted in parentheses "()" immediately after the title or, if it is present, after the subtitle.

E.g.

J. BLENKINSOPP, *A History of Prophecy in Israel* (Revised and Enlarged) (Louisville, KY 1996).

O. EISSFELDT, *Einleitung in das Alte Testament* (NTG; Tübingen ³1964, ⁴1976).

3.8 *Citations Taken from Secondary Sources*

Studies consulted personally (primary sources) should be quoted. However, if it is impossible to access a source directly, a study is to be quoted according to the styles mentioned above (cf. book; article); after a comma and a space, the expression "quoted in" is used and all bibliographical references of the work from which the quotation was taken is then cited.

E.g.

S. ABRAMSKY, *Kingdom of Saul and Kingdom of David* (Jerusalem 1977) 117-125, quoted in S. M. KANG, *Divine War in the Old Testament and in the Ancient Near East* (BZAW 177; Berlin – New York 1989) 213.

3.9 *Classic, Patristic and Medieval Works*

3.9.1 Rules for a Single Work

NAME OF THE AUTHOR – in its most known form.

Title of the work – abbreviated.

Internal notations – divisions and subdivisions of the work, ordinarily established by the author himself.

As for abbreviations of these works, authors lack uniformity of style. If personal abbreviations are used, it is necessary to maintain consistency throughout one's written work.

For a list of the abbreviations, see:

ALEXANDER, *The SBL Handbook of Style*, 237-263.

ALLENBACH, J. et al. (ed.), *Biblia Patristica*. Index des citations et allusions bibliques dans la littérature patristique (Paris 1975-) I-VII.

LIDDELL, H. G. – SCOTT, R., *A Greek-English Lexicon* (Revised and Augmented by H. S. JONES) (Oxford ⁹1925-1940, 1990) xvi-xxxviii; IIDEM, *A Greek-English Lexicon*. Revised Supplement (ed. E. A. BARBER) (Oxford 1968) vii-x; IIDEM, *A Greek-English Lexicon*. Revised Supplement (ed. P. G. W. GLARE) (Oxford 1996) x-xx.

LAMPE, G. W. H., *A Patristic Greek Lexicon* (Oxford 1961) xi-xlv.

SOUTER, A. et al. (ed.), *Oxford Latin Dictionary* (Oxford 1968) ix-xx.

E.g.

ARISTOTELES, *De mundo*, 391b.2.
PLUTARCHUS, *Tiberius et Caius Gracchus*, XI, 2.3-4.
ATHANASIUS, *Exp. in Ps.* 2,2-3.
AUGUSTINUS, *De doctr. Chr.* II, 16.
HILARIUS, *Tr. in Ps.* 2,1-4.
ALBERTUS MAGNUS, *De animal.* XIII, 2, 1.

3.9.2 Citation of a Series or Multivolume Work

After the elements already indicated above in § 3.9.1 and in the parentheses "()", additional indications are added:

Collection or EDITOR – Preferably the collection. For Church Fathers, critical editions should be used, if they exist.

Volume number – that is preceded by the abbreviation of the collection and a space.

Page number or, sometimes, line number – preceded by a comma and by a space.

E.g.

ARISTOTELES, *De mundo*, 391b.2 (ed. D. J. FURLEY, III, 346).
PLUTARCHUS, *Tiberius et Caius Gracchus*, XI, 2.3-4 (ed. B. PERRIN, X, 170).
ATHANASIUS, *Exp. in Ps.* 2,2-3 (PG 27, 64D-65A).
AUGUSTINUS, *De doctr. Chr.* II, 16 (CChr.SL 32, 42).
HILARIUS, *Tr. in Ps.* 2,1-4 (CSEL 22, 37-40).
ALBERTUS MAGNUS, *De animal.* XIII, 2, 1 (ed. H. STADLER, II, 927-931).

3.10 *Rabbinic, Talmudic, Midrashic Works*

3.10.1 Rules for the Tractates of the Talmud, Mishnah and Tosefta

Title of the work – abbreviated (cf. SCHWERTNER, *IATG²*, xl; see above chap. III, § 12.1) preceded by "b", "y", "t", "m".

Folio number followed, without a space, by "a", indicating a citation for a left page or "b", for a right page; and for Talmud Yerushalmi, "a" and/or "b" for the columns on the front site of the page or "c" and/or "d" for the columns on the back site of the page.

E.g.

bPes 17a.
yHag 77d.

3.10.2 Rules for Midrashim, Targumim, and Collections

Title of the work – Roman type and abbreviated (cf. SCHWERTNER, *IATG²*, xl-xli; see above chap. III, § 12.1).

In case of a commentary on a biblical passage, cite the biblical reference.

EDITOR – in parentheses "()" ("ed." followed by a space, the initial of the name, a period, a space and the SURNAME of the editor; a comma and a space follow, and then the page number, without "p.").

E.g.

MTeh on Ps 72,5 (ed. S. BUBER, 326).
EstR on Esth 3,5 (ed. S. BUBER, 23).
MekhY on Exod 15,1 (ed. H. S. HOROVITZ – I. A. RABIN, 118-119).
Yalq 843 on Ps 92,2 (ed. A. B. HYMAN, 130).
TgPsJ on Exod 20,2.
TgNeof I on Deut 5,6.

3.11 *Qumran*

For numbering, abbreviations and publications of documents from Qumran, Masada, Ḥirbet Mird, Wadi Murabbaʻat, Wadi ed-Daliyeh, Naḥal Šeʼelim (= Wadi Seiyal), Naḥal Ḥever, and other sites, see:

FITZMYER, J. A., *The Dead Sea Scrolls.* Major Publications and Tools for Study (SBL Resources for Biblical Study 20; Atlanta ³1990) 1-93.

REED, S. A., *The Dead Sea Scrolls Catalogue.* Documents, Photographs and Museum Inventory Numbers (SBL Resources for Biblical Study 32; Atlanta 1994).

WASHBURN, D. L., *A Catalog of Biblical Passages in the Dead Sea Scrolls* (SBL Text-Critical Studies 3/2; Atlanta 2002).

3.12 *Electronic Publications*

A few ways of quoting texts published on CD-ROM, DVD and on the Internet are suggested below.

3.12.1 Rules for CD-ROMs and DVDs

AUTHOR – initial of the name + SURNAME.

Title. Subtitle – italics and Roman type, in case of the book; or

"Title. Subtitle" – Roman type in quotation marks, in case of an article, dictionary article, etc.; after a comma and a space, if the document lacks pagination, possible references to the internal division of the document are cited, such as a chapter heading or other divisions.

The title of the collection of texts on CD/DVD as it is written on the title page of the electronic document or on the cover or on the disk (cf. books).

Place of publication – cf. books.

Date – cf. books.

Indicate CD-ROM or DVD in square brackets.

E.g.

G. J. WENHAM, *Genesis 1–15* (WBC; Waco, TX 1987) [CD-ROM].

S. GREENGUS, "Law. Biblical and ANE Law", E. Laws Protecting the Family, *The Anchor Bible Dictionary* (ed. D. N. FREEDMAN) (New York – London – Toronto – Sydney – Auckland 1992) [CD-ROM].

3.12.2 Rules for Web Publications

AUTHOR – initial of the name + SURNAME.

Title. Subtitle – for books, etc.

"Title. Subtitle" – for periodicals, etc.

The Internet address – preceded by a comma and a space.

Accessed – in square brackets; this element is inserted specifically when the year or the date of the publication are not found.

E.g.

P. H. ALEXANDER et al. (ed.), *The SBL Handbook of Style for Ancient Near Eastern, Biblical, and Early Christian Studies* (Peabody, MA 1999) 25-31, http://www.sbl-site.org/assets/pdfs/SBLHS. pdf.

J. J. KILGALLEN, "Hostility to Paul in Pisidian Antioch (Acts 13,45) – Why?", *Bib* 84 (2003) 1-15, http://www.bsw.org/?l=71841&a= Comm01.html.

J. A. SOGGIN, "Il giubileo e l'anno sabatico", http://www.biblico.it/ doc-vari/conferenza_soggin.html [accessed January 9, 2009].

3.13 *Unpublished and Informally Published Works*

Apart of what was already stated in § 3.2 (cf. "Diss.", "Mémoire", "forthcoming"), it is also possible to cite an author's unpublished work in various ways. In a footnote, one of the following expressions is used: "personal communication of the author (date)"; "personal letter of the author (date)"; "statement recorded on..."; (N. N., *Title*...,); "manuscript", etc. In case of a personal communication, a tape recording, or shorthand reports, the printed text should be submitted for the cited person's approval.

3.14 *Nota Bene*

If the same work is quoted several times in a contribution, the first time it is cited in full, whereas afterwards, only essential data are provided: the author's surname is followed by one (or more) significant words from the title. If one refers again to the same work published by an editor, the expression "ed.", and, if necessary, "et al.".

The expressions: op. cit., art. cit. or similar, are not used. An exception to this rule is the expression *ibidem* (in the same work), which is used in the same footnote, immediately after previous quotation of the same work.

E.g.   [12] T. R. HENN, *The Bible as Literature* (London – New York 1970) 9-15.

[16] HENN, *Literature*, 11.

[23] P. H. ALEXANDER et al. (ed.), *The SBL Handbook of Style for Ancient Near Eastern, Biblical, and Early Christian Studies* (Peabody 1999).

[46] ALEXANDER, *The SBL Handbook of Style*, 237-263.

If, in a footnote, bibliographical documentation on a topic is listed, chronological order should be used.

In case of two or more quotations of the same author/s or the same authoress/es in the same footnote, the Latin terms IDEM, IIDEM or EADEM, EAEDEM are used.

4. Bibliography

Each entry should be alphabetized according to the English alphabet. In case of works in foreign languages, the entry should be alphabetized in accordance with the alphabet of the main language used in the publication.

The citation method is the same as in § 3. The author's surname is followed by a comma, a space, and the initial of the first name. At the end of the entry, the inclusive page (or column) numbers of the article or the cited entry; however, this does not apply to a book if it is by the same author.

Alphabetical order is used.

When putting the entries in order, the apostrophe within a surname should not be taken into account.

E.g.   OBRECHTS-TITECA, L.
        O'CALLAGHAN, J.
        OEMING, M.

The division of the bibliography, especially in case of dissertations or books, should be agreed upon with the director of the thesis, or the publisher. In a classical division, there are *sources*, with the entries on which is based the commentary on the disquisition of the work, and *studies* which furnishes other texts on the subject investigated. It is better to avoid numerous subdivisions.

If two or more works of the same author are listed, his name is not repeated, but is replaced by a line: ———.

E.g.   JENNI, E., "עָנָן ʿānān, Wolke", *THAT* II, 351-353.
        ———, "Das Wort ʿōlām im Alten Testament", *ZAW* 64 (1952) 197-248.

5. Alphabets

Even though there are different ways of organizing the names of the authors (or titles, if the work is anonymous) in the bibliography, it is better to keep to an objective and uniform standard, namely, that which applies the rules of each author's own respective language. Otherwise, the writer runs the risk of listing the authors inappropriately, placing, for instance, DE ROSSI under the letter R or DE VAUX under the letter D.

In other words, discerning where an author's name is to be placed in the bibliography requires the identification of the "alphabetizing element" of the surname. In what follows, the first letter of this element will be highlighted in **_Bold Italic_**.

5.1 *Regular Cases*

In alphabetical order.

5.2 *Names with Patronymic Particles*

When the surname is preceded by patronymic particles (Ab, Ap, Bar, Ben, Der, Fitz, Mac, Mc, M', O', Ó, Ter), the latter is the alphabetizing element. Surnames with particles Mac, Mc, M', should be alphabetized as if they were built by the prefix Mac-.

E.g.   Andreas Ab Alpe = *A*B ALPE, A.
Dafydd Rhys Ap-Thomas = *A*P-THOMAS, D. R.
Meir Bar Ilan = *B*AR ILAN, M.
Zafrira Ben-Barak = *B*EN-BARAK, Z.
Sirarpie Der Nersessian = *D*ER NERSESSIAN, S.
François Fitz-James = *F*ITZ-JAMES, F.
Peter Kyle McCarter = *M*CCARTER, P. K.
Thomas M'Crie = *M'*CRIE, T.
Dennis R. MacDonald = *M*ACDONALD, D. R.
Fearghus Ó Fearghail = *Ó* FEARGHAIL, F.

Robert O'Toole = *O*'Toole, R.
Lévon Ter-Pétrossian = *T*er-Pétrossian, L.

5.3 *Articles and Prepositions*

Frequent difficulties can occur when an author's surname is formed by articles and prepositions.

First of all, the original spelling of the prepositions and articles should be respected. In other words, it is necessary to maintain the lower case or capital letter with which they are written.

The rules quoted in the following sections are to be applied.

5.3.1 Names Beginning with the Definite Article

This article is the alphabetizing element (in Dutch and Flemish, "de" is an article, but only in Flemish is it the alphabetizing element).

E.g.   Eugène A. La Verdiere = *L*a Verdiere, E. A.
Carmelo Lo Giudice = *L*o Giudice, C.
Marinus De Jong = *D*e Jong, M.

5.3.2 Names Beginning with a Preposition

When the surname starts with a single preposition, this preposition is not the alphabetizing element (except Italian surnames).

E.g.   Isabelle de Castelbajac = de *C*astelbajac, I.
Gerhard von Rad = von *R*ad, G.

Paolo De Benedetti = *D*e Benedetti, P.

5.3.3 Names with an Uncontracted Preposition and Article

When the surname starts with a preposition and an article that is uncontracted, they are not considered to be alphabetizing elements, except French surnames, for which the article is always an alphabetizing element.

E.g.   Alfonso de la Fuente = DE LA *F*UENTE, A.
         Pieter van der Lugt = VAN DER *L*UGT, P.

         Ignace de la Potterie = DE *LA* POTTERIE, I.

5.3.4 Names with a Contracted Preposition and Article

When the surname starts with a preposition and an article that are contracted into a single term, this term is the alphabetizing element, but only for Italian and French surnames.

E.g.   Gregorio del Olmo Lete = DEL *O*LMO LETE, G.
         José C. dos Santos = DOS *S*ANTOS, J. C.

         Flavio Dalla Vecchia = *D*ALLA VECCHIA, F.
         Antonio Dell'Era = *D*ELL'ERA, A.
         Édouard des Places = *D*ES PLACES, É.

5.3.5 Dutch and Flemish Surnames

In Dutch and Flemish, surnames formed by articles and/or prepositions, and by a significative word, are written and arranged in a different way.

a) Netherlands

The surname (not the particle) is considered to be the alphabetizing element.

E.g.   Johannes Cornelis de Moor = DE *M*OOR, J. C.
         Cornelis Jacobus den Heyer = DEN *H*EYER, C. J.
         Wilhelm Theodor in der Smitten = IN DER *S*MITTEN, W. T.
         Gabriel te Stroete = TE *S*TROETE, G.
         Adam Simon van der Woude = VAN DER *W*OUDE, A. S.

NB If in the text the first name or its initial is omitted, Dutch surnames should be written in this way: De Moor, Den Heyer, In der Smitten, Te Stroete, Van der Woude.

b) Belgium

The particle that precedes the surname is the alphabetizing element.

E.g. Robert De Langhe = DE LANGHE, R.
Damian Van den Eynde = VAN DEN EYNDE, D.

5.4 Double or Composed Surnames

The alphabetizing element is the first surname, except English and Portuguese surnames.

E.g. Luis Alonso Schökel = ALONSO SCHÖKEL, L.
Rosa M. Boixareu i Vilaplana = BOIXAREU I VILAPLANA, R. M.
Rosanna Virgili Dal Prà = VIRGILI DAL PRÀ, R.

Henry Van Dyke Parunak = Van Dyke PARUNAK, H.
Robert Payne Smith = Payne SMITH, R. / SMITH, R. P.
Vânia Moreira Klen = Moreira KLEN, V. / KLEN, V. M.

5.5 Names in non-Latin Characters

Names and surnames of the authors, written with particular script (Arabic, Cyrillic, Hebrew, Greek), they should be transcribed or transliterated, but they should be not translated.
Names of Greek authors are quoted in the Latin transcribed form.

E.g. ATHANASIUS, THEODORETUS.

For Latin transcription of Greek names, it is possible to consult:

LIDDELL – SCOTT, A Greek-English Lexicon, xvi-xxxviii; IIDEM, A Greek-English Lexicon. Revised Supplement (1968) vii-x; IIDEM, A Greek-English Lexicon. Revised Supplement (1996) x-xx.
LAMPE, A Patristic Greek Lexicon, xi-xlv.

5.6 *Names in the Genitive Case*

When the author's name is expressed in the genitive case – it is quoted in the nominative case.

E.g.   HUGO DE SANCTO VICTORE, *De archa Noe*

5.7 *The Same Family Surname*

When the authors of a work have the same surname and are members of the same family, after the surname and the initial of the first name of the first author, follow: a space and the symbol ampersand &; after it a space and the initial of the first name of the second author is placed.

E.g.   ALAND, K. & B., *Der Text des Neuen Testaments*. Einführung in die wissenschaftlichen Ausgaben sowie in Theorie und Praxis der modernen Textkritik (Stuttgart 1982).

BRIGGS, C. A. & E. G., *A Critical and Exegetical Commentary on the Book of Psalms* (ICC; Edinburgh 1906-1907) I-II.

5.8 *Anonymous Publications (Unknown Authorship)*

The first significant element of the title is considered to be the alphabetizing element. Not included are articles, prepositions and numerals written in digits, even though they are also to be quoted.

E.g.   *The **R**evisers and the Greek Text of the New Testament*. By Two Members of the New Testament Company (London 1882).

5.9 *Anonymous Publications (Known Authorship)*

When the author's name can be identified, it acts as the alphabetizing element and is placed before the title in square brackets.

E.g.   [HAYES, C.,] *A Dissertation on the Chronology of the Septuagint* (London 1741).

5.10 *Pseudonymous Works*

When the real name of the author is unknown, the word "pseud." in square brackets follows the pseudonym. This is omitted in the footnote.

E.g.   EMMANUEL [pseud.], *Pour commenter la Genèse* (Paris 1971).

5.11 *Homonyms*

When two surnames of different authors are identical and the names start with the same letter, they are alphabetized by surnames and the names are written in full.

E.g.   BIANCHI, Ferdinando
BIANCHI, Francesco
DELITZSCH, Franz
DELITZSCH, Friedrich
NESTLE, Eberhard
NESTLE, Erwin

In case of two identical surnames and first names, etc., the chronological arrangement should be followed, namely in accordance with biographical data of the author.

E.g.   SMEND, Rudolf, 1851-1913
SMEND, Rudolf, 1932-

5.12 *Jr., Sr., etc.*

In the *text*, commas are not required with Jr. and Sr.[4] However, if they are used, they should be present both before and after the element. A comma is never used with II, III, IV. In the *bibliography*, all these elements are placed after the initial of the first name preceded by a comma.

---

[4] *Chicago Manual*, 254 (no. 6.49).

In Brazilian Portuguese, the surname sometimes appears with the element "Filho", "Júnior" ("son"), "Sobrinho" ("nephew") or "Neto" ("grandson"). These components are quoted in the bibliographical list after the surname followed by a space.

E.g.   Patrick D. Miller Jr. = MILLER, P. D., Jr.
        Leonard L. Hamlin Sr. = HAMLIN, L. L., Sr.
        William R. Herzog II = HERZOG, W. R., II
        Roy A. Harrisville III = HARRISVILLE, R. A., III
        Herbert W. Bateman IV = BATEMAN, H. W., IV

        Leonardo Coimbra Filho = COIMBRA Filho, L.
        Augusto Cardoso Júnior = CARDOSO Júnior, A.
        Serafim da Silva Neto = DA SILVA Neto, S.
        Custódio Gomes Sobrinho = GOMES Sobrinho, C.

5.13 *Titles of Persons*

In general, formal titles are not indicated (Mr., Mrs., Prof., Rev., Fr., Duke, Sir, Lord). However, titles of the nobility are quoted if, from the bibliographical point of view, they are the principal (or unique) denominators.

E.g.   Wolf Wilhelm Graf von Baudissin = Graf VON BAUDISSIN, W. W.

5.14 *Authors Known by (a First) Name*

Authors known by their (first) name (saints, medieval authors, etc.) are arranged by that name, written in full (small capitals).

E.g.   ALI ABOU-ASSAF
        CORNELIUS A LAPIDE
        JOHN PAUL II
        ORTENSIO DA SPINETOLI
        THOMAS AQUINAS

5.15 *Works of Roman Pontiffs Published along with Their Secular Names*

If a Roman pontiff publishes a work signed with his secular sur-name and with his pontiff's name, the latter, after a comma and a space, is placed after the former, which serves as an alphabetizing element.

E.g.   RATZINGER, J., BENEDICT XVI

5.16 *Diacritical Marks*

If, in surnames (or first names) of the authors, particular diacriti-cal marks appear (å, ä, ã, ą, â, ć, č, ď, đ, è, é, ě, ë, ê, ĝ, ğ, ġ, ġ, ħ, ĥ, ḥ, ḫ, î, ī, ļ, ł, ñ, ń, ň, ṇ, ó, ô, õ, ø, ö, ŕ, ŗ, ř, ś, š, ŝ, ş, ṣ, ţ, ť, ŧ, ṭ, ü, ŭ, ů, ų, û, ż, ź, ž), these marks do not effect alphabetization.

In the same manner, *alef* (ʾ) and/or *ayin* (ʿ) do not have an im-pact on the location (of the work) of an author in the bibliographical list.

5.17 *Composed Characters*

Digraphs, trigraphs and tetragraphs, which represent a single speech sound (ch, cz, ea, eau, eaux, gn, ll, nh, ny, ph, rz, sch, sci, sh, sj, sz, th, etc.), are placed in the alphabetical list as if the phonetic transformation had not occurred.

6. Bibliographical and Typographical Terms

At the conclusion of these considerations, a table is included with some bibliographical and typographical terms that have been em-ployed in this book. For the easier consultation, they are cited in six languages.

Table of bibliographical and typographical terms

English	Español	Français	Deutsch	Italiano	Po polsku
ampersand: &	ampersand	esperluette	Et-Zeichen, Und-Zeichen	ampersand, e commerciale	ampersand, etka
angular brackets: ⟨⟩	paréntesis triangulares	parenthèses triangulaires	Winkelklammern, spitzen Klammern	parentesi uncinata	nawiasy trójkątne, ostre
apostrophe: '	apóstrofo	apostrophe	Apostroph	apostrofo	apostrof
article	artículo	article	Artikel	articolo	artykuł
author	autor	auteur	Verfasser	autore	autor
boldface	negrita	gras	halbfett, Halbfettdruck, fett, Fettdruck	grassetto	pogrubiony
brace: {}	corchete, llave	accolade	geschwungene Klammern, Akkolade	parentesi graffa	nawiasy klamrowe, wąsy
capital, upper case	mayúscula	majuscule, capitale	Großbuchstabe	maiuscolo	wersaliki
collection	colección	collection	Reihe, Serie	collezione	zbiór

	dos puntos	deux-points	Doppelpunkt	due punti	dwukropek
colon: :	dos puntos	deux-points	Doppelpunkt	due punti	dwukropek
column	columna	colonne	Spalte	colonna	kolumna
comma: ,	coma	virgule	Komma	virgola	przecinek
dash: –	raya	tiret	(Binde)Strich	lineetta, trattino	półpauza, myślnik
date	fecha	date	Datum	data	data
Diss. (Dissertation)	Dis. (Disertación)	Diss. (Dissertation)	Diss. (Dissertation)	Diss. (Dissertazione)	Dys. (rozprawa pra-ca, doktorska)
ed.	ed.	éd.	Hrsg.	a cura di	red.
edited volume	obra colectiva, obra en colaboración	œuvre collective, collectif	Sammelwerk, Sammelband	opera collettiva	praca zbiorowa, dzieło zbiorowe
edition	edición	édition	Ausgabe	edizione	wydanie
editor	editor, coordinador	éditeur	Herausgeber	curatore	redaktor
em dash: —	guión largo	grand tiret	Geviertstrich	lineato lungo	pauza, myślnik
en dash: –	guión corto	petit tiret	Halb-geviertstrich	lineato breve	półpauza

»

essay	ensayo	essai	Essay, Abhandlung	saggio	esej
exclamation point: !	signo de exclamación	point d'exclamation	Ausrufezeichen	punto esclamativo	wykrzyknik
fascicle number, issue number	fascículo, entrega	fascicule	Heft, Faszikel	fascicolo	fascykuł, zeszyt
folio	pliego	folio	Foliant	foglio	folio, arkusz
footnote	nota	note	Anmerkung	nota	przypis
forthcoming	en prensa	sous presse, à l'impression	im Druck	in corso di stampa	w druku
guillemets: « »	comillas españolas	guillemet	Anführungszeichen – französische Form	virgolette a sergente, a caporale	cudzysłów francuski
hyphen: -	guión	trait d'union, division	Bindstrich, Kurzstrich	trattino	dywiz, łącznik
italics	cursiva, itálica	italique	kursiv, Kursivschrift	corsivo	kursywa, pismo pochyłe
left-hand page	verso, reverso	verso, dos	Rückseite, Kehrseite	pagina pari, verso	strona parzysta, verso

line	línea	ligne	Zeile	riga	linia
lower case	minúscula	minuscule	Kleinbuchstabe	minuscolo	małe litery
n.d. (no date)	s. a. (sin año)	s.d.(sans date)	o. J. (ohne Jahr)	s.a. (senza anno)	b.r. (bez roku)
n.p. (no place)	s. l. (sin lugar)	s.l. (sans lieu)	o. O. (ohne Ort)	s.l. (senza luogo)	b.m. (bez miejsca)
oblique stroke, slash: /	barra oblicua	barre inclinée, barre oblique	Schrägstrich, Bruchstrich	barra obliqua	kreska pochyła, kreska ukośna, ukośnik
page	página	page	Seite	pagina	strona
pagination	paginación	pagination	Seitenzahlen, Seiten-numerierung	paginazione, impaginazione	paginacja
parentheses: ( )	paréntesis (redondo)	parenthèse	runde Klammern	parentesi	nawias (nawiasy okrągłe)
periodical, journal	revista	revue	Zeitschrift	rivista	czasopismo
place	lugar	lieu	Ort	luogo	miejsce
publisher	editorial	éditeur	Verlag	editrice	wydawnictwo
question mark: ?	signo de interrogación	point d'interrogation	Fragezeichen	punto interrogativo	znak zapytania

»

quotation marks, inverted commas: ""	comillas inglesas	griffes	Anführungs-zeichen	virgolette inglesi	cudzysłów
quoted in	citado en	cité en	zitiert von	citato da	cyt. za
period, full stop: .	punto	point	Punkt	punto	kropka
reprint	reedición	réédition	Abdruck	ristampa	dodruk
review	recensión	compte rendu	Rezension	recensione	recenzja
right-hand page	recto, anverso	recto	Recto, Vorderseite	pagina dispari, recto	strona niepa-rzysta, recto
Roman type	redonda	romain	Rundschrift, Grundschrift	tondo	antykwa, pismo proste
semicolon: ;	punto y coma	point-virgule	Strichpunkt	punto e virgola	średnik
series	colección	collection	Reihe	collana	seria
small capital	versalita	petite capital	Kapitälchen	maiuscoletto	kapitaliki
space: [ ]	espacio	espace	Spatium, Leerzeichen	spazio	spacja, odstęp

square brackets: []	corchete, paréntesis cuadrado	crochet	eckige Klammern	parentesi quadra	klamry (nawiasy kwadratowe)
subscript	subíndice	indice	Index	pedice	frakcja dolna, indeks
subtitle	subtítulo	sous-titre	Untertitel	sottotitolo	podtytuł
superscript	superíndice	exposant	Exponent	apice	frakcja górna, wykładnik
title	título	titre	Titel	titolo	tytuł
title page	frontispicio	frontispice	Titelseite, Titelblatt	frontespizio	strona tytułowa
transcription	transcripción	transcription	Umschrift	trascrizione	transkrypcja
transliteration	transliteración	translittération	Transliteration	traslitterazione	transliteracja
volume	tomo, volumen	tome, année	Band, Buch, Jahrgang	volume, annata	tom, numer rocznika
volume in honor of	homenaje	mélanges	Festschrift	in onore di, miscellanea	księga pamiątkowa
year	año	année	Jahr	anno	rok wydania

Index of Names